P9-CJI-398

PENGUIN BOOKS

1900: A FIN-DE-SIÈCLE READER

Mike Jay is also the editor of *Artificial Paradises* (Penguin 1999) and the author of *Blue Tide: The Search for Soma* (1999).

Michael Neve is a historian at the Wellcome Institute for the History of Medicine in London. He teaches and researches the history of psychiatry, the life sciences and the doctor/patient relationship, as well as the impact of European degenerationist writings from the mid nineteenth century.

1900 A Fin-de-siècle Reader

Edited by
MIKE JAY *and* **MICHAEL NEVE**

PENGUIN BOOKS

PENGUIN BOOKS

Published by the Penguin Group
Penguin Books Ltd, 27 Wrights Lane, London w8 5tz, England
Penguin Putnam Inc., 375 Hudson Street, New York, New York 10014, USA
Penguin Books Australia Ltd, Ringwood, Victoria, Australia
Penguin Books Canada Ltd, 10 Alcorn Avenue, Toronto, Ontario, Canada m4v 3b2
Penguin Books (NZ) Ltd, Private Bag 102902, NSMC, Auckland, New Zealand

Penguin Books Ltd, Registered Offices: Harmondsworth, Middlesex, England

First published in Penguin Books 1999
10 9 8 7 6 5 4 3 2

Set in 9.5/12.5 pt PostScript Adobe New Caledonia
Typeset by Rowland Phototypesetting Ltd, Bury St Edmunds, Suffolk
Printed in England by Clays Ltd, St Ives plc

Contents

5 Return of the Repressed: The Unconscious

6 The Arrival of the Deviant: Sexology

List of Illustrations

Introduction

At the end of the twentieth century, it is widely believed that we are entering into a crisis of civilization which is entirely new, a result of considerations which are forcing themselves upon us for the first time. These considerations – the impact of the accelerating growth of science, technology, population, globalization, radical belief systems – form the complex of crises which we have come to associate with the Millennium, with its associated catch-phrases of 'millennial anxiety', 'millennial panic' and 'pre-millennial tension'.

But if we cast back a century, to the period from the 1880s to the 1910s, we discover a parallel complex of crises grouped under the term *fin-de-siècle*. As this reader demonstrates, much of what we think of as the 'new' or 'modern' crisis presents itself to us in the *fin-de-siècle* in strikingly similar form. The future of the human race, the apocalyptic possibilities opened up by science, the crisis of faith, the mass belief in the paranormal, the future role of women, the multicultural 'global village' – all of these were worried over and dissected a century ago. Within these broad areas of concern many specific modern debates, from life on Mars to the 'gay gene' to the Channel Tunnel, find uncanny echoes in the world of the *fin-de-siècle*.

The case can indeed be made that the *fin-de-siècle* was in fact the true Millennium, and what we imagine to be our 'modern' crisis little more than the aftershocks of the *fin-de-siècle* amplified and diffused by an increasingly overwhelming global media. At the beginning of the nineteenth century, the conventional view of human civilization was predicated on ideas of a divinely ordained universe, its mechanisms set not by man but by God, and change itself as no more than fluctuations within an essential stasis. But as discoveries within geology and the physical sciences revealed a past of almost unimaginable antiquity, and the theory of evolution suggested the possibility of continuing and fundamental change, the 'modern' perspective of past and future developed for the first time. As it did so, it revealed the new and profound abilities of humanity to change and control its own destiny: the fundamental sea-change in human thought which remains the underlying challenge of the Millennium.

It was this change which led to another shared dynamic of both the *fin-de-siècle* and the Millennium: self-consciousness. The Millennium has become a catch-all concept within which, it is claimed, every manifestation of the modern world can be interpreted, to the extent that much of the discourse around it ends up disputing and questioning the nature and meaning of Millennium itself: is the Millennium simply a handy conceptual peg for cultural stock-taking, or is the turning of the century playing an active role in crystallizing some crisis? Similarly, *fin-de-siècle* became a term which generated as much interest and debate as the subjects which it purported to illuminate. The term, as broadly used today, has come to designate the work which was most commonly regarded as the symptoms of the *fin-de-siècle* malaise: the 'decadent' arts, with their emphasis on existential agnosticism, the amoral celebration of pleasure and pain; and a self-conscious 'sickness of the soul'. While these are represented here, we have sought to present a *fin-de-siècle* which is both broader and more representative of the time, one which includes the attempts to diagnose the *fin-de-siècle* sickness as well as presenting its most familiar symptoms.

The sense of crisis secular and spiritual, of an unprecedented challenge to civilization, the self-conscious use of the marker presented by End of Century – all these 'millennial' ideas turn out to be present in the *fin-de-siècle*. But perhaps even more illuminating than the similarities are the differences between Millennium and *fin-de-siècle*, for it is these which give us the most accurate measure of the progress of the twentieth century.

The most significant difference is that at the core of the notion of Millennium is the spectre of finality, of apocalypse – the imminent approach of a 'singularity event' which will change the fundamental laws of man and nature for either good or ill, and in the face of which we are simply the victims of Fate. Today, we find apocalyptic tendencies everywhere from the Marian prophecies of Catholicism to the Green movement, from the Evangelical churches to the new cult of the Mayan calendar to the endlessly widening spectrum of new religious movements, and we see its tragic manifestations increasingly from Waco to the Tokyo attacks of Aum Shinri Kyo to Heaven's Gate. The strength of this tendency can perhaps be measured not only in the growing adherence of millions to such movements, but in the failure of imagination which the twenty-first century provokes: we may not believe in any such apocalypse ourselves, but few of us would truly claim the confidence to imagine the century to come. We are on the brink of something – but of what?

Not so the *fin-de-siècle*. The readers of the 1890s were positively engulfed with imaginative constructions of the next century: Utopias, monomanic tracts, dire warnings, technological predictions, blueprints for survival. Even at the time, the sheer number of books and magazines with *New Century* in their titles was remarked upon with ironic amusement or vigorous consternation. The idea that civilization, or humanity itself, would cease to exist was limited to a small handful of apocalyptic movements: the Ghost-Dance religion of the Native Americans, the Canudos commune of Brazil. This was not because there was an absence of apocalyptic belief in the nineteenth century: far from it. The mass hysteria of End Time was a well-recognized phenomenon from the Millerites onwards: the image of the prophet and his followers waiting on a hill for the final judgement was a nineteenth-century cliché, perhaps even more familiar then than now. It was more that the *fin-de-siècle* was pervaded by an urgent sense of the new powers of humanity and of our potential to alter the conditions which were threatening the crisis. In this sense, our mass movement towards fatalism at the end of this century shows that we are not more modern than the *fin-de-siècle* but less: perhaps the *fin-de-siècle* was, after all, the apex of the modern movement, from which this century has witnessed a gradual descent towards some 'new medievalism', or collective blankness about the possible shape of the future.

The *fin-de-siècle*'s claim to its new ability to determine, predict and control the future can be summed up in a single word: science. As such, the struggle between science and other systems of knowledge was the core of the nineteenth-century cultural drama. For the scientist, humanity had to grow up and recognize certain truths. First, that God did not exist. Second, that science meant that we could now understand natural laws correctly. And third, that it was the task of the scientist either to assume the responsibility of putting these truths into practical effect in human society or at least to ensure that others – politicians, doctors, generals – did so.

It must be remembered that science in the *fin-de-siècle* was not so much a 'career' in the modern sense as a state of mind. Scientists were

academics, professional practitioners, commercial writers, men of letters
or of independent means. By no means all of the 'medical experts' in
this volume, for example, had medical degrees. Despite their broad
range of views they were, unsurprisingly, drawn from a limited band of
the social spectrum: adult white males of greater or lesser degrees of
privilege. What united them across all their contradictions and contro-
versies was the humanistic breadth of their belief in the scientific
method, and the possibilities of its application to ever broader areas of
the social world.

If Darwin, to take the most important example, taught that natural
selection was the motor of evolution, then social policy had to recognize
this fact. If Darwin also demonstrated that the means by which the unfit
were weeded out were (from our perspective) cruel, then social policy
had to recognize this too. To hide behind liberal or sentimental anxieties
was to endorse a form of arrested development. Few scientific claims
of the *fin-de-siècle* are as important as this: that the backward and feeble
nature of degenerate human types – and both their biological and
cultural productions – was a bio-medical matter of scientific fact.

This partial but, it was argued, progressive degeneration of the human
race made the 'pathological groups' who displayed it into objects of
scientific curiosity and examination. Whether this examination used the
lens of Darwinian evolution, psychiatric medicine, or mixtures of ethical
and behavioural philosophy, the implication was clear. To resist or
oppose the evidence of degenerationism was to contest the authority
of science itself, to open the door to earlier accounts of human personality
and purpose: accounts religious or in some other form irrational, of the
type which science had now firmly cast as themselves forms of primitive
thought.

The *fin-de-siècle*, then, was more than the end of a century. It was
the end of an era: but whose era? From the scientific point of view, it
was vital that it should be the end of the era of the degenerate or unfit
– for, the thunderous warning came, if it was not the end of the era of
the unfit it was the end of the era of science. If the scientist were not
actively to follow what science had proved to be the case, he would be
giving up his power to stop the human future from being merely a
disastrous re-run of the human past. Such a scientist would be allowing
the twilight world of the degenerate to become the future of us all.

It was this conviction that gave the *fin-de-siècle* its pervading atmosphere of seriousness and gloom; but this atmosphere is in some ways

misleading. The stressing of disaster prepares the way for drastic measures: the insistence on the twilight of humanity can actually be a springboard for the assertion that what is passing away is 'their' world, and what is dawning is 'ours'. 'They' may be examples of various 'types' – the biologically unfit, the criminal classes, the 'lower races', the alcoholic, the syphilitic, the degenerate artist, the idiot, the moron, the masculinizing female, the feminizing male – but as 'we' confront the crisis which they pose, 'we' may use the language of anxiety as a first stage of preparation for a cleansing of the world.

This cleansing – the second stage – also had its language, the specific flip-side of degeneration – 'regeneration'. Even the most flamboyantly pessimistic writer of the period, Max Nordau – whose works pondered both *fin-de-siècle* and degeneration – believed that the time of decadence would pass away, leaving a new world which urgently needed to be anticipated and planned.

But the science which produced this starkest of dichotomies proved too brittle to sustain it. The 'degenerate' tendencies within *fin-de-siècle* thought mounted an increasingly trenchant critique of the scientific credo: whole areas of science itself became tainted with 'degenerate' thinking. Take the great evolutionary writer Alfred Russel Wallace. For him, spiritualism was empirically proven: for other scientists, it was no more than a manifestation of insanity. For Wallace, too, it was scientifically demonstrable that socialism was the politics of the future: for others, socialism was nothing more nor less than the death of politics itself. For Sigmund Freud, the unconscious was a scientific fact: for most of his colleagues, it was a confused, fantastical and dangerous myth. For Edward Carpenter, the liberation of women was the most urgent reform needed to create a healthy future society: for many others, it was the arch degeneracy to be suppressed at all costs. The end of the century saw the slow collapse of the certainties that science had embodied in earlier decades. Not merely did some scientists see their strange fellow-workers as quacks or charlatans, but science itself seemed prone to internal sabotage, to uncertainty. And the messengers of this uncertainty were science's own creatures and discoveries. It seemed that the joke, after all, was on science – that in the end it had no more claim to agreed truth than any other form of knowledge. Perhaps – a famous view held by the philosopher Friedrich Nietzsche – Art was far wiser and closer to rendering truth than science ever would be.

Thinking itself above history, science failed to spot the staying power both of history and of the *fin-de-siècle* categories of degeneracy. It found itself sharing in all the doubts, collapses and strangenesses that once seemed the object of its experimental gaze. Even the physical sciences seemed to conspire in this uncertainty. The invisible electron undermined the certainties of classical science, plunging the nature of nature itself into mystery. The sun was losing heat and dying: the scientific future was an earth cold and uninhabitable. The other planets and stars might be inhabited by beings so advanced in science as to make a mockery of the entire human programme. *Fin-de-siècle*, if properly understood, might after all turn out to be *fin de la science* – even *fin du monde*.

Despite this, the end of the nineteenth century remained a time when almost everyone resolutely believed in a future, even as the consensus about the nature of that future fell into disarray. The practical demonstrations of science, the exponential growth of technologies, were for most people irresistible. Whatever the disasters to come, it was impossible to imagine that they could not be somehow outrun. This led to the development of a range of progressive views whereby the degenerationists themselves were a symptom of atavistic decline, of those who would fall at the present obstacle of the *fin-de-siècle*. Thus the new century would witness the decline of an increasingly disparate range of 'social atavists': men hostile to women voting, doctors hostile to contraception, literary critics unable to tolerate Symbolism, psychiatrists unable to talk about sex, the upper middle classes appalled at the growth of suburbia, commuting and mass holidays by the seaside.

The distinctive need to choose a new future for the new century was given urgency by the spectre of War. Some voices told that war was itself degenerate, and the regeneration following the next war would mean it would be the last. In the socialist view of H. G. Wells and others, war would pit the decaying forces of imperialism against each other and clear the twentieth century for the rest of us. Other voices looked forward with horror or barely concealed satisfaction to a new kind of war – a mechanized, relentless 'total war' which would become the motor for a civilization of the future. Still others combined these views – a future war would be fought by degenerate barbarians with the deadly new weapons of science.

In the *fin-de-siècle* climate, fierce policies were conceived and in many cases brought into effect. As we see in the concluding section of this reader, the segregation, sterilization and elimination of the 'unfit' were all practised – not so much in a desperate defence against degeneration but, perhaps more chillingly, in a progressive and ultimately optimistic spirit of 'regeneration'. A bright future seemed to require vigilance, weeding out, ferocious answers to pressing questions. In this sense, the *fin-de-siècle* is often read as a prelude to the fascism, Nazism and genocide of the twentieth century; but this is a reading which requires the wisdom of hindsight. Much of the *fin-de-siècle* development was progressive, liberal, democratizing, using new knowledge to free ordinary people from misery and degradation. But even *with* hindsight, some of these progressive strands of thought are hard to separate from the now-demonized doctrines of compulsory eugenics and proto-fascism. None the less, the *fin-de-siècle* presented in this reader includes texts and a range of beliefs that have no place at all in any imagined fascist prelude. It is historically important to disconnect such writings from a fictional ending.

The association of the *fin-de-siècle* with the culminating forces of totalitarianism may, in fact, tell us less about the nineteenth century than about our own Millennium. Perhaps it is this association which offers the clue to our millennial fatalism which contrasts so strongly with the *fin-de-siècle*'s energy. For it is now clear to us that there is no such thing as scientifically validated, objectively correct actions for the human race: that whatever form action takes, it will mean someone's destruction. This century has offered too many unthinkable yet all too real examples of the type of social planning, total warfare and biological imperatives which were explored during the *fin-de-siècle* as novelties – possibilities whose implementation lay beyond the horizon. The problem we face is the same, but the idea of taking any 'total action' is made unthinkable by the recent horrors that such actions embody. We see no future civilization, even as the scale of such imagined *fin-de-siècle* futures begins to recede from our view.

This was the heart of the modern crisis as it emerged during the *fin-de-siècle*: that humanity was alone, in a world becoming ever more scrutable to science but only to be improved – itself a good and practical possibility – on a massive and dangerous scale. Dream futures of eugenics, imperialism, science, mechanized production and war locked themselves inextricably with the world of democracy, emancipation, co-operation and peace. The two entered the new century twinned, increasingly well-armed – and yet ever less likely to resolve their struggle.

Acknowledgements

We would like to thank the following for assistance in tracking down sources, sharing thoughts and for general encouragement: Martin Adamson, Jan Bondeson, David Brady, Janet Browne, Bal Croce, Alex Goldbloom, Nicholas Goodrick-Clarke, Mark Gosbee, Lesley Hall, Rhodri Hayward, Paul Keegan (and much else besides), Gary Lachman, Ed Maggs, Michele Minto from Wellcome Trust Reprographics, Michael Moorcock, Charles Peltz, Mark Pilkington, Chandak Sengoopta, Sonu Shamdasani and Anna South. Michael Neve conveys his special thanks to Caroline Overy for her tireless help and to the Wellcome Trust for its support.

1
Faces of the Future:
Evolution and Degeneration

Of all the new understandings of the nineteenth century, the one which offered the most potent model for predicting the course of the next century was that of evolution. A range of evolutionary systems, of which Darwin's and Lamarck's are the best known, helped to create a new discipline within which human history and nature could be scrutinized.

Using these biological frameworks, a range of views of humanity's future evolution was also offered, but the most compelling prediction of Darwin's natural selection was that the human race was separating into two distinct groups: the 'fit' and the 'unfit'. This view forms one of the most striking literary motifs of the period, and is the central idea behind two of its most recognizable literary classics: The Time Machine *and* Dr Jekyll & Mr Hyde.

The novelist H. G. Wells's The Time Machine *is a parable of the future subspeciation of the human race, with its roots specifically located in the* fin-de-siècle *class divide. His future Eloi, the pale, effete creatures of idle leisure, were a recognizable caricature of the Bloomsbury elite, and the subterranean underclass, the Morlocks, of the Victorian working class (Wells's mother, a household servant, lived almost entirely underground).*

H. G. WELLS
The Time Machine

(1895)

Under the new conditions of perfect comfort and security, that restless energy, that with us is strength, would become weakness. Even in our own time certain tendencies and desires, once necessary to survival, are a constant source of failure. Physical courage and the love of battle, for instance, are no great help – may even be hindrances – to a civilized man. And in a state of physical balance and security, power, intellectual as well as physical, would be out of place. For countless years I judged there had been no danger of war or solitary violence, no danger from wild beasts, no wasting disease to require strength of constitution, no need of toil. For such a life, what we should call the weak are as well equipped as the strong, are indeed no longer weak. Better equipped indeed they are, for the strong would be fretted by an energy for which there was no outlet. No doubt the exquisite beauty of the buildings I saw was the outcome of the last surgings of the now purposeless energy of mankind before it settled down into perfect harmony with the conditions under which it lived – the flourish of that triumph which began the last great peace. This has ever been the fate of energy in security; it takes to art and to eroticism, and then come languor and decay.

. . .

'Well, one very hot morning – my fourth, I think – as I was seeking shelter from the heat and glare in a colossal ruin near the great house where I slept and fed, there happened this strange thing: Clambering among these heaps of masonry, I found a narrow gallery, whose end and side windows were blocked by fallen masses of stone. By contrast with the brilliancy outside, it seemed at first impenetrably dark to me. I entered it groping, for the change from light to blackness made spots of colour swim before me. Suddenly I halted spellbound. A pair of eyes, luminous by reflection against the daylight without, was watching me out of the darkness.

'The old instinctive dread of wild beasts came upon me. I clenched my hands and steadfastly looked into the glaring eyeballs. I was afraid to turn. Then the thought of the absolute security in which humanity appeared to be living came to my mind. And then I remembered that strange terror of the dark. Overcoming my fear to some extent, I advanced a step and spoke. I will admit that my voice was harsh and ill-controlled. I put out my hand and touched something soft. At once the eyes darted sideways, and something white ran past me. I turned with my heart in my mouth, and saw a queer little ape-like figure, its head held down in a peculiar manner, running across the sunlight space behind me. It blundered against a block of granite, staggered aside, and in a moment was hidden in a black shadow beneath another pile of ruined masonry.

'My impression of it is, of course, imperfect; but I know it was a dull white, and had strange large greyish-red eyes; also that there was flaxen hair on its head and down its back. But, as I say, it went too fast for me to see distinctly. I cannot even say whether it ran on all-fours, or only with its forearms held very low. After an instant's pause I followed it into the second heap of ruins. I could not find it at first; but, after a time in the profound obscurity, I came upon one of those round well-like openings of which I have told you, half closed by a fallen pillar. A sudden thought came to me. Could this Thing have vanished down the shaft? I lit a match, and, looking down, I saw a small, white, moving creature, with large bright eyes which regarded me steadfastly as it retreated. It made me shudder. It was so like a human spider! It was clambering down the wall, and now I saw for the first time a number of metal foot and hand rests forming a kind of ladder down the shaft. Then the light burned my fingers and fell out of my hand, going out as it dropped, and when I had lit another the little monster had disappeared.

'I do not know how long I sat peering down that well. It was not for some time that I could succeed in persuading myself that the thing I had seen was human. But, gradually, the truth dawned on me: that Man had not remained one species, but had differentiated into two distinct animals: that my graceful children of the Upper-world were not the sole descendants of our generation, but that this bleached, obscene, nocturnal Thing, which had flashed before me, was also heir to all the ages.

. . .

'Here was the new view. Plainly, this second species of Man was subterranean. There were three circumstances in particular which made me think that its rare emergence above ground was the outcome of a long-continued underground habit. In the first place, there was the bleached look common in most animals that live largely in the dark – the white fish of the Kentucky caves, for instance. Then, those large eyes, with that capacity for reflecting light, are common features of nocturnal things – witness the owl and the cat. And last of all, that evident confusion in the sunshine, that hasty yet fumbling and awkward flight towards dark shadow, and that peculiar carriage of the head while in the light – all reinforced the theory of an extreme sensitiveness of the retina.

'Beneath my feet, then, the earth must be tunnelled enormously, and these tunnellings were the habitat of the new race. The presence of ventilating shafts and wells along the hill slopes – everywhere, in fact, except along the river valley – showed how universal were its ramifications. What so natural, then, as to assume that it was in this artificial Under-world that such work as was necessary to the comfort of the daylight race was done? The notion was so plausible that I at once accepted it, and went on to assume the how of this splitting of the human species. I dare say you will anticipate the shape of my theory; though, for myself, I very soon felt that it fell far short of the truth.

'At first, proceeding from the problems of our own age, it seemed clear as daylight to me that the gradual widening of the present merely temporary and social difference between the Capitalist and the Labourer, was the key to the whole position. No doubt it will seem grotesque enough to you – and wildly incredible! – and yet even now there are existing circumstances to point that way. There is a tendency to utilize underground space for the less ornamental purposes of civilization; there is the Metropolitan Railway in London, for instance, there are new electric railways, there are subways, there are underground workrooms and restaurants, and they increase and multiply. Evidently, I thought, this tendency had increased till Industry had gradually lost its birthright in the sky. I mean that it had gone deeper and deeper into larger and ever larger underground factories, spending a still-increasing amount of its time therein, till, in the end –! Even now, does not an East-end worker live in such artificial conditions as practically to be cut off from the natural surface of the earth?

'Again, the exclusive tendency of richer people – due, no doubt, to the increasing refinement of their education, and the widening gulf between them and the rude violence of the poor – is already leading to the closing, in their interest, of considerable portions of the surface of the land. About London, for instance, perhaps half the prettier country is shut in against intrusion. And this same widening gulf – which is due to the length and expense of the higher educational process and the increased facilities for and temptations towards refined habits on the part of the rich – will make that exchange between class and class, that promotion by intermarriage which at present retards the splitting of our species along lines of social stratification, less and less frequent. So, in the end, above ground you must have the Haves, pursuing pleasure and comfort and beauty, and below ground the Have-nots, the Workers getting continually adapted to the conditions of their labour. Once they were there, they would no doubt have to pay rent, and not a little of it, for the ventilation of their caverns; and if they refused, they would starve or be suffocated for arrears. Such of them as were so constituted as to be miserable and rebellious would die; and, in the end, the balance being permanent, the survivors would become as well adapted to the conditions of underground life, and as happy in their way, as the Upper-world people were to theirs. As it seemed to me, the refined beauty and the etiolated pallor followed naturally enough.

'The great triumph of Humanity I had dreamed of took a different shape in my mind. It had been no such triumph of moral education and general co-operation as I had imagined. Instead, I saw a real aristocracy, armed with a perfected science and working to a logical conclusion the industrial system of today. Its triumph had not been simply a triumph over Nature, but a triumph over Nature and the fellow-man.'

Stevenson's parable also finds two separate species present within modern man, but his implication is that the one will never be free from the other.

ROBERT LOUIS STEVENSON
The Strange Case of Dr Jekyll and Mr Hyde
(1886)

With every day, and from both sides of my intelligence, the moral and the intellectual, I thus drew steadily nearer to that truth by whose partial discovery I have been doomed to such a dreadful shipwreck: that man is not truly one, but truly two. I say two, because the state of my own knowledge does not pass beyond that point. Others will follow, others will outstrip me on the same lines; and I hazard the guess that man will be ultimately known for a mere polity of multifarious, incongruous and independent denizens. I, for my part, from the nature of my life, advanced infallibly in one direction and in one direction only. It was on the moral side, and in my own person, that I learned to recognize the thorough and primitive duality of man; I saw that, of the two natures that contended in the field of my consciousness, even if I could rightly be said to be either, it was only because I was radically both; and from an early date, even before the course of my scientific discoveries had begun to suggest the most naked possibility of such a miracle, I had learned to dwell with pleasure, as a beloved daydream, on the thought of the separation of these elements. If each, I told myself, could but be housed in separate identities, life would be relieved of all that was unbearable; the unjust might go his way, delivered from the aspirations and remorse of his more upright twin; and the just could walk steadfastly and securely on his upward path, doing the good things in which he found his pleasure, and no longer exposed to disgrace and penitence by the hands of this extraneous evil. It was the curse of mankind that these incongruous faggots were thus bound together – that in the agonized womb of consciousness these polar twins should be continuously struggling.

It seemed to Henry Maudsley, one of England's foremost psychiatrists, that even the encouragement of the 'fit' would not be enough, as the human race had a stronger tendency to degenerate than to progress.

HENRY MAUDSLEY
Pathology of Mind

(1895)

A physician who had spent his life in ministering to diseased minds might be excused if, asking at the end of it whether he had spent his life well, he accused the fortune of an evil hour which threw him on that track of work. He could not well help feeling something of bitterness in the certitude that one-half the disease [*sic*] he had dealt with never could get well, and something of misgiving in the reflection whether he had done real service to his kind by restoring the other half to do reproductive work. Nor would the scientific interest of his studies compensate entirely for the practical uncertainties, since their revelation of the structure of human nature might inspire a doubt whether, notwithstanding impassioned aims, paeons of progress, endless pageants of self-illusions, its capacity of degeneration did not equal, and might some day exceed, its capacity of development. Fain, though in vain, would he question the Genius of the human race, mute and inscrutable, musing of the seeds of time and dreaming prophetically of things to come.

The ruling metaphor for evolution and degeneration was Darwin's
Malthusian principle of natural selection. Darwin himself was reluctant
to apply his theory to the human race but, in his last book, his account
of the role of worms in the formation of mould shows a sympathy with
the worm's eye view, and a respect for their industriousness.

CHARLES DARWIN
The Formation of Vegetable Mould
(1881)

THE PART WHICH WORMS HAVE PLAYED IN THE
BURIAL OF ANCIENT BUILDINGS

Archaeologists are probably not aware how much they owe
to worms for the preservation of many ancient objects. Coins, gold
ornaments, stone implements, etc., if dropped on the surface of the
ground, will infallibly be buried by the castings of worms in a few years,
and will thus be safely preserved, until the land at some future time is
turned up. For instance, many years ago a grass-field was ploughed on
the northern side of the Severn, not far from Shrewsbury; and a surprising
number of iron arrowheads were found at the bottom of the furrows,
which, as Mr Blakeway, a local antiquary, believed, were relics of the
battle of Shrewsbury in the year 1403, and no doubt had been originally
left strewed on the battlefield. In the present chapter I shall show that
not only implements, etc., are thus preserved, but that the floors and
the remains of many ancient buildings in England have been buried so
effectually, in large part through the action of worms, that they have
been discovered in recent times solely through various accidents. The
enormous beds of rubbish, several yards in thickness, which underlie
many cities, such as Rome, Paris and London, the lower ones being of
great antiquity, are not here referred to, as they have not been in any
way acted on by worms. When we consider how much matter is daily
brought into a great city for building, fuel, clothing and food, and that
in old times when the roads were bad and the work of the scavenger
was neglected, a comparatively small amount was carried away, we may
agree with Elie de Beaumont, who, in discussing this subject, says 'pour

une voiture de matériaux qui en sort, on y en fait entrer cent'.° Nor should we overlook the effects of fires, the demolition of old buildings, and the removal of rubbish to the nearest vacant space.

The cases given in this chapter show that worms have played a considerable part in the burial and concealment of several Roman and other old buildings in England; but no doubt the washing down of soil from the neighbouring higher lands, and the deposition of dust, have together aided largely in the work of concealment. Dust would be apt to accumulate wherever old broken-down walls projected a little above the then existing surface and thus afforded some shelter. The floors of the old rooms, halls and passages have generally sunk, partly from the settling of the ground, but chiefly from having been undermined by worms; and the sinking has commonly been greater in the middle than near the walls. The walls themselves, whenever their foundations do not lie at a great depth, have been penetrated and undermined by worms, and have consequently subsided. The unequal subsidence thus caused, probably explains the great cracks which may be seen in many ancient walls, as well as their inclination from the perpendicular.

° 'Leçons de Géologie pratique', 1845, p. 142.

'Man is but a worm' (Linley Sambourne, *Punch Almanack*, 1882): Darwin's work was satirized for its perceived implication that the 'civilization' of worms was in some ways more robust than our own. (Courtesy of Mary Evans Picture Library)

Informed by this Darwinian perspective, May Kendall playfully exam-ines mankind from the perspective of a trilobite.

MAY KENDALL
'Lay of the Trilobite'

(1887)

A mountain's giddy height I sought
  Because I could not find
Sufficient vague and mighty thought
  To fill my mighty mind;
And as I wandered ill at ease,
  There chanced upon my sight
A native of Silurian seas,
  An ancient Trilobite.

So calm, so peacefully he lay,
  I watched him even with tears:
I thought of Monads far away
  In the forgotten years.
How wonderful it seemed and right,
  The providential plan,
That he should be a Trilobite,
  And I should be a Man!

And then, quite natural and free
  Out of his rocky bed,
That Trilobite he spoke to me,
  And this is what he said:
'I don't know how the thing was done,
  Although I cannot doubt it;
But Huxley – he if anyone
  Can tell you all about it.

'How all your faiths are ghosts and dreams,
    How in the silent sea
Your ancestors were Monotremes
    Whatever these may be;
How you evolved your shining lights
    Of wisdom and perfection
From Jelly-fish and Trilobites
    By Natural Selection.

'You've Kant to make your brains go round,
    Hegel you have to clear them,
You've Mr Browning to confound,
    And Mr Punch to cheer them!
The native of an alien land
    You call a man and brother,
And greet with hymn-book in one hand
    And pistol in the other!

'You've Politics to make you fight
    As if you were possessed;
You've cannon and you've dynamite
    To give the nations rest:
The side that makes the loudest din
    Is surest to be right,
And oh, a pretty fix you're in!'
    Remarked the Trilobite,

'But gentle, stupid, free from woe
    I lived among my nation,
I didn't care – I didn't know
    That I was a Crustacean.°
I didn't grumble, didn't steal,
    I *never* took to rhyme:
Salt water was my frugal meal,
    And carbonate of lime.'

° He was not a Crustacean. He has since discovered that he was an Arachnid, or
something similar. But he says it does not matter. He says they told him wrong once,
and they may again.

Reluctantly I turned away,
   No other word he said;
An ancient Trilobite, he lay
   Within his rocky bed.
I did not answer him, for that
   Would have annoyed my pride:
I merely bowed, and raised my hat,
   But in my heart I cried: –

'I wish our brains were not so good,
   I wish our skulls were thicker,
I wish that Evolution could
   Have stopped a little quicker;
For oh, it was a happy plight,
   Of liberty and ease,
To be a simple Trilobite
   In the Silurian seas!'

*E. Ray Lankester, distinguished biologist and Darwinist, went further
in pointing out the degeneration of certain species in nature and implying
that the human race was in danger of reverting to a passive parasitism.*

E. RAY LANKESTER
Degeneration: A Chapter in Darwinism

(1880)

With regard to ourselves, the white races of Europe, the possibility of degeneration seems to be worth some consideration. In accordance with a tacit assumption of universal progress – an unreasoning optimism – we are accustomed to regard ourselves as necessarily progressing, as necessarily having arrived at a higher and more elaborated condition than that which our ancestors reached, and as destined to progress still further. On the other hand, it is well to remember that we are subject to the general laws of evolution, and are as likely to degenerate as to progress. As compared with the immediate forefathers of our civilization – the ancient Greeks – we do not appear to have improved so far as our bodily structure is concerned, nor assuredly so far as some of our mental capacities are concerned. Our powers of perceiving and expressing beauty of form have certainly *not* increased since the days of the Parthenon and Aphrodite of Melos. In matters of the reason, in the development of intellect, we may seriously enquire how the case stands. Does the reason of the average man of civilized Europe stand out clearly as an evidence of progress when compared with that of the men of bygone ages? Are all the inventions and figments of human superstition and folly, the self-inflicted torturing of mind, the reiterated substitution of wrong for right, and of falsehood for truth, which disfigure our modern civilization – are these evidences of progress? In such respects we have at least reason to fear that we may be degenerate. Possibly we are all drifting, tending to the condition of intellectual Barnacles or Ascidians. It is possible for us – just as the Ascidian throws away its tail and its eye and sinks into a quiescent state of inferiority – to reject the good gift of reason with which every child is born, and to degenerate into a contented life of material enjoyment accompanied by ignorance and superstition. The unprejudiced, all-questioning spirit of childhood may not inaptly be compared to the tadpole tail and eye of the young Ascidian: we have to fear lest the prejudices, preoccupations, and dogmatism of modern civilization should in any way lead to the atrophy and loss of the valuable mental qualities inherited by our young forms from primaeval man.

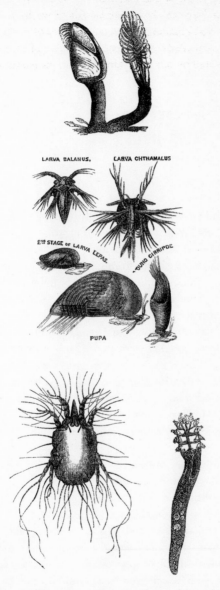

'Degenerate forms': illustrations from Lankester's *Degeneration*.

*The biological model was absorbed into the broader culture along
with its message that man, too, is subject to perverse and retrograde
development. Here, Sherlock Holmes uses it to explain how a man of
high social standing and impeccable reputation can still turn out to be
a master criminal.*

SIR ARTHUR CONAN DOYLE
'The Empty House'

(1905)

He turned over the pages lazily, leaning back in his chair and
blowing great clouds of smoke from his cigar.

'My collection of M's is a fine one,' said he. 'Moriarty himself is
enough to make any letter illustrious, and here is Morgan the poisoner,
and Merridew of abominable memory, and Mathews, who knocked out
my left canine in the waiting-room at Charing Cross, and, finally, here
is our friend of tonight.'

He handed over the book, and I read: '*Moran, Sebastian, Colonel.
Formerly 1st Bengalore Pioneers. Born London, 1840. Son of Sir Augus-
tus Moran, C.B., once British Minister to Persia. Educated Eton and
Oxford. Served in Jowaki Campaign, Afghan Campaign, Charasiab (dis-
patches), Sherpur, and Cabul. Author of Heavy Game of the Western
Himalayas, 1881; Three Months in the Jungle, 1884. Address: Conduit
Street. Clubs: The Anglo-Indian, the Tankerville, the Bagatelle Card
Club.*'

On the margin was written in Holmes' precise hand: 'The second
most dangerous man in London.'

'This is astonishing,' said I, as I handed back the volume. 'The man's
career is that of an honourable soldier.'

'It is true,' Holmes answered. 'Up to a certain point he did well. He
was always a man of iron nerve, and the story is still told in India how
he crawled down a drain after a wounded man-eating tiger. There are
some trees, Watson, which grow to a certain height and then suddenly
develop some unsightly eccentricity. You will see it often in humans. I
have a theory that the individual represents in his development the
whole procession of his ancestors, and that such a sudden turn to good

or evil stands for some strong influence which came into the line of his pedigree. The person becomes, as it were, the epitome of the history of his own family.'

The view that heredity was primarily responsible for degeneration was, like today's assertion that 'it's all in the genes', readily taken up by the popular press. This clipping, like several others in this volume, is from the private scrapbooks of the poet, pederast and sexologist George Ives, who collected newspaper stories of the bizarre, cruel and unusual from the 1890s to the 1930s.

HEREDITARY VICES.

The statistical essay on " Hereditary Alcoholism," which Professor Pellmann, of the University of Bonn, has contributed to the new number of *Prometheus*, contains some amazing tables of ancestry. Amongst the genealogical trees whose roots are drenched with intoxicating liquors, the most remarkable, perhaps, is that of the family of Jurke. A woman named Ada Jurke was born in 1740, and ended her drunken existence during the first decade of our century, when she was between sixty and seventy years old. She was a thief, tramp, and beggar for most of the time, and has left behind her a progeny of 834 persons, down to the present year, and the unpleasant biography of 709 out of her descendants has been authentically compiled from official records. The lives of the remaining 125 cannot be traced. Out of 709 hereditary Jurkes, 106 were born out of wedlock, 142 were beggars, 64 were chronic dependents upon alms; 181 of the women of this unprofitable family were prostitutes ; 76, including males and females, were condemned criminals, 7 of whom were executed for murder. Professor Pellmann has proved that this one single family, during the space of three-quarters of a century, has been far more expensive to the Commonwealth than many a princely and aristocratic family, since it has done nothing but suck up like a sponge, without any pretence of distribution. According to the Professor's sum total of costs of imprisonment, money spent upon the maintenance of the Jurkes, and a list of other payments made to them, or made on their account, the State has expended in seventy-five years about five million marks, or £250,000, upon the precious descendants of the drunken Ada Jurke. And this is but one, though confessedly the worst, amongst a host of documentarily established instances of the curse of " Erblicher Alkoholismus."

Here Prince Zaleski, M. P. Shiel's exotic detective in the mould of Sherlock Holmes, muses on the ways in which the degenerates in society are becoming not the exception but the rule.

M. P. SHIEL
Prince Zaleski

(1928)

Do you know that at this moment your hospitals are crammed with beings in human likeness suffering from a thousand obscure and subtly-ineradicable ills, all of whom, if left alone, would die almost at once, but ninety in the hundred of whom will, as it is, be sent forth 'cured', like missionaries of hell, and the horrent shapes of Night and Acheron, to mingle in the pure river of humanity the poison-taint of their protean vileness? Do you know that in your schools one-quarter of the children are already purblind? Have you gauged the importance of your tremendous consumption of quack catholicons, of the fortunes derived from their sale, of the spread of modern nervous disorders, of toothless youth and thrice loathsome age among the helot-classes? Do you know that in the course of my late journey to London, I walked from Piccadilly Circus to Hyde Park Corner, during which time I observed some five hundred people, of whom twenty-seven only were perfectly healthy, well-formed men, and eighteen healthy, beautiful women?

Similar anxieties were a cause of great concern for the psychiatric profession. Sir James Crichton-Browne was convinced that the current 'liberal' vogue for ambidexterity and left-handedness might signal a disastrous turn away from our civilized development.

SIR JAMES CRICHTON-BROWNE
'Dexterity and the Bend Sinister'

Proceedings at the meetings of the members of the Royal Institution of Great Britain (1907)

There are periodical outbreaks of ambidexterity, or rather, I should say, of feverish attempts to persuade us to adopt ambidexterity or to force it upon us. An innate love of symmetry, which Ruskin refers to as one of the essential constituents of beauty and a symbol of abstract justice, a correlative aversion to lop-sidedness which suggests abnormality, the hope of duplicating the special aptitudes to which the right hand has attained, and the ever-recurring craving for some new thing, have, from time to time during the last 2000 years, led to revolts against the existing state of matters and to efforts to establish what has been regarded as a better system of government in manual affairs.

Plato, I believe, included in his idealism the perfect equipoise of the two sides of the body; and, skipping the innumerable eruptions of ambidextral enthusiasm since his day, down to thirty years ago, I may remind you that at that time the late Mr Charles Reade again stirred up widespread interest in the subject by a series of articles entitled 'The Coming Man'. In those articles the brilliant novelist denounced dextral pre-eminence as wicked and against nature, the outcome of the foolish practices of credulous mothers, silly nurses and hidebound schoolmasters on our sacred bodies in defenceless childhood. He ridiculed biological science, especially as represented by my profession, and promised rich rewards to those who would diligently cultivate either-handedness. But somehow in his passionate philanthropy Mr Charles Reade overstepped the mark, rode roughshod over facts, and indulged in blatant exaggeration and transparent fallacies; and so his advocacy failed, his campaign proved abortive, and 'The Coming Man' did not come. For about a quarter of a century we were left undisturbed in the enjoyment of our lop-sidedness, but some five years ago ambidexterity again popped up, and a new crusade on its behalf is now being carried on under influential auspices. We have now an Ambidextral Culture Society; big books upon ambidexterity have been published, pamphlets and leaflets dealing with it are being circulated, schools are trying to attract pupils by advertising that they give ambidextral training, of course with unparalleled educational successes; and in the most renowned of all our schools the thin edge of the wedge has been introduced, for it has been ordained, we are told, that at Eton the boys who for their transgressions are called upon to write lines, are henceforth to do so with the left hand.

In this present movement in favour of ambidexterity I fancy I detect the old taint of faddism. Some of those who promote it are addicted to vegetarianism, hatlessness, or anti-vaccination, and other aberrant forms of belief; but it must be allowed that beyond that it has the support of a large number of highly educated, intelligent and reasonable people, and of some men of light and leading.

. . .

It is indisputable that right-handedness has been an attribute of his as far back as we have any knowledge of him, and has been one of the main means of lifting him out of darkness and barbarism into light and civilization. Whenever he ceased to be solitary and become gregarious, it became essential that in all co-operative work he should preferentially employ one fore-limb. 'Curious,' exclaims Carlyle, 'to consider the institution of the right hand among universal mankind, probably the very oldest institution that exists, indispensable to all human co-operation whatsoever; he that has seen three mowers, one of whom is left-handed, trying to work together, has witnessed the simplest form of an impossibility which but for the distinction of right hand would have pervaded all human things.'

And in this sentence of Carlyle lies really the quietus of ambidexterity, for if the habitual priority in the use of the right hand from a remote period has controlled industrial development, regulated all systems of associated manual activity, the form of tools, the construction of machinery, the organization of sports and games, and even of dress down to hooks and eyes, and buttons, it is obvious that the general adoption of ambidexterity, if that were practicable, would upset our whole social life, introduce hopeless confusion and multiply accidents of all kinds. And again: if all nations and tribes and races, civilized and savage, have in all time preferentially used the same hand, it is obvious that the origin of the custom cannot be looked for in any acquired habit that can be taken up or laid aside at pleasure. In what other custom, rite, convention, institution, has there been such world-wide consensus and uniformity? We can conceive that every tribe and community, finding the preferential use of one hand convenient and profitable, would adopt one hand and give it established precedence; but we cannot conceive that all tribes and communities should have adopted the same hand; and the fact that they have done so is an irrefragable proof that the source of right-handedness is much deeper than voluntary selection and must be sought in anatomical conformation. Had the selection of one hand as preferential been adopted by any tribe or community as a convention, it is certain that love of change, the spirit of opposition, caprice or pure cussedness would have set the convention at defiance and rendered the use of one hand as common as the use of the other.

And right-handedness is as prevalent today as it has ever been. We have no instance of any tribe, community or people that has grown out of it or broken away from it and found salvation in ambidexterity.

. . .

If human beings were synthesized in the laboratory of the chemist, we should have an equal number of persons with the heart on the right and on the left side; but as they are put together in the laboratory of nature, the left side has it by a gigantic majority.

After all asymmetry is all-embracing; it is a property of the globe we inhabit. Our world rotates on its axis, in one direction from west to east, and shows no ambi-rotary predilection; but that implies the possibility of another, not necessarily a better world rotating in the opposite direction.

I have skimmed the subject of right-handedness. There are a hundred aspects of it on which it has been impossible to touch. I have endeavoured to show that the propaganda of ambidexterity is not according to physiological knowledge, and that either-handedness is not the charter of the coming man.

We have been right-handed for a very long while, the foundation of that human characteristic having been laid down long before the first syllable of recorded time.

We have found our right-handedness very useful, civilization has largely depended on it and the world is full of the treasures it has piled up.

There is not a tittle of evidence that our right-handedness is growing upon us and that we are becoming more and more lop-sided. We are apparently just as right-handed as were the Greeks in their palmy days, neither more nor less; and, indeed, right-handedness seems to be a terminal form in evolution.

We cannot, I believe, get rid of our right-handedness, try how we may. To 'raze out the written troubles of the brain' is no easy matter; to delete its deeply engraven records is a task impossible. Ambidextral culture, useful enough in respect of some few special movements in some few specially employed persons, must on the large scale tend to confusion. Pushed towards that consummation which its ardent apostles tell us is so devoutly to be wished for, when the two hands will be able to write on two different subjects at the same time, it must involve the enormous enlargement of our already overgrown lunatic asylums. Right-handedness is woven in the brain; to change the pattern you must unravel its tissues. My own conviction is that, as regards right-handedness, our best policy is to let well alone and to stick to dexterity and the bend sinister.

'Faces of criminality': The Italian criminologist Cesare Lombroso spent many years on his ambitious project of analysing features of the human physiognomy in his attempt to set down scientific criteria which would distinguish the face of the hereditary criminal. (From *Archivo di psichiatria, antropologia criminale e scienza penale*, 1885.)

*The idea of 'atavism' or 'throwbacks' was commonly pressed into service
to explain the sudden appearance of degeneration. A recurrent theme
for the horror writer Arthur Machen was the existence of atavistic forms,
in this case the pre-Celtic 'little people' of the Welsh mountains.*

ARTHUR MACHEN
The Novel of the Black Seal

(1895)

THE STATEMENT OF WILLIAM GREGG, F.R.S. ETC.

It is many years since the first glimmer of the theory which is
now almost, if not quite, reduced to fact dawned on my mind. A
somewhat extensive course of miscellaneous and obsolete reading had
done a great deal to prepare the way, and, later, when I became
somewhat of a specialist, and immersed myself in the studies known as
ethnological, I was now and then startled by facts that would not square
with orthodox scientific opinion, and by discoveries that seemed to hint
at something still hidden for all our research. More particularly I became
convinced that much of the folklore of the world is but an exaggerated
account of events that really happened, and I was especially drawn to
consider the stories of the fairies, the good folk of the Celtic races.
Here, I thought I could detect the fringe of embroidery and exaggeration,
the fantastic guise, the little people dressed in green and gold sporting
in the flowers, and I thought I saw a distinct analogy between the name
given to this race (supposed to be imaginary) and the description of
their appearance and manners. Just as our remote ancestors called the
dreaded beings 'fair' and 'good' precisely because they dreaded them,
so they had dressed them up in charming forms, knowing the truth to
be the very reverse. Literature, too, had gone early to work, and had
lent a powerful hand in the transformation, so that the playful elves of
Shakespere are already far removed from the true original, and the real
horror is disguised in a form of prankish mischief. But in the older tales,
the stories that used to make men cross themselves as they sat around
the burning logs, we tread a different stage; I saw a widely opposed
spirit in certain histories of children and of men and women who

vanished strangely from the earth. They would be seen by a peasant in the fields walking towards some green and rounded hillock, and seen no more on earth; and there are stories of mothers who have left a child quietly sleeping, with the cottage door rudely barred with a piece of wood, and have returned, not to find the plump and rosy little Saxon, but a thin and wizened creature, with sallow skin and black, piercing eyes, the child of another race. Then, again, there were myths darker still; the dread of witch and wizard, the lurid evil of the Sabbath and the hint of demons who mingled with the daughters of men. And just as we have turned the terrible 'fair folk' into a company of benignant, if freakish elves, so we have hidden from us the black foulness of the witch and her companions under a popular *diablerie* of old women and broomsticks, and a comic cat with tail on end. So the Greeks called the hideous furies benevolent ladies, and thus the northern nations have followed their example. I pursued my investigations, stealing odd hours from other and more imperative labours, and I asked myself the question: Supposing these traditions to be true, who were the demons who are reported to have attended the Sabbaths? I need not say that I laid aside what I may call the supernatural hypothesis of the Middle Ages, and came to the conclusion that fairies and devils were of one and the same race and origin; invention, no doubt, and the Gothic fancy of old days, had done much in the way of exaggeration and distortion; yet I firmly believe that beneath all this imagery there was a black background of truth. As for some of the alleged wonders, I hesitated. While I should be very loath to receive any one specific instance of modern spiritualism as containing even a grain of the genuine, yet I was not wholly prepared to deny that human flesh may now and then, once perhaps in ten million cases, be the veil of powers which seem magical to us – powers which, so far from proceeding from the heights and leading men thither, are in reality survivals from the depths of being. The amoeba and the snail have powers which we do not possess; and I thought it possible that the theory of reversion might explain many things which seem wholly inexplicable.

. . .

Amongst other instances, I remember being struck by the phrase 'articulate-speaking men' in Homer, as if the writer knew or had heard of men whose speech was so rude that it could hardly be termed articulate; and on my hypothesis of a race who had lagged far behind the rest, I could easily conceive that such a folk would speak a jargon but little removed from the inarticulate noises of brute beasts.

. . .

I knew that I should find in Jervase Cradock something of the blood of the 'Little People', and I found later that he had more than once encountered his kinsmen in lonely places in that lonely land. When I was summoned one day to the garden, and found him in a seizure speaking or hissing the ghastly jargon of the Black Seal, I am afraid that exultation prevailed over pity. I heard bursting from his lips the secrets of the underworld, and the word of dread, 'Ishakshar', signification of which I must be excused from giving.

But there is one incident I cannot pass over unnoticed. In the waste hollow of the night I awoke at the sound of those hissing syllables I knew so well; and on going to the wretched boy's room, I found him convulsed and foaming at the mouth, struggling on the bed as if he strove to escape the grasp of writhing demons. I took him down to my room and lit the lamp, while he lay twisting on the floor, calling on the power within his flesh to leave him. I saw his body swell and become distended as a bladder, while the face blackened before my eyes; and then at the crisis I did what was necessary according to the directions on the Seal, and putting all scruple on one side, I became a man of science, observant of what was passing. Yet the sight I had to witness was horrible, almost beyond the power of human conception and the most fearful fantasy. Something pushed out from the body there on the floor, and stretched forth a slimy, wavering tentacle, across the room, grasped the bust upon the cupboard and laid it down on my desk.

When it was over, and I was left to walk up and down all the rest of the night, white and shuddering, with sweat pouring from my flesh, I vainly tried to reason within myself: I said, truly enough, that I had seen nothing really supernatural, that a snail pushing out his horns and drawing them in was but an instance on a smaller scale of what I had witnessed; and yet horror broke through all such reasonings and left me shattered and loathing myself for the share I had taken in the night's work.

*The Scottish psychiatrist Sir Thomas Clouston offered a pathological
description of the 'submerged tenth' of the population who he diagnosed
as degenerate.*

T. S. CLOUSTON
The Neuroses of Development

(1891)

The question of mental degeneracy, quite apart from idiocy or
technical imbecility or insanity, is one of enormous social importance.
For every idiot or insane person we no doubt have ten human beings
in society, and weighing it down, who are so much below or away from
even a minimum standard of humanity that they must be reckoned
among the degenerate. Such persons are the despair of teachers and
parents. They afterwards sink in the social scale through incapacity;
they are left stranded in nooks and corners and eddies in the struggle
for existence; they live at a lower level than average humanity; they
are not an interesting class; they need help always and cannot help
themselves; they easily are drifted over the borderline that separates
the criminal from the non-criminal; they fill poorhouses and are a heavy
burden on the charitably disposed, for they cannot be taught to help
themselves; they are only kept at work by their empty stomachs; they
are fortunately and fittingly situated when they settle down into the
grooves of hewing some of the world's wood and drawing its water; they
are the grown-up children of society who can never attain self-
government; they always do best under the rule of the strong and kindly;
they are responsible to the law and have the liberty of men with the
self-control of children, yet liberty in a complete sense is contraindicated
for them by the tyranny of their organization. It is this class that
unquestionably makes up a considerable part of General Booth's 'submerged tenth'. All of us can recall such men and women – families of
them. If we are scientific enough or curious enough to hunt out their
family histories we shall find the neuroses in abundance – idiocy,
deformity, epilepsy, insanity, criminality, 'ne'er-do-weelness', drinking,
unpracticability, odd religiousness and consumption. If we trace their
mental histories up from babyhood, we shall find that their most marked

deficiencies and peculiarities of body and mind were not very apparent till they got to the age of adolescence. I recall a family where the father is incurably insane and undersized, the mother undersized and not strong minded, all the children dwarfish, ill-formed, ill-favoured, one of them is little above an imbecile, two had attacks of adolescent insanity, one falling into incurable secondary dementia, one has infantile paralysis, and another had chorea; they live as pigs would live, in dirt and disorder; they are asocial but not vicious, except an almost automatic masturbation be counted a vice.

The German philosopher of history, Oswald Spengler, took a broader
perspective, seeing degeneration as part of the same inevitable cycle of
human history which led to the fall of Rome.

OSWALD SPENGLER
The Decline of the West

(1918–22)

Let it be realized, then:

That the secret of historical form does not lie on the surface, that it
cannot be grasped by means of similarities of costume and setting, and
that in the history of men as in that of animals and plants there occur
phenomena showing deceptive similarity but inwardly without any con-
nexion – e.g. Charlemagne and Haroun-al-Raschid, Alexander and
Caesar, the German wars upon Rome and the Mongol onslaughts upon
West Europe – and other phenomena of extreme outward dissimilarity
but of identical import – e.g. Trajan and Rameses II, the Bourbons and
the Attic Demos, Mohammed and Pythagoras.

That the 19th and 20th centuries, hitherto looked on as the highest
point of an ascending straight line of world-history, are in reality a stage
of life which may be observed in every Culture that has ripened to its
limit – a stage of life characterized not by Socialists, Impressionists,
electric railways, torpedoes and differential equations (for these are
only body-constituents of the time), but by a civilized spirituality which
possesses not only these but also quite other creative possibilities.

That, as our own time represents a transitional phase which occurs with
certainty under particular conditions, there are perfectly well-defined
states (such as have occurred more than once in the history of the past)
later than the present-day state of West Europe, and therefore that the
future of the West is not a limitless tending upwards and onwards for
all time towards our present ideals, but a single phenomenon of history,
strictly limited and defined as to form and duration, which covers a few
centuries and can be viewed and, in essentials, calculated from available
precedents.

In Britain, both positive and negative constructions of the direction of history were widely claimed. The distinguished naturalist Alfred Russel Wallace saw the nineteenth century as representing the greatest advance in human achievement since the Stone Age.

ALFRED RUSSEL WALLACE
The Wonderful Century: The Age of New Ideas in Science and Invention

(1898)

Looking back through the long dark vista of human history, the one step in material progress that seems to be really comparable in importance with several of the steps we have just made, was, when Fire was first utilized, and became the servant and the friend instead of being the master and the enemy of man. From that far-distant epoch even down to our day, fire, in various forms and in ever-widening spheres of action, has not only ministered to the necessities and the enjoyments of man, but has been the greatest, the essential factor, in that continuous increase of his power over nature, which has undoubtedly been a chief means of the development of his intellect and a necessary condition of what we term civilization. Without fire there would have been neither a Bronze nor an Iron Age, and without these there could have been no effective tools or weapons, with all the long succession of mechanical discoveries and refinements that depended upon them. Without fire, there could be no rudiment even of chemistry, and all that has arisen out of it. Without fire much of the earth's surface would be uninhabitable by man, and much of what is now wholesome food would be useless to him. Without fire he must always have remained ignorant of the larger part of the world of matter and of its mysterious forces. He might have lived in the warmer parts of the earth in a savage or even in a partially civilized condition, but he could never have risen to the full dignity of intellectual man, the interpreter and master of the laws and forces of nature.

Having thus briefly indicated our standpoint, let us proceed to sketch in outline those great advances in science and the arts which are the glory of our age. In the course of our survey we shall find, that the more important of these are not mere improvements upon, or developments of, anything that had been done before, but that they are entirely New Departures, arising out of our increasing knowledge of and command over the forces of the universe. Many of these advances have already led to developments of the most startling kind, giving us such marvellous powers, and such extensions of our normal senses, as would have been incredible, and almost unthinkable, even to our greatest men of science, a hundred years ago.

. . . while the critic and art historian John Ruskin felt that the latest stage of civilization had placed a 'storm-cloud' over nature which had rendered the appreciation of beauty a thing of the past.

JOHN RUSKIN
The Storm-Cloud of the Nineteenth Century

(lecture delivered in 1884)

So far as the existing evidence, I say, of former literature can be interpreted, the storm-cloud – or more accurately plague-cloud, for it is not always stormy – which I am about to describe to you, never was seen but by now living, or *lately* living eyes. It is not yet twenty years that this – I may well call it, wonderful – cloud has been, in its essence, recognizable. There is no description of it, so far as I have read, by any ancient observer.

. . .

'This wind is the plague-wind of the eighth decade of years in the nineteenth century; a period which will assuredly be recognized in future meteorological history as one of phenomena hitherto unrecorded in the courses of nature, and characterized pre-eminently by the almost ceaseless action of this calamitous wind. While I have been writing these sentences, the white clouds above specified have increased to twice the size they had when I began to write; and in about two hours from this time – say by eleven o'clock, if the wind continue, – the whole sky will be dark with them, as it was yesterday, and has been through prolonged periods during the last five years. I first noticed the definite character of this wind, and of the clouds it brings with it, in the year 1871, describing it then in the July number of *Fors Clavigera*; but little, at that time, apprehending either its universality, or any probability of its annual continuance. I am able now to state positively that its range of power extends from the North of England to Sicily; and that it blows more or less during the whole of the year, except the early autumn. This autumnal abdication is, I hope, beginning: it blew but feebly yesterday, though without intermission, from the north, making every

shady place cold, while the sun was burning; its effect on the sky being
only to dim the blue of it between masses of ragged cumulus. Today it
has entirely fallen; and there seems hope of bright weather, the first for
me since the end of May, when I had two fine days at Aylesbury; the
third, May 28th, being black again from morning to evening. There
seems to be some reference to the blackness caused by the prevalence
of this wind in the old French name of Bise, *"grey* wind"; and, indeed,
one of the darkest and bitterest days of it I ever saw was at Vevay in
1872.'

. . .

Of myself, however, if you care to hear it, I will tell you thus much: that
had the weather when I was young been such as it is now, no book such
as *Modern Painters* [1843] ever would or *could* have been written; for
every argument, and every sentiment in that book, was founded on the
personal experience of the beauty and blessing of nature, all spring and
summer long; and on the then demonstrable fact that over a great
portion of the world's surface the air and the earth were fitted to the
education of the spirit of man as closely as a schoolboy's primer is to
his labour, and as gloriously as a lover's mistress is to his eyes.

That harmony is now broken, and broken the world round: fragments,
indeed, of what existed still exist, and hours of what is past still return;
but month by month the darkness gains upon the day, and the ashes of
the Antipodes glare through the night.

Karl Pearson, professor at University College London, stressed the urgent need to recognize that the decline could only be averted by a systematic programme of population control and racial efficiency.

KARL PEARSON
National Life: From the Standpoint of Science

(1901)

From the standpoint of science there are two questions we can, or, rather, we *must*, ask. First: What, from the scientific standpoint, is the function of a nation? What part from the natural history aspect does the national organization play in the universal struggle for existence? And, secondly, What has science to tell us of the best methods of fitting the nation for its task?

To answer at all effectually the latter question, we must first consider what is the proper answer to be given to the former. I shall therefore endeavour to lay in broad outlines before you what I hold to be the scientific view of a nation, and of the relationship of nations to each other. If at the very offset my statements strike you as harsh, cold, possibly immoral, I would ask you to be patient with me to the end, when some of you may perceive that the public conscience, the moral goodness which you value so highly, is established by science on a firmer and more definite, if a narrower, foundation than you are wont to suppose.

. . .

If you bring the white man into contact with the black, you too often suspend the very process of natural selection on which the evolution of a higher type depends. You get superior and inferior races living on the same soil, and that coexistence is demoralizing for both. They naturally sink into the position of master and servant, if not admittedly or covertly into that of slave-owner and slave. Frequently they intercross, and if the bad stock be raised the good is lowered. Even in the case of Eurasians, of whom I have met mentally and physically fine specimens,

I have felt how much better they would have been had they been pure Asiatics or pure Europeans. Thus it comes about that when the struggle for existence between races is suspended, the solution of great problems may be unnaturally postponed; instead of the slow, stern processes of evolution, cataclysmal solutions are prepared for the future. Such problems in suspense, it appears to me, are to be found in the negro population of the Southern States of America, in the large admixture of Indian blood in some of the South American races, but, above all, in the Kaffir factor in South Africa.

. . .

The struggle means suffering, intense suffering, while it is in progress; but that struggle and that suffering have been the stages by which the white man has reached his present stage of development, and they account for the fact that he no longer lives in caves and feeds on roots and nuts. This dependence of progress on the survival of the fitter race, terribly black as it may seem to some of you, gives the struggle for existence its redeeming features; it is the fiery crucible out of which comes the finer metal. You may hope for a time when the sword shall be turned into the ploughshare, when American and German and English traders shall no longer compete in the markets of the world for their raw material and for their food supply, when the white man and the dark shall share the soil between them, and each till it as he lists. But, believe me, when that day comes mankind will no longer progress; there will be nothing to check the fertility of inferior stock; the relentless law of heredity will not be controlled and guided by natural selection. Man will stagnate; and unless he ceases to multiply, the catastrophe will come again; famine and pestilence, as we see them in the East, physical selection instead of the struggle of race against race, will do the work more relentlessly, and, to judge from India and China, far less efficiently than of old.

. . .

From the standpoint of the nation we want to inculcate a feeling of shame in the parents of a weakling, whether it be mentally or physically unfit. We want parents to grasp that they have given birth to a new *citizen*, and that this involves, on the one hand, a duty towards the community in respect of his breed and nurture, and a claim, on the other hand, of the parents on the State that the latter shall make the conditions of life favourable to the rearing of healthy, mentally vigorous men and women. Bear in mind that one quarter only of the married people of this country – say, a sixth to an eighth of the adult population – produce 50 per cent of the next generation. You will then see how essential it is for the maintenance of a physically and mentally fit race that this one-sixth to one-eighth of our population should be drawn from the best and not the worst stocks. A nation that begins to tamper with its fertility may unconsciously have changed its national character-istics before two generations have passed.

. . .

The national spirit is not a thing to be ashamed of, as the educated man seems occasionally to hold. If that spirit be the mere excrescence of the music-hall, or an ignorant assertion of superiority to the foreigner, it may be ridiculous, it may even be nationally dangerous; but if the national spirit takes the form of a strong feeling of the importance of organizing the nation as a whole, of making its social and economic conditions such that it is able to do its work in the world and meet its fellows without hesitation in the field and in the market, then it seems to me a wholly good spirit – indeed, one of the highest forms of social, that is, moral instinct.

So far from our having too much of this spirit of patriotism, I doubt if we have anything like enough of it. We wait to improve the condition of some class of workers until they themselves cry out or even rebel against their economic condition. We do not better their state because we perceive its relation to the strength and stability of the nation as a whole. Too often it is done as the outcome of a blind class war. The coal-owners, the miners, the manufacturers, the mill-hands, the land-lords, the farmers, the agricultural labourers, struggle by fair means, and occasionally by foul, against each other, and, in doing so, against the nation at large, and our statesmen as a rule look on. That was the correct attitude from the standpoint of the old political economy. It is not the correct attitude from the standpoint of science; for science realizes that the nation is an organized whole, in continual struggle with its competitors. You cannot get a strong and effective nation if many of its stomachs are half fed and many of its brains untrained. We, as a nation, cannot survive in the struggle for existence if we allow class distinctions to permanently endow the brainless and to push them into posts of national responsibility. The true statesman has to limit the internal struggle of the community in order to make it stronger for the external struggle.

. . .

The origin of the world and the purport of life are mysteries alike to the poet, the theologian and the man of science. One who has stood somewhat as the mediator between the three admitted the mystery, saw the cruelty of natural processes when judged from the relative standpoint of man, but found therein an undefinable 'tendency towards righteousness'. If by righteousness he meant wider human sympathies, intenser social instincts, keener pity and clearer principles of conduct, then I believe that tendency, that continual progress of mankind, is the scarcely recognized outcome of the bitter struggle of race with race, the result of man, like all other life, being subject to the stern law of the survival of the fitter, to the victory of the physically and mentally better organized. Mankind as a whole, like the individual man, advances through pain and suffering only. The path of progress is strewn with the wreck of nations; traces are everywhere to be seen of the hecatombs of inferior races, and of victims who found not the narrow way to the greater perfection. Yet these dead peoples are, in very truth, the stepping-stones on which mankind has arisen to the higher intellectual and deeper emotional life of today.

KARL PEARSON
The Scope and Importance to the State of the Science of National Eugenics

(1907)

Now may we not claim Plato as a precursor of the modern Eugenics movement? He grasped the intensity of inheritance, for he appeals to the herd and the flock; he realized the danger to the state of a growing band of degenerates, and he called upon the legislator to purify the state. Plato's purgation, if you will accept the view I have endeavoured to lay before you today, has in fact hitherto been carried out by natural selection, by the struggle of man against man, of man against nature and of state against state. This very cosmical process has so developed our ethical feelings, that we find it difficult to regard the process as benign. A hundred years ago we still hung the greater proportion of our criminals or sent them for life across the seas, not even euphemistically terming it a 'colony'. We shut up our insane, making no attempt at cure; the modern system of hospitals and institutions and charities was scarcely developed; the physically and mentally weak had small chance of surviving and bearing offspring. There was a constant stern selection purifying in Plato's sense the state. The growth of human sympathy – and is not this one of the chief factors of national fitness? – has been so rapid during the century that it has cried Halt! to almost every form of racial purification. Is not this the real opposition which Huxley noticed between the ethical and cosmic processes? One factor – absolutely needful for race survival – sympathy, has been developed in such an exaggerated form that we are in danger, by suspending selection, of lessening the effect of those other factors which automatically purge the state of the degenerates in body and mind.

Do I therefore call for less human sympathy, for more limited charity, and for sterner treatment of the weak? Not for a moment; we cannot go backwards a single step in the evolution of human feeling! But I demand that all sympathy and charity shall be organized and guided into paths where they will promote racial efficiency, and not lead us straight towards national shipwreck. The time is coming when we must consciously carry out that purification of the state and race which has hitherto been the work of the unconscious cosmic process. The higher patriotism and the pride of race must come to our aid in stemming deterioration; the science of Eugenics has not only to furnish Plato's legislator with the facts upon which he can take action, but it has to educate public opinion until without a despotism he may attempt even the mildest purgation. To produce a nation healthy alike in mind and body must become a fixed idea – one of almost religious intensity, as Francis Galton has expressed it – in the minds of the intellectual oligarchy, which after all sways the masses and their political leaders.

H. G. Wells, also using the language of Darwinism, made the case that
Pearson's objectives could be more humanely achieved by a liberal
emphasis on education.

H. G. WELLS
'Human Evolution, An Artificial Process'

(*Fortnightly Review*, 1896)

In civilized man we have (1) an inherited factor, the natural
man, who is the product of natural selection, the culminating ape, and
a type of animal more obstinately unchangeable than any other living
creature; and (2) an acquired factor, the artificial man, the highly plastic
creature of tradition, suggestion and reasoned thought. In the artificial
man we have all that makes the comforts and securities of civilization
a possibility. That factor and civilization have developed, and will develop
together. And in this view, what we call Morality becomes the padding
of suggested emotional habits necessary to keep the round Palaeolithic
savage in the square hole of the civilized state. And Sin is the conflict
of the two factors – as I have tried to convey in my *Island of Dr Moreau.*

If this new view is acceptable it provides a novel definition of Education, which obviously should be the careful and systematic manufacture of the artificial factor in man.

The artificial factor in man is made and modified by two chief
influences. The greatest of these is *suggestion*, and particularly the
suggestion of example. With this tradition is inseparably interwoven.
The second is his reasoned conclusions from additions to his individual
knowledge, either through instruction or experience. The artificial factor
in a man, therefore, may evidently be deliberately affected by a sufficiently intelligent exterior agent in a number of ways: by example
deliberately set; by the fictitious example of the stage and novel; by
sound or unsound presentations of facts, or sound or fallacious arguments
derived from facts, even, it may be, by emotionally propounded precepts.
The artificial factor of mankind – and that is the one reality of civilization
– grows, therefore, through the agency of eccentric and innovating
people, playwrights, novelists, preachers, poets, journalists, and political
reasoners and speakers, the modern equivalents of the prophets who

struggled against the priests – against the social order that is of the barbaric stage. And though from the wider view our most capricious acts are predestinate, yet, at any rate, these developmental influences are exercised as deliberately, are as much a matter of design and choice, as any human act can be. In other words, in a rude and undisciplined way indeed, in an amorphous chaotic way we might say, humanity is even now consciously steering itself against the currents and winds of the universe in which it finds itself. In the future, it is at least conceivable, that men with a trained reason and a sounder science, both of matter and psychology, may conduct this operation far more intelligently, unanimously and effectively, and work towards, and at last attain and preserve, a social organization so cunningly balanced against exterior necessities on the one hand, and the artificial factor in the individual on the other, that the life of every human being, and, indeed, through man, of every sentient creature on earth, may be generally happy. To me, at least, that is no dream, but a possibility to be lost or won by men, as they may have or may not have the greatness of heart to consciously shape their moral conceptions and their lives to such an end.

This view, in fact, reconciles a scientific faith in evolution with optimism. The attainment of an unstable and transitory perfection only through innumerable generations of suffering and 'elimination' is not necessarily the destiny of humanity. If what is here advanced is true, in Education lies the possible salvation of mankind from misery and sin . . . We need not clamour for the Systematic Massacre of the Unfit, nor fear that degeneration is the inevitable consequence of security.

Like Spengler, 'Darwin's bulldog' T. H. Huxley felt that a collapse on the order of the Fall of Rome was imminent, but he blamed it not on progress but on the lack of it – the persistence of irrationalism.

T. H. HUXLEY
'Mr Balfour's Attack on Agnosticism'

Nineteenth Century (1895)

In the second century of the existence of Imperial Rome, anyone interested in the future of that vast and ancient society would have done well to take careful note of certain movements of thought and drifts of opinion which, however overlooked, perhaps despised, by the mere administrator, bent on the maintenance of civil order, or by the mere politician, thirsting for a profitable proconsulship, might loom larger than patrician conspiracies, or the massing of barbarians on the frontier, to a statesman.

Generation after generation of hard-headed, hard-fisted, eminently practical Quirites had held together; and, by courage, intelligence, industry, frugality, force, fraud – whichever came handiest – had raised an aggregation of obscure hamlets on and about the Palatine hill by the Tiber, into the sovereign city of the largest and, in spite of all shortcomings, the best-organized, realm the world had ever known. It had been of immense service to these singular Romans that they held a common faith, which inspired them with both piety and enthusiasm. And though the piety was not incompatible with calculation, and the enthusiasm generally had an eye to business, these qualities were none the less efficient. Their *religio* really bound the individual lives into a common life, and subordinated personal interests to those of the community.

But, in the second century, this theory of the nature of the things and of the human obligations consequent upon it, was far advanced in a process of decay. It had long been difficult for reasonably honest people even to pretend to believe in the mythological fables held sacred by their forefathers; and, for a considerable time, the Augurs had been suspected of smiling, perhaps of winking, at one another during the performance of their sacred office. There was much refined depravity among the upper classes, much ignorance, suffering and sheer brutality among the lower; though it is greatly to be doubted if the Rome of Hadrian was one whit worse than the Paris of Louis the Fifteenth, the London of George the Second or the Petersburg of Catherine the Second; to say nothing of the Papal Rome of thirteen centuries later.

As confidence in the old, and somewhat cold, national religion had waned, foreign, chiefly Oriental, superstitions of a more emotional cast had found wide acceptance. From mystic, quasi-philosophical theosophies to the vulgarest corybantic revivalisms, there were creeds to suit every taste, and missionaries and ministers thereof to draw upon every believer's purse. Thiasoi and sodalities of Isis, of Mithra, of Serapis; Israelite synagogues, each with its gentile zone of half-proselyte 'fearers of God'; Christian ecclesiae, Catholic, Schismatic, Gnostic; answered to the motley variety of churches and chapels with which we Britons have been said to compensate ourselves for the uniformitarianism of our cooks. Beside all these, more or less (too often less!) serious and respectable embodiments of the religious spirit, swarmed a wretched brood, full of superstitious and magical practices, many of them honest survivals of savagery; but many more gross and criminal impostures, analogous to so much of modern spirit-rapping and table-turning. Flourishing prototypes of our Cagliostros and Blavatskys abounded; while for these wolves and foxes, innumerable sheep and geese had been prepared by the over-civilization which, then as now, sapped manhood and debased and distorted womanhood.

2
Pandora's Box: Science

The main catalyst for the crisis of civilization was the advancement of science. The fin-de-siècle witnessed an incredible and relentlessly accelerating proliferation of invention. The era saw transport revolutionized by everything from the bicycle to the tram, the motor car to the Zeppelin. Electrification of the cities of Europe and America began in the 1890s, and around the same time the telephone, telegram and wireless radio opened up the world of electrical communication. Predictions for the further advancement of science in the next century offered marvel upon marvel.

This piece is typical of the optimistic view of the new century which was being offered by the propagandists of science – though exceptional in its remarkably specific prediction of the mobile phone.

W. J. WINTLE
'Life in Our New Century: The Most Striking of New Inventions'

Harmsworth's Magazine (1901)

In this age of progress no one will dispute that the twentieth century, on which we have now entered, will see marvellous advances and improvements on every hand.

To try to peep into the future is the work of the seer or the prophet, and we make no claim to be either the one or the other. But there are certain tendencies of modern progress and discovery which will become translated into actual facts within a very few years, and it needs no prophet to forecast what these will be.

In the present article we shall indulge in no imaginative speculation, but shall restrict ourselves to the task of recording various wonders that have already been accomplished in the laboratory, and that only await further development and testing to be introduced to the world.

The man of the twentieth century will no longer confine his travels to land and sea – he will navigate the air as well. It is beyond question that the flying-machine will soon become a practical reality.

. . .

There can be little doubt that the successful flying-machine will be constructed on the principle of the flying bird. After all, nature has shown us how to fly, and it only remains for us to copy her methods. Our artist has drawn a machine on these lines, the louvres in the wings being designed to act in much the same way as the large feathers of a bird. We present this idea gratis to the capitalist in search of some pleasant way of getting rid of a little superfluous cash!

On land, also, the twentieth century will see great advances in the way of locomotion. It is now an established fact that a suitably designed electric car can be safely run at a speed of 120 miles an hour on the monorail system, and such a line will shortly be constructed in England. At present it does not appear possible to go any faster than this with safety, but, no doubt, greater things will be achieved in the future.

The motor car is already a familiar sight, and there can be no question that, before the century is far advanced, automobiles will be the usual, rather than the exceptional, vehicles seen in our streets. But there is no reason to suppose that they will altogether supersede the horse, nor is that useful quadruped likely to be relegated to a paddock in the Zoological Gardens.

The ocean greyhound of the present day will be quite eclipsed by the rapid ships of the future. The latest step in advance is seen in the adoption of the turbine propeller for steamship purposes. Quite a sensation has been caused in nautical circles by the performances of H.M.S. *Viper*, which travels at the rate of forty-three miles an hour. This extraordinary speed has been obtained by fitting her with steam turbines.

Up to the present no passenger ship has been fitted on this principle, but such an ocean liner has been designed, and it is contemplated to fit some of the future Channel packets with turbines.

There seems to be no reason why in ten years' time we should not be crossing the Atlantic at a pace of forty miles an hour, or even more.

The new method not only vastly increases the speed but reduces the size and weight of the engines, practically annihilates vibration and economizes fuel.

The last point is one of vital importance, for the fastest liners of the present day carry 2500 tons of coal for a trip across the Atlantic. A greater speed would mean more coal, and this would increase the size of the vessel to an impracticable extent. Probably the twentieth century will see liquid air used in marine engines instead of steam, and then this difficulty will be overcome.

We have already indicated electricity as the great power of the future, and it is from this source that the greatest wonders may be expected. The discovery of the Hertzian waves – which are really a kind of invisible light – and the transmission of telegraphic messages without wires have marked an enormous stride in advance.

Mr A. Rosenberg, one of the most brilliant electricians of the day, has invented a system of pocket telegraphy, by means of which a man may carry his own apparatus in his pocket and receive messages even from people who do not know where he is.

The inventor takes his small receiver with him when he goes out to lunch, and places it beside him on the restaurant table. If his clerks need him they simply depress a key connected with the transmitter in the office, and the bell of the receiver in the restaurant at once rings.

. . .

Will the world be better and happier in the new century? To us it seems that the answer should be unquestionably in the affirmative. Scientific progress tends to moral advancement.

A moment's reflection will show that aerial navigation, rapid transit, the electroscope and other inventions that we have named, will all tend to make crime and war more difficult, while improved social conditions will make them less attractive.

The facts we have stated in this article are but a few of the many that might be adduced in evidence of the immense progress in all directions which the new century will witness.

During the 1890s, the eccentric electrical genius Nikola Tesla had given the world alternating current, robotics, teleautomation and the high-voltage Tesla coil; in this profile, he offers a remarkable series of demonstrations, followed by predictions which range from the prescient to the fantastic:

CHAUNCEY MONTGOMERY McGOVERN
'The New Wizard of the West'

Pearson's Magazine (1899)

*A*n *Interview with Tesla, the Modern Miracle-worker, who is Harnessing the Rays of the Sun; has Discovered Ways of Transmitting Power without Wires and of Seeing by Telephone; has Invented a Means of Employing Electricity as a Fertilizer; and, Finally, is Able to Manufacture Artificial Daylight.*

Not to stagger on being shown through the laboratory of Nikola Tesla requires the possession of an uncommonly sturdy mind. No person can escape a feeling of giddiness when permitted to pass into this miracle-factory and contemplate for a moment the amazing feats which this young man can accomplish by the mere turning of a hand.

Fancy yourself seated in a large, well-lighted room, with mountains of curious-looking machinery on all sides. A tall, thin young man walks up to you, and by merely snapping his fingers creates instantaneously a ball of leaping red flame, and holds it calmly in his hands. As you gaze you are surprised to see it does not burn his fingers. He lets it fall upon his clothing, on his hair, into your lap and, finally, puts the ball of flame into a wooden box. You are amazed to see that nowhere does the flame leave the slightest trace, and you rub your eyes to make sure you are not asleep.

The odd flame having been extinguished as miraculously as it appeared, the tall, thin young man next signals to his assistants to close up all the windows. When this has been done the room is as dark as a cave. A moment later you hear the young man say in the laboured accentuation of the foreigner: 'Now, my friends, I will make for you some daylight.' Quick as a flash the whole laboratory is filled with a strange light as beautiful as that of the moon, but as strong as that of old Sol. As you glance up at the closed shutters on each window, you see that each of them is as tight as a vice, and that no rays are coming through them. Cast your eyes wherever you will you can see no trace of the source of the odd light.

Scarcely have you begun to marvel when the light goes out by a touch on a button by the young man's hand. The room is in darkness again until the same laboured accentuation causes the reopening of all the shutters. Some animal is now brought out from a cage, it is tied to a platform, an electric current is applied to its body and in a second the animal is dead. The tall young man calls your attention to the fact that the indicator registers only one thousand volts, and the dead animal being removed, he jumps upon the platform himself, and his assistants apply the same current to the dismay of the spectators.

You feel a creeping sensation course up your back, and you see the indicator slowly mounting up to nine hundred, and then one thousand volts, and you involuntarily close your eyes, expecting the young man to fall dead before you the very next minute. But he does not budge. Quickly the indicator goes up, up, up, until presently it shows that ten thousand volts of electricity are pouring through the frame of the tall young man, who does not move a muscle.

At a sign, the current is stopped, the room is again made dark as night, and presently the visitor sees the sharply-defined black silhouette of the young man, with a beautiful halo of electricity in the background, formed by myriads of tongues of electric flame which are darting out from every quarter of the tall, thin frame. The place is lighted once more, and as the young man comes up to you and shakes your hand, you twist it about in the same fashion as you have seen people do who hold the handles of a strong electric battery. The young man is literally a human electric 'live wire'.

To tell of these and a thousand other wonders that Tesla does in a trice gives only a faint conception of their effect on the visitor. To really appreciate them one must see, hear and feel them in the flesh. It is a scientific treat of a lifetime, but it is a treat that few can enjoy, for the laboratory of Tesla is securely locked against everyone not provided with an introduction from a personal friend of the audacious wizard.

'Oh pshaw! these are only a few playthings,' Nikola Tesla replies when the visitor puts into words the astonishment he has experienced: 'none of these amount to anything – they are of no value to the great world of science. But come over here and I will show you something that will make a big revolution in every business and home as soon as I am able to get the thing into working form,' and then he leads the way through a forest of queer-looking discs and mysterious coils of copper and steel, until the party reaches a raised wall of masonry, on which reposes a long cylinder of glass filled with water, and surrounded by a circle of large mirrors. The roof over this apparatus is of glass, and as the sun pours its rays through this, the rays strike the mirrors and are reflected again towards the glass cylinder, magnifying glasses intensifying the heat of the rays before they strike the cylinder.

'This is the experimental model of the apparatus with which I hope some day to so harness the rays of the sun that that heavenly body will operate every machine in our factories, propel every train and carriage in our streets, and do all the cooking in our homes, as well as furnish all the light that man may need by night as well as by day. It will, in short, replace all wood and coal as a producer of motive power and heat and electric lighting.'

The plan of Nikola Tesla to harness the rays of the sun to do man's bidding is probably the boldest engineering feat that he or anyone else has ever attempted. Though the idea is so great, its principle is so simple that a schoolboy can readily comprehend it. It consists of concentrating the heat of the sun on one spot (the glass cylinder) by the series of complicated mirrors and magnifying glasses until the resulting heat is something terrific.

. . .

It is, of course, not the intention of Mr Tesla that one sun-station will provide all the electricity for the whole world. His scheme is that in every city and town the local authorities shall build one or more of these sun-stations by public taxation for the use of the whole population, just as these cities now have waterworks and gas plants. Each factory and home will then get its supply of electricity from the nearest sun-station by ordinary electric wires.

. . .

Not the least ingenious of Tesla's great schemes is his invention to fertilize impoverished land by electricity. When Tesla has a company formed to put this invention on the market it will no longer be necessary for the farmer to spend half his year's receipts in purchasing fertilizers. He has only to buy an electric fertilizer of his own, which he can secure for a trifle at the nearest town.

Dumping a few loads of loose earth into the fertilizer, it comes out at the other end ready to be spread over the surface of the impoverished ground, where it will ensure for the following season the luxurious crop of the virgin soil.

. . .

Nikola Tesla is a young man yet, and on this account many of his promises have been looked upon by older scientists as but fanciful dreams of a youthful mind. He has scarcely ever made any invention which the scientific world has accepted as possible on the first public announcement. But sooner or later the scientific wiseacres have been compelled to admit that Tesla has proven their theories to be wrong.

How these conservative scientists sneered at Tesla's 'Utopian audacity' when he first suggested that man should harness the great Niagara Falls! But they humbled their pride sufficiently to be present when the enterprise was formally completed. Again, when he announced the invention of the 'Tesla coil' they set him down as 'pipe-dreamer'. But a few of the brightest of them set to work seriously on the 'coil', with the result that one of them – Röntgen – discovered his famous X-Rays.

No one who is privileged to know Tesla personally, to have heard him explain his plans, and to have been shown through his unique workshop, has the slightest doubt that every one of his promises will be fulfilled in an equally successful way.

There were, of course, dissenting voices, such as the inhabitants of the
French village of Saint-Etienne des Gres, who in 1903 refused en masse
to have the telephone connected. (From Ives scrapbook.)

Star 6THE DEVILPHONE. aug, 03.

It has been found impossible to establish
the telephone at Saint-Etienne des Gres, in
the Tarascon district, says the Paris correspondent of the "Telegraph."

Under the odd impression that the invention was the work of the Evil One,
the inhabitants determined to oppose its
entry and resolved to arm themselves with
their agricultural implements and to make
a fight for it.

The carter conveying the apparatus thereupon said he would not risk his life in the
adventure and the cart has been left at
Tarascon.

Oliver Wendell Holmes's poem both captured and reinforced the popular association of electricity with the forces of witchcraft and devilry, partly by suggesting male technological control over female primitivism.

OLIVER WENDELL HOLMES
'The Broomstick Train, or The Return of the Witches'

Atlantic Magazine (1890)

They came, of course, at their master's call,
The witches, the broomsticks, the cats and all;
He led the hags to a railway train
The horses were trying to drag in vain.
'Now, then,' says he, 'you've had your fun.
And here are the cars you've got to run.
The driver may just unhitch his team.
We don't want horses, we don't want steam;
You may keep your old black cats to hug.
But the loaded train you've got to lug.'
Since then on many a car you'll see
A broomstick plain as plain can be;
On every stick there's a witch astride –
The string you see to her leg is tied.
She will do a mischief if she can,
But the string is held by a careful man,
And whenever the evil-minded witch
Would cut some caper, he gives a twitch.
As for the hag, you can't see her.
But hark! You can hear the black cat's purr,
And now and then, as a car goes by,
You may catch a gleam from her wicked eye.
Often you've looked on a rushing train,
But just what moved it was not so plain.
It couldn't be those wires above,
For they could neither pull nor shove;
Where was the motor that made it go?
You couldn't guess. BUT NOW YOU KNOW.

. . . and a young Robert Louis Stevenson lamented the transition from the homely gas lamp to the harsh new electric lighting of the cities.

ROBERT LOUIS STEVENSON
'A Plea for Gas Lamps'

(1881)

When gas first spread along a city, mapping it forth about evenfall for the eye of observant birds, a new age had begun for sociality and corporate pleasure-seeking, and begun with proper circumstance, becoming its own birthright. The work of Prometheus had advanced by another stride. Mankind and its supper parties were no longer at the mercy of a few miles of sea-fog; sundown no longer emptied the promenade; and the day was lengthened out to every man's fancy. The city-folk had stars of their own; biddable, domesticated stars.

It is true that these were not so steady, nor yet so clear, as their originals; nor indeed was their lustre so elegant as that of the best wax candles. But then the gas stars, being nearer at hand, were more practically efficacious than Jupiter himself. It is true, again, that they did not unfold their rays with the appropriate spontaneity of the planets, coming out along the firmament one after another, as the need arises. But the lamplighters took to their heels every evening, and ran with a good heart. It was pretty to see man thus emulating the punctuality of heaven's orbs; and though perfection was not absolutely reached, and now and then an individual may have been knocked on the head by the ladder of the flying functionary, yet people commended his zeal in a proverb, and taught their children to say, 'God bless the lamplighter!' And since his passage was a piece of the day's programme, the children were well pleased to repeat the benediction, not, of course, in so many words, which would have been improper, but in some chaste circumlocution, suitable for infant lips.

God bless him, indeed! For the term of his twilight diligence is near at hand; and for not much longer shall we watch him speeding up the street and, at measured intervals, knocking another luminous hole into the dusk. The Greeks would have made a noble myth of such a one; how he distributed starlight, and, as soon as the need was over, recollected it; and the little bull's-eye, which was his instrument, and held enough fire to kindle a whole parish, would have been fitly commemorated in the legend. Now, like all heroic tasks, his labours draw towards apotheosis, and in the light of victory himself shall disappear. For another advance has been effected. Our tame stars are to come out in future, not one by one, but all in a body and at once. A sedate electrician somewhere in a back office touches a spring – and behold! from one end to another of the city, from east to west, from the Alexandra to the Crystal Palace, there is light! *Fiat Lux*, says the sedate electrician. What a spectacle, on some clear, dark nightfall, from the edge of Hampstead Hill, when in a moment, in the twinkling of an eye, the design of the monstrous city flashes into vision – a glittering hieroglyph many square miles in extent; and when, to borrow and debase an image, all the evening street-lamps burst together into song! Such is the spectacle of the future, preluded the other day by the experiment in Pall Mall. Star-rise by electricity, the most romantic flight of civilization; the compensatory benefit for an innumerable array of factories and bankers' clerks. To the artistic spirit exercised about Thirlmere, here is a crumb of consolation; consolatory, at least, to such of them as look out upon the world through seeing eyes, and contentedly accept beauty where it comes.

But the conservative, while lauding progress, is ever timid of innovation; his is the hand upheld to counsel pause; his is the signal advising slow advance. The word *electricity* now sounds the note of danger. In Paris, at the mouth of the Passage des Princes, in the place before the Opera portico, and in the Rue Drouot at the *Figaro* office, a new sort of urban star now shines out nightly, horrible, unearthly, obnoxious to the human eye; a lamp for a nightmare! Such a light as this should shine only on murders and public crime, or along the corridors of lunatic asylums, a horror to heighten horror. To look at it only once is to fall in love with gas, which gives a warm domestic radiance fit to eat by. Mankind, you would have thought, might have remained content with what Prometheus stole for them and not gone fishing the profound heaven with kites to catch and domesticate the wildfire of the storm. Yet here we have the levin brand at our doors, and it is proposed that we should henceforward take our walks abroad in the glare of permanent lightning. A man need not be very superstitious if he scruple to follow his pleasures by the light of the Terror that Flieth, nor very epicurean if he prefer to see the face of beauty more becomingly displayed. That ugly blinding glare may not improperly advertise the home of slanderous *Figaro*, which is a back-shop to the infernal regions; but where soft joys prevail, where people are convoked to pleasure and the philosopher looks on smiling and silent, where love and laughter and deifying wine abound, there, at least, let the old mild lustre shine upon the ways of man.

But alongside the triumphalism, the physical and mathematical sciences were delivering another message. Mankind's place in the universe was becoming ever smaller, more peripheral and more precarious. Lord Kelvin's calculations showed that the heat death of the sun would occur far sooner than previously imagined. This stark prediction – only revised by the discovery of radioactivity, and the nature of the sun's nuclear reaction, in the 1910s – cast a long shadow over the newly evolved idea of a triumphant future.

WILLIAM THOMSON, FIRST BARON KELVIN
'On the Dissipation of Energy'

(1892)

Within a finite period of time the earth must have been, and within a finite period of time must again be, unfit for the habitation of man as at present constituted, *unless operations have been and are to be performed which are impossible under the laws governing the known operations going on at present in the material world.*

This prediction spread a pall of gloom across vast expanses of fin-de-siècle *thought. We find it in Sir James Frazer's massive ethnographic survey,* The Golden Bough . . .

JAMES FRAZER
The Golden Bough:
A Study of Comparative Religions

(1890)

The dreams of magic may one day be the waking realities of science. But a dark shadow lies athwart the far end of this fair prospect. For however vast the increase of knowledge and of power which the future may have in store for man, he can scarcely hope to stay the sweep of those great forces which seem to be making silently but relentlessly for the destruction of all this starry universe in which our earth swims as a speck or mote. In the ages to come man may be able to predict, perhaps even to control, the wayward courses of the winds and clouds, but hardly will his puny hands have strength to speed afresh our slackening planet in its orbit or rekindle the dying fire of the sun. Yet the philosopher who trembles at the idea of such distant catastrophes may console himself by reflecting that these gloomy apprehensions, like the earth and the sun themselves, are only part of that unsubstantial world which thought has conjured up out of the void, and that the phantoms which the subtle enchantress has evoked today she may ban tomorrow. They too, like so much that to common eyes seems solid, may melt into air, into thin air.

. . . and it demonstrated a power over the Victorian dream (here in the account of feminist and anti-vivisectionist Frances Power Cobbe) at least as potent as the message of scientific triumph.

FRANCES POWER COBBE
Darwinism in Morals and Other Essays

(1872)

I dreamed that I was standing on a certain broad grassy space in the park of my old home. It was totally dark, but I was sure that I was in the midst of an immense crowd. We were all gazing upward into the murky sky and a sense of some fearful calamity was over us, so that no one spoke aloud. Suddenly overhead appeared through a rift in the black heavens, a branch of stars which I recognized as the belt and sword of Orion. Then went forth a cry of despair from all our hearts! We knew, though no one said, that these stars proved it was not a cloud or mist which, as we had somehow believed, was causing the darkness. No; the air was clear; it was high noon, and *the sun had not risen*! That was the tremendous reason why we beheld the skies. The sun would never rise again!

A contemporary visualization of the End of the World by Camille Flammarion, featuring the death of the sun. (*La fin du monde,* 1893.)

The death of the sun was the ineluctable final image of Wells's Time Machine.

H. G. WELLS
The Time Machine

(1895)

'I cannot convey the sense of abominable desolation that hung over the world. The red eastern sky, the northward blackness, the salt Dead Sea, the stony beach crawling with these foul, slow-stirring monsters, the uniform poisonous-looking green of the lichenous plants, the thin air that hurts one's lungs: all contributed to an appalling effect. I moved on a hundred years, and there was the same red sun – a little larger, a little duller – the same dying sea, the same chill air and the same crowd of earthy crustacea creeping in and out among the green weed and the red rocks. And in the westward sky I saw a curved pale line like a vast new moon.

'So I travelled, stopping ever and again, in great strides of a thousand years or more, drawn on by the mystery of the earth's fate, watching with a strange fascination the sun grow larger and duller in the westward sky, and the life of the old earth ebb away. At last, more than thirty million years hence, the huge red-hot dome of the sun had come to obscure nearly a tenth part of the darkling heavens. Then I stopped once more, for the crawling multitude of crabs had disappeared, and the red beach, save for its livid green liverworts and lichens, seemed lifeless. And now it was flecked with white. A bitter cold assailed me. Rare white flakes ever and again came eddying down. To the north-eastward, the glare of snow lay under the starlight of the sable sky, and I could see an undulating crest of hillocks pinkish white. There were fringes of ice along the sea margin, with drifting masses further out; but the main expanse of that salt ocean, all bloody under the eternal sunset, was still unfrozen.

'I looked about me to see if any traces of animal life remained. A certain indefinable apprehension still kept me in the saddle of the machine. But I saw nothing moving, in earth or sky or sea. The green slime on the rocks alone testified that life was not extinct. A shallow sand-bank had appeared in the sea and the water had receded from the beach. I fancied I saw some black object flopping about upon this bank, but it became motionless as I looked at it, and I judged that my eye had been deceived, and that the black object was merely a rock. The stars in the sky were intensely bright and seemed to me to twinkle very little.

'Suddenly I noticed that the circular westward outline of the sun had changed; that a concavity, a bay, had appeared in the curve. I saw this grow larger. For a minute perhaps I stared aghast at this blackness that was creeping over the day, and then I realized that an eclipse was beginning. Either the moon or the planet Mercury was passing across the sun's disk. Naturally, at first I took it to be the moon, but there is much to incline me to believe that what I really saw was the transit of an inner planet passing very near to the earth.

'The darkness grew apace; a cold wind began to blow in freshening gusts from the east, and the showering white flakes in the air increased in number. From the edge of the sea came a ripple and whisper. Beyond these lifeless sounds the world was silent. Silent? It would be hard to convey the stillness of it. All the sounds of man, the bleating of sheep, the cries of birds, the hum of insects, the stir that makes the background of our lives – all that was over. As the darkness thickened, the eddying flakes grew more abundant, dancing before my eyes; and the cold of the air more intense. At last, one by one, swiftly, one after the other, the white peaks of the distant hills vanished into blackness. The breeze rose to a moaning wind. I saw the black central shadow of the eclipse sweeping towards me. In another moment the pale stars alone were visible. All else was rayless obscurity. The sky was absolutely black.

'A horror of this great darkness came on me. The cold, that smote to my marrow, and the pain I felt in breathing, overcame me. I shivered, and a deadly nausea seized me. Then like a red-hot bow in the sky appeared the edge of the sun. I got off the machine to recover myself. I felt giddy and incapable of facing the return journey. As I stood sick and confused I saw again the moving thing upon the shoal – there was no mistake now that it was a moving thing – against the red water of the sea. It was a round thing, the size of a football perhaps, or, it may be, bigger, and tentacles trailed down from it; it seemed black against the weltering blood-red water, and it was hopping fitfully about. Then I felt I was fainting. But a terrible dread of lying helpless in that remote and awful twilight sustained me while I clambered upon the saddle.'

The idea of mankind's ultimate precariousness was further suggested by the popular interest in the possibility of life on Mars. This was given impetus by Schiaparelli's discovery of the Martian channels, which he referred to in Italian as 'canali' and which were interpreted by the astronomer Percival Lowell as 'canals'. From this inference Lowell, in a series of best-selling books, conjured a powerful image of the dying Martian race.

PERCIVAL LOWELL
Mars as the Abode of Life

(1896)

ORGANISMS EVOLVE AS A PLANET AGES

As a planet ages, any organisms upon it would share in its development. They must evolve with it, indeed, or perish. At first they change only as environment offers opportunity, in a lowly, unconscious way. But, as brain develops, they rise superior to such occasioning. Originally the organism is the creature of its surroundings; later it learns to make them subservient to itself. In this way the organism avoids unfavourableness in the environment, or turns unpropitious fortune to good use. Man has acquired something of the art here on the earth, and what with clothing himself in the first place, and yoking natural forces in the second, lives in comfort now where, in a state of nature, he would incontinently perish.

Such adaptation in mind, making it superior to adaptation in body, is bound to occur in the organic life on any planet, if it is to survive at all. For conditions are in the end sure to reach a pass where something more potent than body is required to cope with them.

ONE SPECIES SUPPLANTS ALL OTHERS

It is possible to apply a test to tell whether such life existed or not. For certain signs would be forthcoming were such intellect there. Increase of intelligence would cause one species in the end to prevail over all others, as it had prevailed over its environment. What it found inconvenient or unnecessary to enslave, it would exterminate, as we have obliterated the bison and domesticated the dog. This species will thus become lord of the planet and spread completely over its face. Any action it might take would, in consequence, be planet-wide in its showing.

Now, such is precisely what appears in the world-spread system of canals. That it joins the surface from pole to pole and girdles it at the equator betrays a single purpose there at work. Not only does one species possess the planet but even its subdivisions must labour harmoniously to a common aim. Nations must have sunk their local patriotisms in a wider breadth of view and the planet be a unit to the general good.

TO DIE OF THIRST

As the being has conquered all others, so will it at last be threatened itself. In the growing scarcity of water will arise the premonitions of its doom. To secure what may yet be got will thus become the forefront of its endeavour, to which all other questions are secondary. Thus, if these beings are capable of making their presence noticeable at all, their great occupation should be that of water-getting, and should be the first, because the most fundamental, trace of their existence an outsider would be privileged to catch.

The last stage in the expression of life upon a planet's surface must be that just antecedent to its dying of thirst. Whether it came to this pass by simple exhaustion, as is the case with Mars, or by rotary retardation, as is the case with Mercury and Venus, the result would be all one to the planet itself. Failure of its water-supply would be the cause. To procure this indispensable would be its last conscious effort . . .

OUR LIFE NOT UNIQUE

Thus, not only do the observations we have scanned lead us to the conclusion that Mars at this moment is inhabited, but they land us at the further one that these denizens are of an order whose acquaintance was worth the making. Whether we ever shall come to converse with them in any more instant way is a question upon which science at present has no data to decide. More important to us is the fact that they exist, made all the more interesting by their precedence of us in the path of evolution. Their presence certainly ousts us from any unique or self-centred position in the solar system, but so with the world did the Copernican system the Ptolemaic, and the world survived this deposing change. So may man. To all who have a cosmoplanetary breadth of view it cannot but be pregnant to contemplate extra-mundane life and to realize that we have warrant for believing that such life now inhabits the planet Mars.

MARTIAN LIFE NEARING ITS END

A sadder interest attaches to such existence: that it is, cosmically speaking, soon to pass away. To our eventual descendants life on Mars will no longer be something to scan and interpret. It will have lapsed beyond the hope of study or recall. Thus to us it takes on an added glamour from the fact that it has not long to last. For the process that brought it to its present pass must go on to the bitter end, until the last spark of Martian life goes out. The drying up of the planet is certain to proceed until its surface can support no life at all. Slowly but surely time will snuff it out. When the last ember is thus extinguished, the planet will roll a dead world through space, its evolutionary career forever ended.

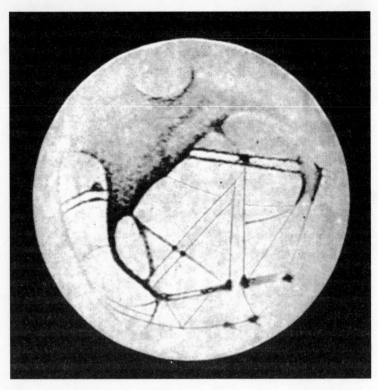

The 'canals' of Mars, as conceived by Lowell and drawn by Schiaparelli (1890). (Courtesy of Mary Evans Picture Library)

H. G. Wells used Lowell's suppositions as the springboard for War of
the Worlds, *taking not just the scenario of Mars as a dying planet but
also the implication that the human race might as a result have to
re-evaluate its own scientific progress in the face of brutal colonization.
At the same time, the image of the Martians as brains encased in machines
suggested a grotesque possibility for our own technocratic future.*

H. G. WELLS
The War of the Worlds

(1898)

No one would have believed, in the last years of the nineteenth
century, that human affairs were being watched keenly and closely by
intelligences greater than man's and yet as mortal as his own; that as
men busied themselves about their affairs they were scrutinized and
studied, perhaps almost as narrowly as a man with a microscope might
scrutinize the transient creatures that swarm and multiply in a drop of
water. With infinite complacency men went to and fro over this globe
about their little affairs, serene in their assurance of their empire over
matter. It is possible that the infusoria under the microscope do the
same. No one gave a thought to the older worlds of space as sources of
human danger, or thought of them only to dismiss the idea of life upon
them as impossible or improbable. It is curious to recall some of the
mental habits of those departed days. At most, terrestrial men fancied
there might be other men upon Mars, perhaps inferior to themselves
and ready to welcome a missionary enterprise. Yet, across the gulf of
space, minds that are to our minds as ours are to those of the beasts
that perish, intellects vast and cool and unsympathetic, regarded this
earth with envious eyes, and slowly and surely drew their plans against
us. And early in the twentieth century came the great disillusionment.

The planet Mars, I scarcely need remind the reader, revolves about
the sun at a mean distance of 140,000,000 miles, and the light and heat
it receives from the sun is barely half of that received by this world. It
must be, if the nebular hypothesis has any truth, older than our world,
and long before this earth ceased to be molten, life upon its surface
must have begun its course. The fact that it is scarcely one-seventh

of the volume of the earth must have accelerated its cooling to the temperature at which life could begin. It has air and water, and all that is necessary for the support of animated existence.

Yet so vain is man, and so blinded by his vanity, that no writer, up to the very end of the nineteenth century, expressed any idea that intelligent life might have developed there far, or indeed at all, beyond its earthly level. Nor was it generally understood that since Mars is older than our earth, with scarcely a quarter of the superficial area, and remoter from the sun, it necessarily follows that it is not only more distant from life's beginning but nearer its end.

The secular cooling that must some day overtake our planet has already gone far indeed with our neighbour. Its physical condition is still largely a mystery, but we know now that even in its equatorial region the mid-day temperature barely approaches that of our coldest winter. Its air is much more attenuated than ours, its oceans have shrunk until they cover but a third of its surface, and as its slow seasons change huge snowcaps gather and melt about either pole, and periodically inundate its temperate zones. That last stage of exhaustion, which to us is still incredibly remote, has become a present-day problem for the inhabitants of Mars. The immediate pressure of necessity has brightened their intellects, enlarged their powers, and hardened their hearts. And looking across space, with instruments and intelligences such as we have scarcely dreamt of, they see, at its nearest distance only 35,000,000 of miles sunward of them, a morning star of hope, our own warmer planet, green with vegetation and grey with water, with a cloudy atmosphere eloquent of fertility, with glimpses through its drifting cloud-wisps of broad stretches of populous country and narrow navy-crowded seas.

And we men, the creatures who inhabit this earth, must be to them at least as alien and lowly as are the monkeys and lemurs to us. The intellectual side of man already admits that life is an incessant struggle for existence, and it would seem that this too is the belief of the minds upon Mars. Their world is far gone in its cooling, and this world is still crowded with life, but crowded only with what they regard as inferior animals. To carry warfare sunward is indeed their only escape from the destruction that generation after generation creeps upon them.

And before we judge of them too harshly, we must remember what ruthless and utter destruction our own species has wrought, not only upon animals, such as the vanished bison and the dodo, but upon its own inferior races. The Tasmanians, in spite of their human likeness, were entirely swept out of existence in a war of extermination waged by European immigrants, in the space of fifty years. Are we such apostles of mercy as to complain if the Martians warred in the same spirit?

The Martians seem to have calculated their descent with amazing subtlety – their mathematical learning is evidently far in excess of ours – and to have carried out their preparations with a well-nigh perfect unanimity. Had our instruments permitted it, we might have seen the gathering trouble far back in the nineteenth century. Men like Schiaparelli watched the red planet – it is odd, by the by, that for countless centuries Mars has been the star of war – but failed to interpret the fluctuating appearances of the markings they mapped so well. All that time the Martians must have been getting ready.

But not all scientists were convinced that life on Mars was plausible.

ALFRED RUSSEL WALLACE
'Man's Place in the Universe'

(1903)

When we consider that the temperature of space is about $-273°$ C., while that of the outer surface of the sun is about 9000 C., we realize what a combination of favourable conditions must exist to preserve on the surface of a planet a degree of heat which shall never for any considerable time fall below 0° C., or rise above, say, 75° C., and that these narrow limits must be *continuously maintained* not for hundreds or thousands only, but for millions, perhaps for *hundreds of millions of years*, if life is to be developed there. It is the maintenance of this comparatively uniform surface temperature for such enormous periods – during, in fact, the whole time covered by the geological record – that most writers have overlooked as among the necessary conditions for the development of the higher forms of life on a planet; and this omission vitiates all their reasoning, since they have to show not only that the requisite conditions of temperature *may* exist now, but that there is even a probability that they have existed or will exist for a sufficiently extended period to allow of the development of a complex system of organic life comparable with our own. Let us, then, enumerate the chief favourable conditions, which in their combination appear to have rendered this development possible on our earth. These are:

(1) A distance from the sun such as to keep up the temperature of the soil to the required amount, by sun-heat alone, and to evaporate sufficient water to produce clouds, rain and a system of river circulation.

(2) An atmosphere of sufficient extent and density to allow of the production and circulation of aqueous vapour in the form of clouds, mists and dews, and to serve also as an equalizer of sun heat during day and night, winter and summer, and also between the tropical and temperate zones. This amount of atmosphere is held to be largely dependent upon the mass of a planet, and this one feature alone probably renders Mars quite unsuitable, since its mass is less than one-eighth that of the earth.

(3) The very large proportion of the surface covered by deep oceans, so that they surround and interpenetrate the land, and by their tides and currents keep up a continuous circulation, and are thus the chief agents in the essential equalization of temperatures. This, again, is largely dependent on our possessing so large a satellite capable of producing a regular but not excessive tidal action. The want of such a satellite may alone render Venus quite unsuitable for the development of high forms of life, even if other conditions were favourable, which seems in the highest degree improbable.

(4) The enormous average depth of these oceans, so that the bulk of water they contain is about thirteen times that of the land which rises above their level. This indicates that they are *permanent features of the earth's surface*, thus ensuring the maintenance of continuous land areas and of uniform temperatures during the whole period of the development of life upon the earth. (The evidence which demonstrates this permanence is set forth in my *Island Life* [1880], Chap. VI, and enforced by additional arguments in my *Studies Scientific and Social* [1900], Vol. I, Chap. 2.) It is extremely improbable that this remarkable condition obtains in any other planet.

(5) Lastly, one of the most peculiar and least generally considered features of our earth, but one which is also essential to the development and maintenance of the rich organic life it possesses, is the uninterrupted supply of atmospheric dust, which is now known to be necessary for the production of rain-clouds and beneficial rains and mists, and without which the whole course of meteorological phenomena would be so changed as to endanger the very existence of a large portion of the life upon the earth.

Nevertheless, the idea of intelligent life on other planets began to colour popular consciousness. Here Théodore Flournoy, Swiss philosopher, professor and mentor to Carl Jung, records a vision of Martian life received during a seance.

THÉODORE FLOURNOY
From India to the Planet Mars: A Case of Multiple Personality with Imaginary Languages

(1899)

From the beginning, says the report of the seance, Mlle Smith perceived, in the distance and at a great height, a bright light. Then she felt a tremor which almost caused her heart to cease beating, after which it seemed to her as though her head were empty and as if she were no longer in the body. She found herself in a dense fog, which changed successively from blue to a vivid rose colour, to grey, and then to black: she is floating, she says; and the table, supporting itself on one leg, seemed to express a very curious floating movement. Then she sees a star, growing larger, always larger, and become finally, 'as large as our house'. Hélène feels that she is ascending; then the table gives, by raps: 'Lemaître, that which you have so long desired!' Mlle Smith, who had been ill at ease, finds herself feeling better; she distinguishes three enormous globes, one of them very beautiful. 'On what am I walking?' she asks. And the table replies: 'On a world – Mars.' Hélène then began a description of all the strange things which presented themselves to her view, and caused her as much surprise as amusement. Carriages without horses or wheels, emitting sparks as they glided by; houses with fountains on the roof; a cradle having for curtains an angel made of iron with outstretched wings, etc. What seemed less strange, were people exactly like the inhabitants of our earth, save that both sexes wore the same costume, formed of trousers very ample, and a long blouse, drawn tight about the waist and decorated with various designs. The child in the cradle was exactly like our children, according to the sketch which Hélène made from memory after the seance.

Finally, she saw upon Mars a sort of vast assembly hall, in which was Professor Raspail, having in the first row of his hearers the young Alexis Mirbel, who, by a typtological dictation, reproached his mother for not having followed the medical prescription which he gave her a month previously: 'Dear mamma, have you, then, so little confidence in us? You have no idea how much pain you have caused me!' Then followed a conversation of a private nature between Mme Mirbel and her son, the latter replying by means of the table; then everything becomes quiet, the vision of Mars effaces itself little by little; the table takes the same rotary movement on one foot which it had at the commencement of the seance; Mlle Smith finds herself again in the fogs and goes through the same process as before in an inverse order. Then she exclaims: 'Ah! here I am back again!' and several loud raps on the table mark the end of the seance.

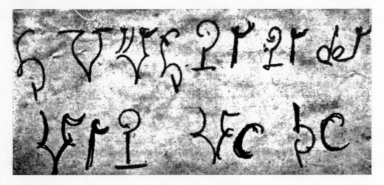

The 'Martian language' transcribed by Flournoy. He notes: 'It is not always easy to represent a language and its pronunciation by means of the typographical characters of another. Happily the Martian, in spite of its strange appearance and the fifty millions of leagues which separate us from the red planet, is in reality so near neighbour to French that there is scarcely any difficulty in this case.' ('From India to the Planet Mars'.)

This poem by the physicist James Clerk-Maxwell vividly conveys the realization of science that the cosmos has surprises in store to dwarf our own technological achievements.

JAMES CLERK-MAXWELL
'To the Chief Musician upon Nabla*: A Tyndallic Ode'

(written 1874; 1882)

I come from fields of fractured ice,
   Whose wounds are cured by squeezing,
Melting they cool, but in a trice,
   Get warm again by freezing.
Here, in the frosty air, the sprays
   With fern-like hoar-frost bristle,
There, liquid stars their watery rays
   Shoot through the solid crystal.

I come from empyrean fires –
   From microscopic spaces,
Where molecules with fierce desires,
   Shiver in hot embraces.
The atoms clash, the spectra flash,
   Projected on the screen,
The double D, magnesian b,
   And Thallium's living green.

We place our eye where these dark rays
   Unite in this dark focus,
Right on the source of power we gaze,

° Nabla was the name of an Assyrian harp of the shape ∇. ∇ is a quaternion operator $\left(i\dfrac{d}{dx} + j\dfrac{d}{dy} + k\dfrac{d}{dz} \right)$ invented by Sir W. R. Hamilton, whose use and properties were first fully discussed by Professor Tait, who is therefore called the 'Chief Musician upon Nabla'.

Without a screen to cloak us.
Then where the eye was placed at first,
   We place a disc of platinum,
It glows, it puckers! will it burst?
   How ever shall we flatten him!

This crystal tube the electric ray
   Shows optically clean,
No dust or haze within, but stay!
   All has not yet been seen.
What gleams are these of heavenly blue?
   What air-drawn form appearing,
What mystic fish, that, ghostlike, through
   The empty space is steering? . . .

. . . and here Conan Doyle's irascible but stoical hero of science, Professor Challenger, lays down the law on the proper response of the scientific mind to cosmic catastrophe.

SIR ARTHUR CONAN DOYLE
'The Poison Belt'

(1913)

'With your permission I will say a few words upon that subject.' He seated himself upon his desk, his short, stumpy legs swinging in front of him. 'We are assisting at a tremendous and awful function. It is, in my opinion, the end of the world.'

The end of the world! Our eyes turned to the great bow-window and we looked out at the summer beauty of the countryside, the long slopes of heather, the great country houses, the cosy farms, the pleasure-seekers upon the links. The end of the world! One had often heard the words, but the idea that they could ever have an immediate practical significance, that it should not be at some vague date, but now, today, that was a tremendous, a staggering thought. We were all struck solemn and waited in silence for Challenger to continue. His overpowering presence and appearance lent such force to the solemnity of his words that for a moment all the crudities and absurdities of the man vanished, and he loomed before us as something majestic and beyond the range of ordinary humanity. Then to me, at least, there came back the cheering recollection of how twice since we had entered the room he had roared with laughter. Surely, I thought, there are limits to mental detachment. The crisis cannot be so great or so pressing, after all.

'You will conceive a bunch of grapes,' said he, 'which are covered by some infinitesimal but noxious bacillus. The gardener passes it through a disinfecting medium. It may be that he desires his grapes to be cleaner. It may be that he needs space to breed some fresh bacillus less noxious than the last. He dips it into the poison and they are gone. Our Gardener is, in my opinion, about to dip the solar system, and the human bacillus, the little mortal vibrio which twisted and wriggled upon the outer rind of the earth, will in an instant be sterilized out of existence.'

. . .

'The true scientific mind is not to be tied down by its own conditions of time and space. It builds itself an observatory erected upon the borderline of present, which separates the infinite past from the infinite future. From this sure post it makes its sallies even to the beginning and to the end of all things. As to death, the scientific mind dies at its post working in normal and methodic fashion to the end. It disregards so petty a thing as its own physical dissolution as completely as it does all other limitations upon the plane of matter. Am I right, Professor Summerlee?'

Summerlee grumbled an ungracious assent.

'With certain reservations, I agree,' said he.

'The ideal scientific mind,' continued Challenger – 'I put it in the third person rather than appear to be too self-complacent – the ideal scientific mind should be capable of thinking out a point of abstract knowledge in the interval between its owner falling from a balloon and reaching the earth. Men of this strong fibre are needed to form the conquerors of Nature and the bodyguard of truth.'

3
The Death of God: Atheism

The ascending power and authority of science was seen by almost all cultural commentators as the most striking fact of the nineteenth-century world; it was widely recognized, too, that science was encroaching irresistibly on areas which had previously been the exclusive domain of religion. Even subtle theologians – of whom there were many – had to absorb the lessons of science within new structures of religious belief. But for the evangelical materialists of science, it seemed plain that the era of religion was over – the only question was whether the rest of humanity had the courage to 'grow up' and recognize the fact.

The classic formulation of atheism – 'God is Dead' – was delivered by Nietzsche.

FRIEDRICH NIETZSCHE
Thus Spoke Zarathustra: A book for Everyone and No One

(1883-5)

When Zarathustra was thirty years old, he left his home and the lake of his home and went into the mountains. Here he had the enjoyment of his spirit and his solitude and he did not weary of it for ten years. But at last his heart turned – and one morning he rose with the dawn, stepped before the sun and spoke to it thus:

Great star! What would your happiness be, if you had not those for whom you shine!

You have come up here to my cave for ten years: you would have grown weary of your light and of this journey, without me, my eagle and my serpent.

But we waited for you every morning, took from you your superfluity and blessed you for it.

Behold! I am weary of my wisdom, like a bee that has gathered too much honey; I need hands outstretched to take it.

I should like to give it away and distribute it, until the wise among men have again become happy in their folly and the poor happy in their wealth.

To that end, I must descend into the depths: as you do at evening, when you go behind the sea and bring light to the underworld too, superabundant star!

Like you, I must *go down* – as men, to whom I want to descend, call it.

So bless me then, tranquil eye, that can behold without envy even an excessive happiness!

Bless the cup that wants to overflow, that the waters may flow golden from him and bear the reflection of your joy over all the world!

Behold! This cup wants to be empty again, and Zarathustra wants to be man again.

Thus began Zarathustra's down-going.

Zarathustra went down the mountain alone, and no one met him. But when he entered the forest, an old man, who had left his holy hut to look for roots in the forest, suddenly stood before him. And the old man spoke thus to Zarathustra:

'This wanderer is no stranger to me: he passed by here many years ago. He was called Zarathustra; but he has changed.

'Then you carried your ashes to the mountains: will you today carry your fire into the valleys? Do you not fear an incendiary's punishment?

'Yes, I recognize Zarathustra. His eyes are clear, and no disgust lurks about his mouth. Does he not go along like a dancer?

'How changed Zarathustra is! Zarathustra has become – a child, an awakened-one: what do you want now with the sleepers?

'You lived in solitude as in the sea, and the sea bore you. Alas, do you want to go ashore? Alas, do you want again to drag your body yourself?'

Zarathustra answered: 'I love mankind.'

'Why,' said the saint, 'did I go into the forest and the desert? Was it not because I loved mankind all too much?

'Now I love God: mankind I do not love. Man is too imperfect a thing for me. Love of mankind would destroy me.'

Zarathustra answered: 'What did I say of love? I am bringing mankind a gift.'

'Give them nothing,' said the saint. 'Rather take something off them and bear it with them – that will please them best; if only it be pleasing to you!

'And if you want to give to them, give no more than an alms, and let them beg for that!'

'No,' answered Zarathustra, 'I give no alms. I am not poor enough for that.'

The saint laughed at Zarathustra, and spoke thus: 'See to it that they accept your treasures! They are mistrustful of hermits, and do not believe that we come to give.

'Our steps ring too lonely through their streets. And when at night they hear in their beds a man going by long before the sun has risen, they probably ask themselves: Where is that thief going?

'Do not go to men, but stay in the forest! Go rather to the animals! Why will you not be as I am – a bear among bears, a bird among birds?'

'And what does the saint do in the forest?' asked Zarathustra.

The saint answered: 'I make songs and sing them, and when I make songs, I laugh, weep and mutter: thus I praise God.

'With singing, weeping, laughing and muttering I praise the God who is my God. But what do you bring us as a gift?'

When Zarathustra heard these words, he saluted the saint and said: 'What should I have to give you! But let me go quickly, that I may take nothing from you!' And thus they parted from one another, the old man and Zarathustra, laughing as two boys laugh.

But when Zarathustra was alone, he spoke thus to his heart: 'Could it be possible! This old saint has not yet heard in his forest that *God is dead*!'

Freud, a great admirer of Nietzsche, felt that psychoanalysis stripped away illusory ideas of the self from humanity, and exposed religion as 'the universal obsessive neurosis of mankind'.

SIGMUND FREUD
'The Future of an Illusion'

(1928)

Your religious doctrines will have to be discarded, no matter whether the first attempts fail, or whether the first substitutes prove to be untenable. You know why: in the long run nothing can withstand reason and experience, and the contradiction which religion offers to both is all too palpable. Even purified religious ideas cannot escape this fate, so long as they try to preserve anything of the consolation of religion. No doubt if they confine themselves to a belief in a higher spiritual being, whose qualities are indefinable and whose purposes cannot be discerned, they will be proof against the challenge of science; but then they will also lose their hold on human interest.

And secondly: observe the difference between your attitude to illusions and mine. You have to defend the religious illusion with all your might. If it becomes discredited – and indeed the threat to it is great enough – then your world collapses. There is nothing left for you but to despair of everything, of civilization and the future of mankind. From that bondage I am, we are, free. Since we are prepared to renounce a good part of our infantile wishes, we can bear it if a few of our expectations turn out to be illusions.

Education freed from the burden of religious doctrines will not, it may be, effect much change in men's psychological nature. Our god Λόγος is perhaps not a very almighty one, and he may only be able to fulfil a small part of what his predecessors have promised. If we have to acknowledge this we shall accept it with resignation. We shall not on that account lose our interest in the world and in life, for we have one sure support which you lack. We believe that it is possible for scientific work to gain some knowledge about the reality of the world, by means of which we can increase our power and in accordance with which we can arrange our life. If this belief is an illusion, then we are in the same position as you. But science has given us evidence by its numerous and important successes that it is no illusion. Science has many open enemies, and many more secret ones, among those who cannot forgive her for having weakened religious faith and for threatening to overthrow it.

In The War of the Worlds, *Wells offered a parable of the inability of religion to sustain its traditional claims in the face of the future.*

H. G. WELLS
The War of the Worlds
(1898)

I do not clearly remember the arrival of the curate, so that I probably dozed. I became aware of him as a seated figure in soot-smudged shirt-sleeves, and with his upturned clean-shaven face staring at a faint flickering that danced over the sky. The sky was what is called a mackerel sky, rows and rows of faint down-plumes of cloud, just tinted with the midsummer sunset.

I sat up, and at the rustle of my motion he looked at me quickly.

'Have you any water?' I asked abruptly.

He shook his head.

'You have been asking for water for the last hour,' he said.

For a moment we were silent, taking stock of one another. I dare say he found me a strange enough figure, naked save for my water-soaked trousers and socks, scalded, and my face and shoulders blackened from the smoke. His face was a fair weakness, his chin retreated and his hair lay in crisp, almost flaxen curls on his low forehead; his eyes were rather large, pale blue and blankly staring. He spoke abruptly, looking vacantly away from me.

'What does it mean?' he said. 'What do these things mean?'

I stared at him and made no answer.

He extended a thin white hand and spoke in almost a complaining tone.

'Why are these things permitted? What sins have we done? The morning service was over, I was walking through the roads to clear my brain for the afternoon, and then – fire, earthquake, death! As if it were Sodom and Gomorrah! All our work undone, all the work . . . What are these Martians?'

'What are we?' I answered, clearing my throat.

He gripped his knees and turned to look at me again. For half a minute, perhaps, he stared silently.

'I was walking through the roads to clear my brains,' he said. 'And suddenly fire, earthquake, death!'

He relapsed into silence, with his chin now sunken almost to his knees.

Presently he began waving his hand:

'All the work – all the Sunday-schools. What have we done – what has Weybridge done? Everything gone – everything destroyed. The Church! We rebuilt it only three years ago. Gone! – swept out of existence! Why?'

Another pause, and he broke out again like one demented.

'The smoke of her burning goeth up for ever and ever!' he shouted.

His eyes flamed, and he pointed a lean finger in the direction of Weybridge.

By this time I was beginning to take his measure. The tremendous tragedy in which he had been involved – it was evident he was a fugitive from Weybridge – had driven him to the very verge of his reason.

'Are we far from Sunbury?' I said in a matter-of-fact tone.

'What are we to do?' he asked. 'Are these creatures everywhere? Has the earth been given over to them?'

'Are we far from Sunbury?'

'Only this morning I officiated at early celebration . . .'

'Things have changed,' I said quietly. 'You must keep your head. There is still hope.'

'Hope!'

'Yes; plentiful hope – for all this destruction!'

I began to explain my view of our position. He listened at first, but as I went on the interest in his eyes changed to their former stare, and his regard wandered from me.

'This must be the beginning of the end,' he said, interrupting me. 'The end! The great and terrible day of the Lord! When men shall call upon the mountains and the rocks to fall upon them and hide them – hide them from the face of Him that sitteth upon the throne!'

I began to understand the position. I ceased my laboured reasoning, struggled to my feet, and, standing over him, laid my hand on his shoulder.

'Be a man,' said I. 'You are scared out of your wits. What good is religion if it collapses at calamity? Think of what earthquakes and floods, wars and volcanoes, have done before to men. Did you think God had exempted Weybridge? . . . He is not an insurance agent, man.'

. . . and, with the death of God, the underpinning of conventional morality and the social contract of civilization seemed in danger of being swept away.

FRIEDRICH NIETZSCHE
On the Genealogy of Morality

(1887)

Unconditional, honest atheism (– that alone is the air we more spiritual men of the age breathe!) is . . . one of the ideal's last phases of development, one of its final forms and inherent logical conclusions, – it is the awe-inspiring *catastrophe* of a two-thousand-year discipline in truth-telling, which finally forbids itself the *lie entailed in the belief in God*. (The same process of development in India, completely independently, which therefore proves something; the same ideal forcing the same conclusion; the decisive point was reached five centuries before the European era began, with Buddha or, more precisely: already with the Sankhya philosophy which Buddha then popularized and made into a religion.) *What*, strictly speaking, has actually *conquered* the Christian God? The answer is in my *Joyful Science* [1882] (section 357): 'Christian morality itself, the concept of truthfulness which was taken more and more seriously, the confessional punctiliousness of Christian conscience, translated and sublimated into scientific conscience, into intellectual purity at any price. Regarding nature as though it were a proof of God's goodness and providence; interpreting history in honour of divine reason, as a constant testimonial to an ethical world order and ethical ultimate purpose; explaining all one's own experiences in the way pious folk have done for long enough, as though everything were providence, a sign, intended, and sent for the salvation of the soul: now all that is *over*, it has conscience *against* it, every sensitive conscience sees it as indecent, dishonest, as a pack of lies, feminism, weakness, cowardice, – this severity makes us *good* Europeans if anything does, and heirs to Europe's most protracted and bravest self-overcoming!' . . . All great things bring about their own demise through an act of self-sublimation: that is the law of life, the law of *necessary* 'self-overcoming' in the essence of life, – the lawgiver himself is always ultimately exposed to the cry: *'patere legem, quam ipse tulisti'*. ['Submit to the law you have yourself made'.] In this way, Christianity *as a dogma* was destroyed by its own morality, in the same way Christianity *as a morality* must also be destroyed, – we stand on the threshold of *this* occurrence. After Christian truthfulness has drawn one conclusion after another, it will finally draw the *strongest conclusion*, that *against* itself; this will, however, happen when it asks itself, *'What does all will to truth mean?'* . . . and here I touch on my problem again, on *our* problem, my *unknown* friends (– because I don't *know* of any friend as yet): what meaning does *our* being have, if it were not that that will to truth has become conscious of itself *as a problem* in us? . . . Without a doubt, from now on, morality will be *destroyed* by the will to truth's becoming-conscious-of-itself: that great drama in a hundred acts reserved for Europe in the next two centuries, the most terrible, most dubious drama but perhaps also the one most rich in hope . . .

Although careful about his public pronouncements on religion, Darwin nevertheless confessed his own abandonment of Christianity.

CHARLES DARWIN

Autobiography of Charles Darwin

(1887; 1958)

The fact that many false religions have spread over large portions of the earth like wildfire had some weight with me. Beautiful as is the morality of the New Testament, it can hardly be denied that its perfection depends in part on the interpretation which we now put on metaphors and allegories. But I was very unwilling to give up my belief. – I feel sure of this for I can well remember often and often inventing day-dreams of old letters between distinguished Romans and manuscripts being discovered at Pompeii or elsewhere which confirmed in the most striking manner all that was written in the Gospels. But I found it more and more difficult, with free scope given to my imagination, to invent evidence which would suffice to convince me. Thus disbelief crept over me at a very slow rate, but was at last complete. The rate was so slow that I felt no distress, and have never since doubted even for a single second that my conclusion was correct. I can indeed hardly see how anyone ought to wish Christianity to be true; for if so, the plain language of the text seems to show that the men who do not believe, and this would include my Father, Brother and almost all my best friends, will be everlastingly punished.

And this is a damnable doctrine.

In the generation since the flowering of decadence in Europe, poets, artists and iconoclasts had been dancing gleefully on religion's grave.

COMTE DE LAUTRÉAMONT
Maldoror

(1868)

It was a spring day. The birds were pouring forth their warbling songs, and human beings were going about their different duties, bathed in the holiness of toil. Everything was working towards its destiny: trees, planets, dogfish. Everything, that is, except the Creator! He was lying stretched out on the road, with his clothes all torn. His lower lip was hanging down like a heavy chain; his teeth had not been cleaned, and the blond waves of his hair were full of dust. His body, benumbed by heavy sluggishness, pinned down on the stones, was making futile attempts to get up. His strength had deserted him and he was lying there, weak as an earthworm, impassive as the bark of a tree. Floods of wine filled the ruts which had been hollowed out by the nervous jerkings of his shoulders. Pig-snouted brutishness covered him with its protective wings and cast loving glances at him. His legs, their muscles slack, swept across the ground like two flapping sails. Blood flowed from his nostrils: as he fell he had knocked his face against a post . . . He was drunk! Horribly drunk! Drunk as a bug which in one night has gorged three barrels of blood; his incoherent words resounded all around; I shall refrain from repeating them here, for even if the supreme drunkard has no self-respect, I must respect men. Did you know that the Creator was drunk?

Anarchists attack a religious procession in Barcelona in 1898. (Courtesy of Mary Evans Picture Library)

There was, of course, strong opposition to the atheist movement from many traditional voices within the church and society – but also from others arguing from more 'progressive' standpoints. The psychologist William James expressed the view that the religious impulse wasn't to be so simply abandoned.

WILLIAM JAMES
'The Will to Believe'

(1897)

The deepest difference, practically, in the moral life of man is the difference between the easy-going and the strenuous mood. When in the easy-going mood, the shrinking from present ill is our ruling consideration. The strenuous mood, on the contrary, makes us quite indifferent to present ill, if only the greater ideal be attained. The capacity for the strenuous mood probably lies slumbering in every man, but it has more difficulty in some than in others in waking up. It needs the wilder passions to arouse it, the big fears, loves and indignations; or else the deeply penetrating appeal of some one of the higher fidelities, like justice, truth or freedom. Strong relief is a necessity of its vision; and a world where all the mountains are brought down and all the valleys are exalted is no congenial place for its habitation. This is why in a solitary thinker this mood might slumber on for ever without waking. His various ideals, known to him to be mere preferences of his own, are too nearly of the same denominational value: he can play fast or loose with them at will. This too is why, in a merely human world without a God, the appeal to our moral energy falls short of its maximal stimulating power. Life, to be sure, is even in such a world a genuinely ethical symphony; but it is played in the compass of a couple of poor octaves, and the infinite scale of values fails to open up. Many of us, indeed, – like Sir James Stephen in those eloquent 'Essays by a Barrister', – would openly laugh at the very idea of the strenuous mood being awakened in us by those claims of remote posterity which constitute the last appeal of the religion of humanity. We do not love these men of the future keenly enough; and we love them perhaps the less the more we hear of their evolutionized perfection, their high average longevity and education, their freedom from war and crime, their relative immunity from pain and zymotic disease, and all their other negative superiorities. This is all too finite, we say; we see too well the vacuum beyond. It lacks the note of infinitude and mystery, and may all be dealt with in the don't-care mood. No need of agonizing ourselves or making others agonize for these good creatures just at present.

When, however, we believe that a God is there, and that he is one of the claimants, the infinite perspective opens out. The scale of the symphony is incalculably prolonged. The more imperative ideals now begin to speak with an altogether new objectivity and significance, and to utter the penetrating, shattering, tragically challenging note of appeal. They ring out like the call of Victor Hugo's alpine eagle, 'qui parle au précipice et que le gouffre entend', and the strenuous mood awakens at the sound. It saith among the trumpets, ha, ha! it smelleth the battle afar off, the thunder of the captains and the shouting. Its blood is up; and cruelty to the lesser claims, so far from being a deterrent element, does but add to the stern joy with which it leaps to answer to the greater. All through history, in the periodical conflicts of puritanism with the don't-care temper, we see the antagonism of the strenuous and genial moods, and the contrast between the ethics of infinite and mysterious obligation from on high, and those of prudence and the satisfaction of merely finite need.

The capacity of the strenuous mood lies so deep down among our natural human possibilities that even if there were no metaphysical or traditional grounds for believing in a God, men would postulate one simply as a pretext for living hard, and getting out of the game of existence its keenest possibilities of zest. Our attitude towards concrete evils is entirely different in a world where we believe there are none but finite demanders, from what it is in one where we joyously face tragedy for an infinite demander's sake. Every sort of energy and endurance, of course and capacity for handling life's evils, is set free in those who have religious faith. For this reason the strenuous type of character will on the battle-field of human history always outwear the easy-going type, and religion will drive irreligion to the wall.

. . . and the poet A. E. Housman insisted that simply to dismiss the laws of God was not enough to make the laws of man a real alternative. Both were 'foreign' but 'strong'.

A. E. HOUSMAN
'The laws of God, the laws of man'

(written *c*. 1900; 1922)

The laws of God, the laws of man,
He may keep that will and can;
Not I: let God and man decree
Laws for themselves and not for me;
And if my ways are not as theirs
Let them mind their own affairs.
Their deeds I judge and much condemn,
Yet when did I make laws for them?
Please yourselves, say I, and they
Need only look the other way.
But no, they will not; they must still
Wrest their neighbour to their will,
And make me dance as they desire
With jail and gallows and hell-fire.
And how am I to face the odds
Of man's bedevilment and God's?
I, a stranger and afraid
In a world I never made.
They will be master, right or wrong;
Though both are foolish, both are strong.
And since, my soul, we cannot fly
To Saturn nor to Mercury,
Keep we must, if keep we can,
These foreign laws of God and man.

If religion can't simply be abandoned, the question still arises as to what will offer firmer moral guidance in its place. To many scientists, the answer was clear – science itself.

E. RAY LANKESTER
Degeneration: A Chapter in Darwinism

(1880)

There is only one means of estimating our position, only one means of so shaping our conduct that we may with certainty avoid degeneration and keep an onward course. We are as a race more fortunate than our ruined cousins – the degenerate Ascidians. For us it is possible to ascertain what will conduce to our higher development, what will favour our degeneration. To us has been given the power to *know the causes of things*, and by the use of this power it is possible for us to control our destinies. It is for us by ceaseless and ever hopeful labour to try to gain a knowledge of man's place in the order of nature. When we have gained this fully and minutely, we shall be able by the light of the past to guide ourselves in the future. In proportion as the whole of the past evolution of civilized man, of which we at present perceive the outlines, is assigned to its causes, we and our successors on the globe may expect to be able duly to estimate that which makes for, and that which makes against, the progress of the race. The full and earnest cultivation of Science – the Knowledge of Causes – is that to which we have to look for the protection of our race – even of this English branch of it – from relapse and degeneration.

The Coming Race, Bulwer-Lytton's fantasy of a race of highly evolved subterranean beings published in 1871, became an influential model of how a technocratic society – based on the mysterious 'vril' power – might simply witness the withering away of the religious impulse.

SIR EDWARD BULWER-LYTTON
The Coming Race

(1871)

This people have a religion, and, whatever may be said against it, at least it has these strange peculiarities: firstly, that they all believe in the creed they profess; secondly, that they all practise the precepts which the creed inculcates. They unite in the worship of the one divine Creator and Sustainer of the universe. They believe that it is one of the properties of the all-permeating agency of vril, to transmit to the well-spring of life and intelligence every thought that a living creature can conceive; and though they do not contend that the idea of a Deity is innate, yet they say that the An (man) is the only creature, so far as their observation of nature extends, to whom *the capacity of conceiving that idea*, with all the trains of thought which open out from it, is vouchsafed. They hold that this capacity is a privilege that cannot have been given in vain, and hence that prayer and thanksgiving are acceptable to the divine Creator, and necessary to the complete development of the human creature. They offer their devotions both in private and public. Not being considered one of their species, I was not admitted into the building or temple in which the public worship is rendered; but I am informed that the service is exceedingly short, and unattended with any pomp of ceremony. It is a doctrine with the Vril-ya, that earnest devotion or complete abstraction from the actual world cannot, with benefit to itself, be maintained long at a stretch by the human mind, especially in public, and that all attempts to do so either lead to fanaticism or to hypocrisy.

. . .

They say that in ancient times there was a great number of books written upon speculations as to the nature of the Deity, and upon the forms of belief or worship supposed to be most agreeable to Him. But these were found to lead to such heated and angry disputations as not only to shake the peace of the community and divide families before the most united, but in the course of discussing the attributes of the Deity, the existence of the Deity Himself became argued away, or, what was worse, became invested with the passions and infirmities of the human disputants. 'For,' said my host, 'since a finite being like an An cannot possibly define the Infinite, so, when he endeavours to realize an idea of the Divinity, he only reduces the Divinity into an An like himself.' During the later ages, therefore, all theological speculations, though not forbidden, have been so discouraged as to have fallen utterly into disuse.

. . . and, in Germany, the biologist Ernst Haeckel formulated a system whereby science can represent Nature in such a way as to satisfy the religious impulse rationally – 'Monism'.

ERNST HAECKEL
The Riddle of the Universe: At the Close of the Nineteenth Century

(1899)

This progress of modern times in knowledge of the true and enjoyment of the beautiful expresses, on the one hand, a valuable element of our monistic religion, but is, on the other hand, in fatal opposition to Christianity. For the human mind is thus made to live on this side of the grave; Christianity would have it ever gaze beyond. Monism teaches that we are perishable children of the earth, who for one or two, or, at the most, three generations, have the good fortune to enjoy the treasures of our planet, to drink of the inexhaustible fountain of its beauty, and to trace out the marvellous play of its forces. Christianity would teach us that the earth is 'a vale of tears', in which we have but a brief period to chasten and torment ourselves in order to merit the life of eternal bliss beyond. Where this 'beyond' is, and of what joys the glory of this eternal life is compacted, no revelation has ever told us. As long as 'heaven' was thought to be the blue vault that hovers over the disk of our planet, and is illumined by the twinkling light of a few thousand stars, the human imagination could picture to itself the ambrosial banquets of the Olympic gods above or the laden tables of the happy dwellers in Valhalla. But now all these deities and the immortal souls that sat at their tables are 'houseless and homeless', as David Strauss has so ably described; for we know from astrophysical science that the immeasurable depths of space are filled with a prosaic ether, and that millions of heavenly bodies, ruled by eternal laws of iron, rush hither and thither in the great ocean, in their eternal rhythm of life and death.

The places of devotion, in which men seek the satisfaction of their religious emotions and worship the objects of their reverence, are regarded as sacred 'churches'. The pagodas of Buddhistic Asia, the

Greek temples of classical antiquity, the synagogues of Palestine, the mosques of Egypt, the Catholic cathedrals of the south, and the Protestant cathedrals of the north, of Europe – all these 'houses of God' serve to raise man above the misery and the prose of daily life, to lift him into the sacred, poetic atmosphere of a higher, ideal world. They attain this end in a thousand different ways, according to their various forms of worship and their age. The modern man who 'has science and art' – and, therefore, 'religion' – needs no special church, no narrow, enclosed portion of space. For through the length and breadth of free nature, wherever he turns his gaze, to the whole universe or to any single part of it, he finds, indeed, the grim 'struggle for life', but by its side are ever 'the good, the true, and the beautiful'; his church is commensurate with the whole of glorious nature.

. . . *but the formulations of a new 'scientific religion' sometimes demon-strated a tendency to become as baroque and irrational as the religion they sought to replace. Dr Lanz von Liebenfelz, an early German racial theorist and contributor to Haeckel's magazine* Das Freie Wort, *contrived to combine modern electrical science, the Holy Grail, the newly discovered electron and a bizarre myth of human evolution into his system of 'Theozoology'.*

JÖRG LANZ VON LIEBENFELZ
Theozoology, or the Science of the Sodom-Apelings and the Electron of the Gods

(1905)

The gods are earlier evolutionary forms of mankind and its races, so is it not possible that they were equipped with archaic sensory instruments? Modern man possesses several sensory instruments, the apparently superfluous remains of old organs. But these archaic organs have marvellous influences on many vital processes. The pituitary gland (hypophysis) is the remnant of a long-vanished sensory organ linked to the oral cavity. The adrenal gland is the cause of Addison's Disease . . . its ancient anatomy resembles arrangements in fish and the amphibians. Close to the pituitary is a second mysterious old organ, the pineal gland, the seat of the soul according to the ancients and Descartes. Recent scientific investigators explain the pineal as the remnant of the third eye in the Stegocephalians. This organ appears to be still active today among certain species of deep-sea fish. Many a lizard displays on the crown of its head a sensory organ which must be regarded as an eye in the light of its microscopic structure. Several scholars claim to have discovered an electrical (or magnetic) organ in the third eye of the saurians . . . My view that the pituitary and the pineal were electrical organs is confirmed by Professor London's experiments in St Petersburg, which demonstrated that blind subjects 'see' radium emissions in the centre of their brain . . .

Anthropologists have important observations concerning the cranium of diluvial man. 'Taubach, Chelles and Rutot Man were surely superior to modern man in many abilities. How else, with low technology, could mankind have survived the murderous struggle against the prehistoric monsters? Prediluvial man had a strongly developed occipital lobe. Science has recently attributed the centres for optical impressions to this area of the brain and so it is believed that prediluvial hunters had specially sharp powers of observation' (Klaatsch). This accords with ancient records: Moses, the great prophet, has a heavy tongue, the Pythia – obviously half-human, half-beast – delivered her oracle in a stammer, and the Bible frequently mentions the *gastromythoi*, the spirits that speak from the belly . . . When the cave-paintings of diluvial man were found in France, they were initially regarded as forgeries, as they depicted animals with an astonishing faculty of observation and perception. This art disappears in later periods. Moreover, the older artistic creations, even in Babylon and Egypt, are more original and ingenious, in the historic period. This would be inexplicable, if one did not accept the view of the Bible, which full of wisdom says: God's spirit does not dwell in the [racial inferiors] (Gen. VI. 3). Clairvoyants, of whose existence one can have no doubt, even if there are many hoaxers, are chiefly found among whites today, and precisely in the most racially pure white persons, Friesians and Westphalians. On the other hand, the only winged animals, bats, have organs and instincts, which still puzzle scientists (Brehm). Blinded bats can avoid all obstacles, even suspended fine wires (Claus). A flying animal is more suited as a receiver of electrical waves than a land creature. As is well known, wireless telegraphy uses several high, vertically suspended aerials.

According to Ohm's Law conductive resistance is inversely related to temperature. Electricity is conducted better through a cold conductor than by a warm conductor. Cold chemical rays are the best conductors of electricity, and it is remarkable that telegraphy functions better by night in the fog than on a clear and sunny day. Through my experiments I have obtained the following law: 'Chemical cooled ultraviolet rays correspond to an electric current in a wire, regarding their behaviour and effects. The opposite holds for infrared rays of warmth. All laws which apply to currents in wires also apply to rays. Interruption or amplification of any ray induces currents in a neighbouring parallel ray.' On the basis of this law one will in future be able to construct light machines, in which all iron components in electric motors will be replaced by cooled (using liquid air) ultraviolet rays, while infrared, warm rays will replace the coils.

Electrical sensory organs are chiefly developed in creatures which live in the dark. Deep-sea squid, bats, the clairvoyant Friesians in the foggy North, the saurians with their electrical cranial eye in a twilit misty world, the wise dwarves of the Nibelungs all make sense in the light of the most recent scientific discoveries.

. . .

Among the ancient Celts was a people who could see better by night than by day. Heimdall-Jring, born on Atlantis 'where the sun sinks', could see for a hundred leagues. Oracles are given in caves and in the darkness. The wise take counsel in the night. Electricity is the 'revelation' and the 'inspiration'. What we strive to see with the eye of science reflected in a glass, the ancients saw through another vision. Thus their astonishing knowledge of prehistory. Divine electricity transmitted it to them! The gods were not only living electrical receiver stations, but also electrical generators and transmitters . . . And if I am asked what I understand by divinity, I say: The creatures of ultraviolet and infrared energies and worlds. They walked upon this earth in prehistoric times as physical and racially pure beings. Today they still live in man. The gods slumber in the racially debased bodies of men, but the day will come when they arise again. We were electrical, we will be electrical, electricity and divinity is one and the same! Early man was omniscient through his electrical eye and omnipotent through his electrical energy. The all-knowing, all-powerful has the right to call himself God!

[A new era of racial eugenics is coming.] Soon the time will come, when a new priesthood will arise in the land of the electron and the Holy Grail . . . just as the rays of the spirit once descended upon its messengers at the first Whitsun, so the electrical swans of the gods will come again at the great Whitsun of Humanity . . . Great princes, doughty warriors, inspired priests, eloquent bards and visionary sages will arise from the ancient holy soil of Germany, once again enchain the [inferior races], establish the Church of the Holy Spirit and transform the earth into a paradise.

4
Beyond Reason?:
Spiritualism and the New Age

Many of the battles between competing systems of belief were fought over the contentious subject of spiritualism which, since the 1850s, had developed into a vast popular movement. There were many in the scientific community who found the claims of spiritualism persuasive. Not only could the new science defend itself in entirely empirical terms, it also offered the possibility for science to extend its remit still further.

ALFRED RUSSEL WALLACE
On Miracles and Modern Spiritualism

(1875)

The assertion so often made, that Spiritualism is the survival or revival of old superstitions, is so utterly unfounded as to be hardly worth notice. A science of human nature which is founded on observed facts; which appeals only to facts and experiment; which takes no beliefs on trust; which inculcates investigation and self-reliance as the first duties of intelligent beings; which teaches that happiness in a future life can be secured by cultivating and developing to the utmost the higher faculties of our intellectual and moral nature *and by no other method*, – is and must be the natural enemy of all superstition. Spiritualism is an experimental science, and affords the only sure foundation for a true philosophy and a pure religion. It abolishes the terms 'supernatural' and 'miracle' by an extension of the sphere of law and the realm of nature; and in doing so it takes up and explains whatever is true in the superstitions and so-called miracles of all ages. It and it alone, is able to harmonize conflicting creeds; and it must ultimately lead to concord among mankind in the matter of religion, which has for so many ages been the source of unceasing discord and incalculable evil; – and it will be able to do this because it appeals to evidence instead of faith, and substitutes facts for opinions; and is thus able to demonstrate the source of much of the teaching that men have so often held to be divine.

It will thus be seen, that those who can form no higher conception of the uses of Spiritualism, 'even if true', than to detect crime or to name in advance the winner of the Derby, not only prove their own ignorance of the whole subject, but exhibit in a marked degree that partial mental paralysis, the result of a century of materialistic thought, which renders so many men unable seriously to conceive the possibility of a natural continuation of human life after the death of the body. It will be seen also that Spiritualism is no mere 'psychological' curiosity, no mere indication of some hitherto unknown 'law of nature'; but that it is a science of vast extent, having the widest, the most important and the most practical issues, and as such should enlist the sympathies alike of moralists, philosophers and politicians, and of all who have at heart the improvement of society and the permanent elevation of human nature.

. . .

My position, therefore, is that the phenomena of Spiritualism in their entirety do *not* require further confirmation. They are proved, quite as well as any facts are proved in other sciences; and it is not denial or quibbling that can disprove any of them, but only fresh facts and accurate deductions from those facts. When the opponents of Spiritualism can give a record of their researches approaching in duration and completeness to those of its advocates; and when they can discover and show in detail, either how the phenomena are produced or how the many sane and able men here referred to have been deluded into a coincident belief that they have witnessed them; and when they can prove the correctness of their theory by producing a like belief in a body of equally sane and able unbelievers, – then, and not till then, will it be necessary for spiritualists to produce fresh confirmation of facts which are, and always have been, sufficiently real and indisputable to satisfy any honest and persevering enquirer.

This being the state of the case as regards evidence and proof, we are fully justified in taking the *facts* of modern Spiritualism (and with them the spiritual theory as the only tenable one) as being fully established.

It was in this spirit that a group of Cambridge scientists set up the Society for Psychical Research in 1882.

HENRY SIDGWICK
Presidential Address to the Society for Psychical Research

(1882)

As this is the first general meeting of our new Society since the time it was definitely constituted, it has been thought that I should make a few brief remarks on the aims and methods of the Society, which will form a kind of explanation in supplement to our prospectus defining those aims and methods, – which, I suppose, has been seen by all the members, and perhaps by some who are not as yet members. This prospectus has not been subjected to much instructive public criticism. It has been received, either with entire cordiality, or with guarded neutrality, or with uninstructive contempt. Still, several private criticisms on that prospectus and questions suggested by it have come to my notice; and it seems to me that I might perhaps employ the few minutes of your time that I wish to take up in no better way than in replying to these criticisms and objections.

The first question I have heard is, Why form a Society for Psychical Research at all at this time, including in its scope not merely the phenomena of thought-reading (to which your attention will be directed chiefly this afternoon), but also those of clairvoyance and mesmerism, and the mass of obscure phenomena commonly known as Spiritualistic? Well, in answering this, the first question, I shall be able to say something on which I hope we shall all agree; meaning by 'we', not merely we who are in this room, but we and the scientific world outside; and as, unfortunately, I have but few observations to make on which so much agreement can be hoped for, it may be as well to bring this into prominence, namely, that we are all agreed that the present state of things is a scandal to the enlightened age in which we live. That the dispute as to the reality of these marvellous phenomena, – of which it is quite impossible to exaggerate the scientific importance, if only a tenth part of what has been alleged by generally credible witnesses could be shown to be true, – I say it is a scandal that the dispute as to the reality of these phenomena should still be going on, that so many competent witnesses should have declared their belief in them, that so many others should be profoundly interested in having the question determined, and yet that the educated world, as a body, should still be simply in the attitude of incredulity.

Now the primary aim of our Society, the thing which we all unite to promote, whether as believers or non-believers, is to make a sustained and systematic attempt to remove this scandal in one way or another.

Taken in the library at Combermere in 1891, this photograph shows a
seated figure resembling the late Lord Combermere at the exact time
of his burial. (Proceedings of the Society for Psychical Research, 1895.)
(Courtesy of Mary Evans Picture Library)

The scientists of spiritualism surveyed a disorientating variety of phenomena with the 'impartial eye of science'. The physician and hypnotist Baron von Schrenck-Notzing recorded the materialization of vaginal ectoplasm under hypnosis.

BARON VON SCHRENCK-NOTZING

Phenomena of Materialization: A Contribution to the Investigation of Mediumistic Teleplastics

(1923)

On my expressing a wish, the medium parted her thighs and I saw that the material assumed a curious shape, resembling an orchid, decreased slowly, and entered the vagina. During the whole process I held her hands. Eva then said, 'Wait, we will try to facilitate the passage.' She rose, mounted on the chair, and sat down on one of the arm-rests, her feet touching the seat. Before my eyes, and with the curtain open, a large spherical mass, about 8 inches in diameter, emerged from the vagina and quickly placed itself on her left thigh while she crossed her legs. I distinctly recognized in the mass a still unfinished face, whose eyes looked at me. As I bent forward in order to see better, this head-like structure rose before my eyes, and suddenly vanished into the dark of the cabinet away from the medium, disappearing from my view.

. . .

Yesterday I hypnotized Eva as usual, and she unexpectedly began to produce phenomena. As soon as they began, Eva allowed me to undress her completely. I then saw a thick thread emerge from the vagina. It changed its place, left the genitals and disappeared in the navel depression. More material emerged from the vagina, and with a sinuous serpentine motion of its own it crept up the girl's body, giving the impression as it were about to rise into the air. Finally it ascended to her head, entered Eva's mouth and disappeared. Eva then stood up, and again a mass of material appeared at the genitals, spread out and hung suspended between her legs. A strip of it rose, took a direction towards me, receded and disappeared.

. . .

Thereupon the phenomena commenced again in the bed, the material again emerging from the vagina, as some days before. Eva lay stretched on her back, and I knelt in front of the bed. The mass emerging from the genitals had the shape of a thick and solid strip, passing along the thigh, and appearing to recede into her body. Suddenly she exclaimed, 'Look, look, it comes again; I feel a head.' Then a round and fairly solid sphere, of the shape and size of a billiard ball, fell into my hand as it lay with the palm upwards between her legs. Also another, quite small, one. The sphere was attached to her body by a ribbon. I thus held in my hand this mysterious living mass, which moved on the palm of my hand.

. . .

On 23rd July 1913 (in La Baule), at 3 p.m., several completely formed fingers wrapped in material, three of which showed nails, emerged from the vagina of the hypnotized medium, moved upwards over her skin, and disappeared without a trace at the moment when Eva awoke spontaneously with a cry of terror.

But spiritualism had its enemies in the professions. The British psy-
chiatrist and author Forbes Winslow regarded spiritualism in all its
forms as delusional and dangerous, and a major contributor to the
increase in the asylum population.

L. S. FORBES WINSLOW
Spiritualistic Madness

(1877)

Spiritualism has from time to time been prominently brought
before the public, and it might have been supposed that, after the many
exposures of collusion, self-deception and imposture in connection with
the so-called 'spirit mediums', the world in general would have by this
time learnt common sense, and the mania for it have died a natural
death; but it has again crept up, and is darkening, by its superstition,
the human mind, which, under its influence, falls into an abyss of
mysticism of an unnaturally unfathomable depth.

It is the curse of our age, and one of the principal causes of the
increase of insanity in England, and especially of that desponding and
melancholic type known as 'religious insanity', so prevalent in the present
century. One of the chief objects I have in view in writing is to show
the terrible consequences which are produced by tolerating such exhi-
bitions of charlatanism, and I trust that I may succeed in persuading a
few weak-minded individuals who believe in its reality to abandon its
dangerous proclivities, dogmas and doctrines before it is too late.

This form of delusion is very prevalent in America, and the asylums
contain many of its victims; nearly ten thousand persons having gone
insane on the subject are confined in the public asylums of the United
States.

. . .

The facile credulity in spiritualism which is spreading widely at the
present day must be considered as one of the principal causes of
the increase of insanity; and, as previously stated, it produces a form
of mental alienation known as religious insanity, associated with

melancholic and suicidal symptoms, rendering many of its victims dangerous to be free agents for their own protection, and that of society in general. The community of believers contains a large proportion of weak-minded hysterical women, in whom the seeds of mental disorder, though for a time latent, are only waiting for a new excitement to ripen into maturity. The persevering charlatanism of spiritualism has indeed much to answer for, and has been the means of causing many a blank in a family circle, the victim of its power being gradually entangled within its meshes, and so severed from ordinary intercourse, and this at a period when we should look for an advancement of civilization and education, and not for the pernicious practices of arrant impostors and humbugs.

*Spiritualist phenomena also offered a critique of science, one which was
vigorously developed by Christians, occultists and spiritualists alike. In
the view of the Anglo-Catholic C. G. Harrison, for example, the mass
popularity of spiritualism was proof that scientific rationalism itself was
on the wane.*

C. G. HARRISON

The Transcendental Universe: Six Lectures on Occult Science, Theosophy and the Catholic Faith

(1894)

The latter half of the century which is now drawing towards its
close has been eminently a period of unrest. In all departments of
human activity – in politics, in science and religion – principles, formerly
accepted without question as fundamental, have been thrown down
into the arena of controversy and subjected to a rigorous examination.
And the results of this sifting process are a profound discontent, a
restless chafing at the bounds of our present knowledge, which find
expression in, and are peculiarly characteristic of, the art of the period.
'Light, more light!' were the dying words of Goethe, the pioneer of the
nineteenth century, and the dying century re-echoes them.

Nothing is more remarkable than the change which has come over
our habits of thought within the last few years. Until quite recently, it
was considered a sign of intellectual superiority to rest content with the
position of an 'Agnostic' in regard to the most important subjects which
can engage the attention of man. It was asserted that not only do we
not know anything about God, the soul or a future life, but that it is
idle to enquire – that true wisdom consists in denial of the possibility
of any such knowledge, and that every revelation which professes to
give information on these subjects is the product of a distempered fancy.
But this curious form of intellectual pride led the Agnostics, like the
Puritans in *Hudibras*, to

> Compound for sins they were inclined to,
> By damning those they had no mind to,

and did not hinder them from indulging in the wildest speculations about the origin of life on the planet and gravely asserting that the chief difference between a man and a monkey is that phosphorus is present in larger quantities in the brain of the former.

It was inevitable that the pendulum should swing back in the opposite direction, and the reaction from Agnosticism has resulted in a very strange phenomenon – the recrudescence of Gnosticism, a veritable revival of Alexandrian thought in the nineteenth century.

. . .

We have outgrown (or, at least, are outgrowing) a scientific method which, in practice, excludes from the domain of knowledge all experience not derived through the avenues of sense, and a theology based on imperialism and elaborated in accordance with the principles of Roman jurisprudence. Materialism has fallen into disrepute, partly because its foundations have been shaken by the phenomena of the seance room and the recognition of the faculty of hypnotism as a curative agent, and partly because it is felt to be unsatisfactory as an explanation of the universe.

Madame Blavatsky, whose mythology of the spiritual descent of man became hugely influential, claimed that scientific discourse lacked even the language to understand the spirit world.

H. P. BLAVATSKY
Studies in Occultism

Lucifer Magazine (1887–91)

It is intensely interesting to follow season after season the rapid evolution and change of public thought in the direction of the mystical. The educated mind is most undeniably attempting to free itself from the heavy fetters of materialism. The ugly caterpillar is writhing in the agonies of death, under the powerful efforts of the psychic butterfly to escape from its science-built prison, and every day brings some new glad tidings of one or more such mental births to light.

. . .

In our highly civilized West, where modern languages have been formed, and words coined, in the wake of ideas and thoughts – as happened with every tongue – the more the latter became materialized in the cold atmosphere of Western selfishness and its incessant chase after the goods of this world, the less was there any need felt for the production of new terms to express that which was tacitly regarded as obsolete and exploded 'superstition'. Such words could answer only to ideas which a cultured man was scarcely supposed to harbour in his mind. 'Magic', a synonym for jugglery; 'Sorcery', an equivalent for crass ignorance; and 'Occultism', the sorry relic of crack-brained, medieval Fire-philosophers, of the Jacob Boehmes and the St Martins, are expressions believed more than amply sufficient to cover the whole field of 'thimble-rigging'. They are terms of contempt, and used generally only in reference to the dross and residues of the Dark Ages and its preceding aeons of paganism. Therefore have we no terms in the English tongue to define and shade the difference between such abnormal powers, or the sciences that lead to the acquisition of them, with the nicety possible in the Eastern languages – pre-eminently the Sanskrit.

*The growing anti-rationalist view which encompassed spiritualism,
occultism and the revival of ancient traditions of magic found its classic
expression in Eliphas Levi's* Transcendental Magic, *translated into English by A. E. Waite, the occult scholar and member of the Order of the
Golden Dawn, in 1899. Despite magic's association in the popular mind
with devil-worship, Levi states explicitly that he foresees the forces of
magic and Christianity rejoining.*

ELIPHAS LEVI
Transcendental Magic: Its Doctrine and Ritual

(1899)

Behind the veil of all the hieratic and mystical allegories of
ancient doctrines, behind the darkness and strange ordeals of all
initiations, under the seal of all sacred writings, in the ruins of Nineveh
or Thebes, on the crumbling stones of old temples and on the blackened
visage of the Assyrian or Egyptian sphinx, in the monstrous or marvellous
paintings which interpret to the faithful of India the inspired pages of
the Vedas, in the cryptic emblems of our old books on alchemy, in the
ceremonies practised at reception by all secret societies, there are found
indications of a doctrine which is everywhere the same and everywhere
carefully concealed. Occult philosophy seems to have been the nurse
or godmother of all intellectual forces, the key of all divine obscurities
and the absolute queen of society in those ages when it was reserved
exclusively for the education of priests and of kings. It reigned in Persia
with the Magi, who perished in the end, as perish all masters of the
world, because they abused their power; it endowed India with the
most wonderful traditions and with an incredible wealth of poesy, grace
and terror in its emblems; it civilized Greece to the music of the lyre
of Orpheus; it concealed the principles of all sciences, all progress of the
human mind, in the daring calculations of Pythagoras; fable abounded in
its miracles, and history, attempting to estimate this unknown power,
became confused with fable; it undermined or consolidated empires by
its oracles, caused tyrants to tremble on their thrones and governed all
minds, either by curiosity or by fear. For this science, said the crowd,

there is nothing impossible; it commands the elements, knows the language of the stars and directs the planetary courses; when it speaks, the moon falls blood-red from heaven; the dead rise in their graves and mutter ominous words, as the night wind blows through their skulls. Mistress of love or of hate, occult science can dispense paradise or hell at its pleasure to human hearts; it disposes of all forms and confers beauty or ugliness; with the wand of Circe it changes men into brutes and animals alternately into men; it disposes even of life and death, can confer wealth on its adepts by the transmutation of metals and immortality by its quintessence or elixir, compounded of gold and light.

Such was Magic from Zoroaster to Manes, from Orpheus to Apollonius of Tyana, when positive Christianity, victorious at length over the brilliant dreams and titanic aspirations of the Alexandrian school, dared to launch its anathemas publicly against this philosophy, and thus forced it to become more occult and mysterious than ever. Moreover, strange and alarming rumours began to circulate concerning initiates or adepts; they were surrounded everywhere by an ominous influence, and they destroyed or distracted those who allowed themselves to be beguiled by their honeyed eloquence or by the sorcery of their learning. The women whom they loved became Stryges and their children vanished at nocturnal meetings, while men whispered shudderingly and in secret of blood-stained orgies and abominable banquets. Bones had been found in the crypts of ancient temples, shrieks had been heard in the night, harvests withered and herds sickened when the magician passed by. Diseases which defied medical skill appeared at times in the world, and always, it was said, beneath the envenomed glance of the adepts. At length an universal cry of execration went up against Magic, the mere name became a crime and the common hatred was formulated in this sentence: 'Magicians to the flames!' – as it was shouted some centuries earlier: 'To the lions with the Christians!' Now the multitude never conspires except against real powers; it does not know what is true, but it has the instinct of what is strong. It remained for the eighteenth century to deride both Christians and Magic, while infatuated with the disquisitions of Rousseau and the illusions of Cagliostro.

. . .

The original alliance between Christianity and the Science of the Magi, once demonstrated fully, will be a discovery of no second-rate

importance, and we do not doubt that the serious study of Magic and
the Kabalah will lead earnest minds to a reconciliation of science and
dogma, of reason and faith, heretofore regarded as impossible.

Dr William Price, the self-proclaimed Last of the Welsh Druids. Pagan revivals formed another strand of the anti-rationalist *fin-de-siècle*. (From *Gwylellis Yn Nayd,* 1871.)

The poet W. B. Yeats, another member of the Golden Dawn, did much to reacquaint poetry with the language and symbolism of alchemy and the esoteric arts.

W. B. YEATS
'The Poet pleads with the Elemental Powers'

(written 1892; 1899)

The Powers whose name and shape no living creature knows
Have pulled the Immortal Rose;
And though the Seven Lights bowed in their dance and wept,
The Polar Dragon slept,
His heavy rings uncoiled from glimmering deep to deep:
When will he wake from sleep?

Great Powers of falling wave and wind and windy fire,
With your harmonious choir
Encircle her I love and sing her into peace,
That my old care may cease;
Unfold your flaming wings and cover out of sight
The nets of day and night.

Dim Powers of drowsy thought, let her no longer be
Like the pale cup of the sea,
When winds have gathered and sun and moon burned dim
Above its cloudy rim;
But let a gentle silence wrought with music flow
Whither her footsteps go.

It was not merely that science was attempting to claim the spiritual: transcendental thinkers were also colonizing the borderlands of the new sciences for their own ideas. While much esoteric thinking was predicated on 'ancient' wisdom, much was also claiming that science would eventually corroborate the wisdom of the 'New Age'. An example of this fusion of the esoteric and the modern was the Fourth Dimension, originally 'discovered' by the maverick mathematician Charles Howard Hinton.

CHARLES HOWARD HINTON
A New Era of Thought

(1888)

Our space as we ordinarily think of it is conceived as limited – not in extent, but in a certain way which can only be realized when we think of our ways of measuring space objects. It is found that there are only three independent directions in which a body can be measured – it must have height, length and breadth, but it has no more than these dimensions. If any other measurement be taken in it, this new measurement will be found to be compounded of the old measurements. It is impossible to find a point in the body which could not be arrived at by travelling in combinations of the three directions already taken.

But why should space be limited to three independent directions?

Geometers have found that there is no reason why bodies should be thus limited. As a matter of fact all the bodies which we can measure are thus limited. So we come to this conclusion, that the space which we use for conceiving ordinary objects in the world is limited to three dimensions. But it might be possible for there to be beings living in a world such that they would conceive a space of four dimensions. All that we can say about such a supposition is, that it is not demanded by our experience. It may be that in the very large or the very minute a fourth dimension of space will have to be postulated to account for parts – but with regard to objects of ordinary magnitudes we are certainly not in a four-dimensional world.

And this was the point at which about ten years ago I took up the inquiry.

It is possible to say a great deal about space of higher dimensions than our own, and to work out analytically many problems which suggest themselves. But can we conceive four-dimensional space in the same way in which we can conceive our own space? Can we think of a body in four dimensions as a unit having properties in the same way as we think of a body having a definite shape in the space with which we are familiar?

Now this question, as every other with which I am acquainted, can only be answered by experiment. And I commenced a series of experiments to arrive at a conclusion one way or the other.

It is obvious that this is not a scientific inquiry – but one for the practical teacher.

And just as in experimental researches the skilful manipulator will demonstrate a law of nature, the less skilled manipulator will fail; so here, everything depended on the manipulation. I was not sure that this power lay hidden in the mind, but to put the question fairly would surely demand every resource of the practical art of education.

And so it proved to be; for after many years of work, during which the conception of four-dimensional bodies lay absolutely dark, at length, by a certain change of plan, the whole subject of four-dimensional existence became perfectly clear and easy to impart.

There is really no more difficulty in conceiving four-dimensional shapes, when we go about it the right way, than in conceiving the idea of solid shapes, nor is there any mystery at all about it.

When the faculty is acquired – or rather when it is brought into consciousness, for it exists in every one in imperfect form – a new horizon opens. The mind acquires a development of power, and in this use of ampler space as a mode of thought, a path is opened by using that very truth which, when first stated by Kant, seemed to close the mind within such fast limits. Our perception is subject to the condition of being in space. But space is not limited as we at first think.

The next step after having formed this power of conception in ampler space, is to investigate nature and see what phenomena are to be explained by four-dimensional relations.

But this part of the subject is hardly one for the same worker as the one who investigates how to think in four-dimensional space. The work of building up the power is the work of the practical educator, the work of applying it to nature is the work of the scientific man. And it is not possible to accomplish both tasks at the same time. Consequently the crown is still to be won. Here the method is given of training the mind;

it will be an exhilarating moment when an investigator comes upon phenomena which show that external nature cannot be explained except by the assumption of a four-dimensional space.

The thought of the past ages has used the conception of a three-dimensional space, and by that means has classified many phenomena and has obtained rules for dealing with matters of great practical utility. The path which opens immediately before us in the future is that of applying the conception of four-dimensional space to the phenomena of nature, and of investigating what can be found out by this new means of apprehension.

In fact, what has been passed through may be called the three-dimensional era; Gauss and Lobatchewski have inaugurated the four-dimensional era.

The notion of the Fourth Dimension was popularized by Edwin Abbott, the headmaster of the City of London school, in Flatland.

A. SQUARE [EDWIN A. ABBOTT]

Flatland: A Romance of Many Dimensions

(1884)

I Nay, gracious Teacher, deny me not what I know it is in thy power to perform. Grant me but one glimpse of thine interior, and I am satisfied for ever, remaining henceforth thy docile pupil, thy unemancipable slave, ready to receive all thy teachings and to feed upon the words that fall from thy lips.

SPHERE   Well, then, to content and silence you, let me say at once. I would shew you what you wish if I could; but I cannot. Would you have me turn my stomach inside out to oblige you?

I   But my Lord has shewn me the intestines of all my countrymen in the Land of Two Dimensions by taking me with him into the Land of Three. What therefore more easy than now to take his servant on a second journey into the blessed region of the Fourth Dimension, where I shall look down with him once more upon this land of Three Dimensions, and see the inside of every three-dimensional house, the secrets of the solid earth, the treasures of the mines in Spaceland and the intestines of every solid living creature, even of the noble and adorable Spheres.

SPHERE   But where is this land of Four Dimensions?

I   I know not: but doubtless my Teacher knows.

SPHERE   Not I. There is no such land. The very idea of it is utterly inconceivable.

I   Not inconceivable, my Lord, to me, and therefore still less inconceivable to my Master. Nay, I despair not that, even here, in this region of Three Dimensions, your Lordship's art may make the Fourth Dimension visible to me; just as in the Land of Two Dimensions my Teacher's skill would fain have opened the eyes of his blind servant to the invisible presence of a Third Dimension, though I saw it not.

Let me recall the past. Was I not taught below that when I saw a Line and inferred a Plane, I in reality saw a Third unrecognized Dimension, not the same as brightness, called 'height'? And does it not now follow that, in this region, when I see a Plane and infer a Solid, I really see a Fourth unrecognized Dimension, not the same as colour, but existent, though infinitesimal and incapable of measurement?

And besides this, there is the Argument from Analogy of Figures.

SPHERE   Analogy! Nonsense: what analogy?

I   Your Lordship tempts his servant to see whether he remembers the revelations imparted to him. Trifle not with me, my Lord; I crave, I thirst, for more knowledge. Doubtless we cannot *see* that other higher Spaceland now, because we have no eye in our stomachs. But, just as there *was* the realm of Flatland, though that poor puny Lineland Monarch could neither turn to left nor right to discern it, and just as there *was* close at hand, and touching my frame, the land of Three Dimensions, though I, blind senseless wretch, had no power to touch it, no eye in my interior to discern it, so of a surety there is a Fourth Dimension, which my Lord perceives with the inner eye of thought. And that it must exist my Lord himself has taught me. Or can he have forgotten what he himself imparted to his servant?

In One Dimension, did not a moving Point produce a Line with *two* terminal points?

In Two Dimensions, did not a moving Line produce a Square with *four* terminal points?

In Three Dimensions, did not a moving Square produce – did not this eye of mine behold it – that blessed Being, a Cube, with *eight* terminal points?

And in Four Dimensions shall not a moving Cube – alas, for Analogy, and alas for the Progress of Truth, if it be not so – shall not, I say, the motion of a divine Cube result in a still more divine Organization with *sixteen* terminal points?

Behold the infallible confirmation of the Series, 2, 4, 8, 16: is not this a Geometrical Progression? Is not this – if I might quote my Lord's own words – 'strictly according to Analogy'?

Again, was I not taught by my Lord that as in a Line there are *two* bounding Points, and in a Square there are *four* bounding Lines, so in a Cube there must be *six* bounding Squares? Behold once more the confirming Series, 2, 4, 6: is not this an Arithmetical

Progression? And consequently does it not of necessity follow that the more divine offspring of the divine Cube in the Land of Four Dimensions, must have 8 bounding Cubes: and is not this also, as my Lord has taught me to believe, 'strictly according to Analogy'?

O, my Lord, my Lord, behold, I cast myself in faith upon conjecture, not knowing the facts; and I appeal to your Lordship to confirm or deny my logical anticipations. If I am wrong, I yield, and will no longer demand a Fourth Dimension; but, if I am right, my Lord will listen to reason.

I ask therefore, is it, or is it not, the fact, that ere now your countrymen also have witnessed the descent of Beings of a higher order than their own, entering closed rooms, even as your Lordship entered mine, without the opening of doors or windows, and appearing and vanishing at will? On the reply to this question I am ready to stake everything. Deny it, and I am henceforth silent. Only vouchsafe an answer.

SPHERE (*after a pause*) It is reported so. But men are divided in opinion as to the facts. And even granting the facts, they explain them in different ways. And in any case, however great may be the number of different explanations, no one has adopted or suggested the theory of a Fourth Dimension. Therefore, pray have done with this trifling, and let us return to business.

I I was certain of it. I was certain that my anticipations would be fulfilled. And now have patience with me and answer me yet one more question, best of Teachers! Those who have thus appeared – no one knows whence – and have returned – no one knows whither – have they also contracted their sections and vanished somehow into that more Spacious Space, whither I now entreat you to conduct me?

SPHERE (*moodily*) They have vanished, certainly – if they ever appeared. But most people say that these visions arose from the thought – you will not understand me – from the brain; from the perturbed angularity of the Seer.

I Say they so? Oh, believe them not. Or if it indeed be so, that this other Space is really Thoughtland, then take me to that blessed Region where I in Thought shall see the insides of all solid things. There, before my ravished eye, a Cube, moving in some altogether new direction, but strictly according to Analogy, so as to make every particle of his interior pass through a new kind of Space, with a wake of its own – shall create a still more perfect perfection than himself, with sixteen terminal Extra-solid angles, and Eight solid Cubes for his Perimeter. And once there, shall we stay our upward course? In that blessed region of Four Dimensions, shall we linger on the threshold of the Fifth, and not enter therein? Ah, no! Let us rather resolve that our ambition shall soar with our corporal ascent. Then, yielding to our intellectual onset, the gates of the Sixth Dimension shall fly open; after that a Seventh, and then an Eighth –

How long I should have continued I know not. In vain did the Sphere, in his voice of thunder, reiterate his command of silence, and threaten me with the direst penalties if I persisted. Nothing could stem the flood of my ecstatic aspirations. Perhaps I was to blame; but indeed I was intoxicated with the recent draughts of Truth to which he himself had introduced me. However, the end was not long in coming. My words were cut short by a crash outside, and a simultaneous crash inside me, which impelled me through space with a velocity that precluded speech. Down! down! down! I was rapidly descending; and I knew that return to Flatland was my doom. One glimpse, one last and never-to-be-forgotten glimpse I had of that dull level wilderness – which was now to become my Universe again – spread out before my eye. Then a darkness. Then a final, all-consummating thunder-peal; and, when I came to myself, I was once more a common creeping Square, in my Study at home, listening to the Peace-Cry of my approaching Wife.

But, despite its mathematical basis, the Fourth Dimension was often more enthusiastically espoused by artists and mystics than by scientists. Here the esoteric Russian philosopher P. D. Ouspensky recruits Hinton's ideas of the Fourth Dimension to produce a fusion of science and mysticism which anticipates much current New Age thinking.

P. D. OUSPENSKY
Tertium Organum: The Third Canon of Thought, A Key to the Enigmas of the World

(1912)

Four-dimensional space, if we try to imagine it to ourselves, will be the infinite repetition of our space, of our infinite three-dimensional sphere, as a line is the infinite repetition of a point.

Many things that have been said before will become much clearer to us when we dwell on the fact that the fourth dimension must be sought for *in time*.

It will become clear what is meant by the fact that it is possible to regard a four-dimensional body as the tracing of the movement in space of a three-dimensional body in a direction not confined within that space. Now the direction not confined in three-dimensional space in which any three-dimensional body moves – this is the direction of time. Any three-dimensional body, *existing*, is at the same time moving in time and leaves as a tracing of its movement the temporal, or four-dimensional body. We never see or feel this body, because of the limitations of our receptive apparatus, but we see the *section* of it only, which section we call the three-dimensional body. Therefore we are in error in thinking that the three-dimensional body is in itself something real. It is the *projection* of the four-dimensional body – its picture – the image of it *on our plane*.

The four-dimensional body is the infinite number of three-dimensional bodies. That is, the four-dimensional body is the infinite number of *moments of existence* of the three-dimensional one – its states and positions. The three-dimensional body which we see appears as a single figure – one of a series of pictures on a cinematographic film as it were.

. . .

Newton came to the conclusion that *constant quantities* do not exist in nature. Variables do exist – *flowing, fluents* only. The velocities with which different fluents change were called by Newton *fluxions*.

From the standpoint of this theory all things known to us – men, plants, animals, planets – are fluents, and they differ by the magnitude of their fluxions. But the *thing*, changing continuously in time, sometimes very much, and quickly, as in the case of a living body for example, still remains *one and the same*. The body of a man in youth, and the body of a man in senility – these are one and the same, though we know that in the old body there is not one atom left that was in the young one. The matter changes, but *something* remains one under all changes, this something is the *Linga-Sharîra*. Newton's theory is valid for the three-dimensional world existing in time. In this world there is nothing constant. All is variable because every consecutive moment the thing is already not that which it was before. We never see the *Linga-Sharîra*, we see always its parts, and they appear to us variable. But if we observe more attentively we shall see that it is an illusion. Things of three dimensions are unreal and variable. They cannot be real because they do not exist in reality, just as the *imaginary sections* of a solid do not exist. Four-dimensional bodies alone are real.

5
Return of the Repressed: The Unconscious

*Spiritualism, along with Mesmer's work on 'animal magnetism'
and other manifestations of 'abnormal psychology', such as sleep-
walking and automatic writing, had been studied by a mar-
ginalized but well-organized group of medical writers throughout
the century. When coupled with evolutionary theory, their work
gradually began to suggest that the workings of the conscious mind
were surrounded by a dynamic but repressed 'world underneath' –
the unconscious.*

This world was dramatically (and theatrically) made manifest by the celebrated Parisian neurologist J. M. Charcot at the Salpêtrière Infirmary in the 1870s and 1880s.

J. M. CHARCOT
Clinical Lectures on Diseases of the Nervous System

(1877–89)

On the 15th of March, four days after becoming our patient, we diligently searched, what had not been done up to this date, to find whether there existed in him any hysterogenetic zones. We found one situated under the left breast, another in each of the iliac regions and a fourth on the right testicle. It was noticed that even a slight excitation of the sub-mammary zone easily determined the diverse phenomena of the aura – a sensation of constriction of the thorax, and then of the neck, beating in the temples, and buzzing sounds, especially in the left ear. But on insisting a little more P— was suddenly noticed to lose consciousness, to throw himself backwards, to stiffen his limbs and then we witnessed *the first attack of hystero-epilepsy* which the patient ever experienced. This attack was absolutely classic; to the epileptoid phase immediately succeeded that of the greater movements. These were of an extreme violence; the patient, in the movements of salutation, went so far as almost to strike his face against his knees. Shortly afterwards he tore the sheets, the curtains of his bed, and turning his fury against himself, he bit his left arm. The phase of passionate attitudes immediately followed, and P— became a prey to a furious delirium; he became abusive, and cited imaginary persons to murder, – 'Hold! Take your knife . . . Quick . . . Strike!' Ultimately he came to himself, and he affirmed that he had no remembrance of what had occurred. It is remarkable that during the whole of that first attack the *left superior extremity took no part in the convulsions*; it remained flaccid and perfectly inert. During the following days the attacks recurred spontaneously many times, always presenting the same characters as the provoked attack. In one of them, which took place during the night of the 17th March, the patient passed his urine in bed. Two other attacks followed on the 19th. On the 21st a fit occurred, *during which the left arm was agitated*. On awakening, the patient found to his great astonishment that he was able voluntarily to move the various segments of the limb, *of which he had not had the use for a single instant during the long period of close on ten months*. The motor paralysis was not completely cured, without doubt, for there remained a certain degree of paresis, but it was considerably improved. Only the perversions of sensibility remained in the same degree as before.

This cure, gentlemen, – or, to speak more properly, this partial cure – after the diagnosis at which we arrived, ought not to be a matter of surprise to you. But, from our point of view, it had occurred prematurely. Indeed, it was evidently no longer possible to afford to you ocular demonstration of the characters in detail of that monoplegia, so worthy of study. The idea, therefore, occurred to me that, perhaps by acting on the mind of the patient, by *means of suggestion*, even in the waking state – we had learned previously that the subject was not hypnotizable – we might reproduce the paralysis, for a time at least. Thus it was that the following day, finding P— just coming out of an attack which had not modified the state of matters, I endeavoured to persuade him that he was paralysed anew. 'You believe yourself cured,' I said to him, with an accent of entire conviction, 'it is an error; you are not able to raise your arm, nor to bend it, nor to move the fingers; see, you are unable to grasp my hand,' etc. The experiment succeeded marvellously, for at the end of a few minutes' discussion the monoplegia returned. I was not anxious on this account, it may be said in passing, for I know from long experience, that *what one has done, one can undo*. Unfortunately this did not persist for more than twenty-four hours. The following day a new attack supervened, in consequence of which the voluntary movements became definitely re-established. On this occasion all the attempts at suggestion which we made were found useless. Today it only remains for me to apprise you of the modifications which, as far as voluntary movement is concerned, have taken place, in consequence of the fits, in a limb which was at one time completely paralysed.

The Austrian doctor Josef Breuer built on Charcot's demonstrations of hysteria with the landmark case of 'Anna O.', which he wrote up in 1895.

JOSEF BREUER AND SIGMUND FREUD
'The Case of Fräulein Anna O.'

Studies on Hysteria (1895)

Although I have suppressed a large number of quite interesting details, this case history of Anna O. has grown bulkier than would seem to be required for a hysterical illness that was not in itself of an unusual character. It was, however, impossible to describe the case without entering into details, and its features seem to be of sufficient importance to excuse this extensive report. In just the same way, the eggs of the echinoderm are important in embryology, not because the sea-urchin is a particularly interesting animal but because the protoplasm of its eggs is transparent and because what we observe in them thus throws light on the probable course of events in eggs whose protoplasm is opaque. The interest of the present case seems to me above all to reside in the extreme clarity and intelligibility of its pathogenesis.

There were two psychical characteristics present in the girl while she was still completely healthy which acted as predisposing causes for her subsequent hysterical illness:

(1) Her monotonous family life and the absence of adequate intellectual occupation left her with an unemployed surplus of mental liveliness and energy, and this found an outlet in the constant activity of her imagination.

(2) This led to a habit of day-dreaming (her 'private theatre'), which laid the foundations for a dissociation of her mental personality. Nevertheless a dissociation of this degree is still within the bounds of normality. Reveries and reflections during a more or less mechanical occupation do not in themselves imply a pathological splitting of consciousness, since if they are interrupted – if, for instance, the subject is spoken to – the normal unity of consciousness is restored; nor, presumably, is any amnesia present. In the case of Anna O., however, this habit prepared the ground upon which the affect of anxiety and dread was able to establish itself in the way I have described, when once that affect had

transformed the patient's habitual day-dreaming into a hallucinatory *absence*. It is remarkable how completely the earliest manifestation of her illness in its beginnings already exhibited its main characteristics, which afterwards remained unchanged for almost two years. These comprised the existence of a second state of consciousness which first emerged as a temporary *absence* and later became organized into a '*double conscience*'; an inhibition of speech, determined by the affect of anxiety, which found a chance discharge in the English verses; later on, paraphasia and loss of her mother-tongue, which was replaced by excellent English; and lastly the accidental paralysis of her right arm, due to pressure, which later developed into a contractural paresis and anaesthesia on her right side. The mechanism by which this latter affection came into being agreed entirely with Charcot's theory of traumatic hysteria – a slight trauma occurring during a state of hypnosis.

But whereas the paralysis experimentally provoked by Charcot in his patients became stabilized immediately, and whereas the paralysis caused in sufferers from traumatic neuroses by a severe traumatic shock sets in at once, the nervous system of this girl put up a successful resistance for four months. Her contracture, as well as the other disturbances which accompanied it, set in only during the short *absences* in her *condition seconde* and left her during her normal state in full control of her body and possession of her senses; so that nothing was noticed either by herself or by those around her, though it is true that the attention of the latter was centred upon the patient's sick father and was consequently diverted from her.

. . .

Throughout the entire illness her two states of consciousness persisted side by side: the primary one in which she was quite normal psychically, and the secondary one which may well be likened to a dream in view of its wealth of imaginative products and hallucinations, its large gaps of memory and the lack of inhibition and control in its associations. In this secondary state the patient was in a condition of alienation. The fact that the patient's mental condition was entirely dependent on the intrusion of this secondary state into the normal one seems to throw considerable light on at least one class of hysterical psychosis. Every one of her hypnoses in the evening afforded evidence that the patient was entirely clear and well-ordered in her mind and normal as regards her feeling and volition so long as none of the products of her secondary state was acting as a stimulus 'in the unconscious'. The extremely marked psychosis which appeared whenever there was any considerable interval in this unburdening process showed the degree to which those products influenced the psychical events of her 'normal' state. It is hard to avoid expressing the situation by saying that the patient was split into two personalities of which one was mentally normal and the other insane. The sharp division between the two states in the present patient only exhibits more clearly, in my opinion, what has given rise to a number of unexplained problems in many other hysterical patients. It was especially noticeable in Anna O. how much the products of her 'bad self', as she herself called it, affected her moral habit of mind. If these products had not been continually disposed of, we should have been faced by a hysteric of the malicious type – refractory, lazy, disagreeable and ill-natured; but, as it was, after the removal of those stimuli her true character, which was the opposite of all these, always re-appeared at once.

Breuer passed the case of Anna O. over to Freud, who broke with him over Breuer's reluctance to accept the sexual origin of hysteria: Freud saw this as an inability to come to terms with the looming truths of psychoanalysis. Freud's analysis of the case of 'Dora' dramatically demonstrates his leap into a world of dreams and sexual life previously uncharted by science.

SIGMUND FREUD

'Fragment of an Analysis of a Case of Hysteria'

(1905)

An opportunity very soon occurred for interpreting Dora's nervous cough in this way by means of an imagined sexual situation. She had once again been insisting that Frau K. only loved her father because he was *'ein vermögender Mann'* ['a man of means']. Certain details of the way in which she expressed herself (which I pass over here, like most other purely technical parts of the analysis) led me to see that behind this phrase its opposite lay concealed, namely, that her father was *'ein unvermögender Mann'* ['a man without means']. This could only be meant in a sexual sense – that her father, as a man, was without means, was impotent. Dora confirmed this interpretation from her conscious knowledge; whereupon I pointed out the contradiction she was involved in if on the one hand she continued to insist that her father's relation with Frau K. was a common love-affair, and on the other hand maintained that her father was impotent, or in other words incapable of carrying on an affair of such a kind. Her answer showed that she had no need to admit the contradiction. She knew very well, she said, that there was more than one way of obtaining sexual gratification. (The source of this piece of knowledge, however, was once more untraceable.) I questioned her further, whether she referred to the use of organs other than the genitals for the purpose of sexual intercourse, and she replied in the affirmative. I could then go on to say that in that case she must be thinking of precisely those parts of the body which in her case were in a state of irritation, – the throat and the oral cavity. To be sure, she would not hear of going so far as this in recognizing her own thoughts; and indeed, if the occurrence of the symptom was to be made possible at all, it was essential that she should not be completely clear on the subject. But the conclusion was inevitable that with her spasmodic cough, which, as is usual, was referred for its exciting stimulus to a tickling in her throat, she pictured to herself a scene of sexual gratification *per os* between the two people whose love-affair occupied her mind so incessantly. A very short time after she had tacitly accepted this explanation her cough vanished – which fitted in very well with my view; but I do not wish to lay too much stress upon this development, since her cough had so often before disappeared spontaneously.

. . .

A few weeks after the first dream the second occurred, and when it had been dealt with the analysis was broken off. It cannot be made as completely intelligible as the first, but it afforded a desirable confirmation of an assumption which had become necessary about the patient's mental state, it filled up a gap in her memory, and it made it possible to obtain a deep insight into the origin of another of her symptoms.

Dora described the dream as follows: *'I was walking about in a town which I did not know. I saw streets and squares which were strange to me.*° *Then I came into a house where I lived, went to my room, and found a letter from Mother lying there. She wrote saying that as I had left home without my parents' knowledge she had not wished to write to me to say that Father was ill. "Now he is dead and if you like*† *you can come." I then went to the station [*"Bahnhof"*] and asked about a hundred times: "Where is the station?" I always got the answer: "Five minutes." I then saw a thick wood before me which I went into and there I asked a man whom I met. He said to me: "Two and a half hours more."*‡ *He offered to accompany me. But I refused and went alone. I saw the station in front of me and could not reach it.'*

. . .

° To this she subsequently made an important addendum: *'I saw a monument in one of the squares.'*
† To this came the addendum: *'There was a question-mark after this word, thus: "like?".'*
‡ In repeating the dream she said: *'Two hours.'*

At this point a certain suspicion of mine became a certainty. The use of *'Bahnhof'* ['station'; literally, 'railway-court']° and *'Friedhof'* ['cemetery'; literally, 'peace-court'] to represent the female genitals was striking enough in itself, but it also served to direct my awakened curiosity to the similarly formed *'Vorhof'* ['vestibulum'; literally, 'fore-court'] – an anatomical term for a particular region of the female genitals. This might have been no more than mistaken ingenuity. But now, with the addition of 'nymphs' visible in the background of a 'thick wood', no further doubts could be entertained. Here was a symbolic geography of sex!

° Moreover, a 'station' is used for purposes of *'Verkehr'* ['traffic', 'intercourse', 'sexual intercourse']: this fact determines the psychical coating in a number of cases of railway phobia.

The figure of the hypnotist became a potent popular symbol of menace and control. In Bram Stoker's Dracula *(1897), where Charcot is cited, we are offered the idea that the world may be infected by individuals who have irresistible access to the hidden parts of our minds; and in George du Maurier's* Trilby, *we are introduced to the mesmeric impresario Svengali.*

GEORGE DU MAURIER
Trilby

(1894)

Svengali was a bolder wooer. When he cringed, it was with a mock humility full of sardonic threats; when he was playful, it was with a terrible playfulness, like that of a cat with a mouse – a weird, ungainly cat, and most unclean; a sticky, haunting, long, lean, uncanny, black spider-cat, if there is such an animal outside a bad dream.

It was a great grievance to him that she had suffered from no more pains in her eyes. She had; but preferred to endure them rather than seek relief from *him.*

So he would playfully try to mesmerize her with his glance, and sidle up nearer and nearer to her, making passes and counter-passes, with stern command in his eyes, till she would shake and shiver and almost sicken with fear, and all but feel the spell come over her, as in a nightmare, and rouse herself with a great effort and escape.

If Taffy were there he would interfere with a friendly 'Now then, old fellow, none of that!' and a jolly slap on the back, which would make Svengali cough for an hour, and paralyse his mesmeric powers for a week.

Svengali had a stroke of good-fortune. He played at three grand concerts with Gecko, and had a well-deserved success. He even gave a concert of his own, which made a furore, and blossomed out into beautiful and costly clothes of quite original colour and shape and pattern, so that people would turn round and stare at him in the street – a thing he loved. He felt his fortune was secure, and ran into debt with tailors, hatters, shoemakers, jewellers, but paid none of his old debts to his friends. His pockets were always full of printed slips – things

that had been written about him in the papers – and he would read
them aloud to everybody he knew, especially to Trilby, as she sat darning
socks on the model-throne while the fencing and boxing were in train.
And he would lay his fame and his fortune at her feet, on condition that
she should share her life with him.

'Ach, himmel, Drilpy!' he would say, 'you don't know what it is to be
a great pianist like me – *hein*? What is your Little Billee, with his stinking
oil-bladders, sitting mum in his corner, his mahlstick and his palette in
one hand, and his twiddling little footle pig's-hair brush in the other!
What noise does *he* make? When his little fool of a picture is finished
he will send it to London, and they will hang it on a wall with a lot of
others, all in a line, like recruits called out for inspection, and the
yawning public will walk by in procession and inspect, and say "damn!"
Svengali will go to London *himself*. Ha! ha! He will be all alone on a
platform, and play as nobody else can play; and hundreds of beautiful
Engländerinnen will see and hear and go mad with love for him –
Prinzessen, Comtessen, Serene English Altessen. They will soon lose
their Serenity and their Highness when they hear Svengali! They will
invite him to their palaces, and pay him a thousand francs to play for
them; and after, he will loll in the best armchair, and they will sit all
round him on footstools, and bring him tea and gin and *küchen* and
marrons glacés, and lean over him and fan him – for he is tired after
playing them for a thousand francs of Chopin! Ha, ha! I know all about
it – *hein*?

'And he will not look at them, even! He will look inward, at his own
dream – and his dream will be about Drilpy – to lay his talent, his glory,
his thousand francs at her beautiful white feet!

'Their stupid, big, fat, tow-headed, putty-nosed husbands will be mad
with jealousy, and long to box him, but they will be afraid. Ach! those
beautiful Anclaises! they will think it an honour to mend his shirts, to
sew buttons on his pantaloons; to darn his socks, as you are doing now
for that sacred imbecile of a Scotchman who is always trying to paint
toréadors, or that sweating, pig-headed bullock of an Englander who is
always trying to get himself dirty and then to get himself clean again! –
e da capo!'

The unconscious, and the techniques for its control, represented a numinous idea which seemed to presage a sea-change in humanity itself. In his autobiographical Inferno, *the dramatist August Strindberg feels the intimations of its arrival among himself and his circle.*

AUGUST STRINDBERG
Inferno

(1898)

Six months have ebbed away and I still take my walk on the ramparts. As I let my eyes stray over the lunatic asylum, and try to catch sight of the blue streak in the distance that is the sea, I fancy that I am on the look-out for the new era that is coming, the new religion of which the world is dreaming.

Dark winter is buried, the fields are growing green, the trees are in blossom, the nightingale is singing in the Observatory Gardens, but the melancholy of winter still weighs upon our spirits because of the many ominous things that are happening, the many inexplicable things that make even the sceptical uneasy. Cases of sleeplessness are increasing, serious nervous disorders are multiplying, invisible presences are of common occurrence, real miracles are taking place. People are waiting for something to happen.

A young man came to visit me. He asked:

'What ought I to do to sleep peacefully at night?'

'What has happened?'

'Upon my word, I cannot tell you, but I have a horror of my bedroom, and I am moving elsewhere tomorrow.'

'Young man, you are an atheist and a believer in naturalism. What has happened?'

'Devil take it! When I got home last night and opened my door someone took hold of my arm and shook me.'

'So there was someone in your room.'

'Why, no! I lit the candles and I could not see anyone.'

'Young man, there is one whom we cannot see by the light of a candle.'

'What manner of thing is he?'

'He is the Unseen, young man. Have you taken sulphonal, potassium bromide, morphia or chloral?'

'I have tried them all.'

'And the Unseen won't decamp? Well, then, you want to sleep peacefully at night, and you have come to ask me how to do so. Listen to me, young man. I am no doctor, nor am I a prophet; I am an old sinner, doing penance. Do not expect any sermons or prophecies from a ruffian who needs all the time he can spare to preach sermons to himself. I too have suffered from sleepless nights and deep dejection. I too have fought face to face with the Unseen, and I have at last regained the power of sleep and got back my health. Do you know how? Guess!'

The young man guessed what I meant and lowered his eyes.

'So you have guessed. Depart in peace and sleep well.'

*Systematic medical exploration of the world of the unconscious generated
languages – and rumours – that infiltrated the general media and public
debate. Many of these representations expressed anxieties about the
extent of strange and uncontrollable lunacies beneath the façade of daily
life. (From Ives scrapbook.)*

INCREASE OF INSANITY.

Mr. E. W. White, Professor of Psychological
Medicine at King's College, delivered his annual
address at 11, Chandos-street, W., yesterday, as
president of the Medico-Psychological Association.
The subject of his paper was "Legal and General
Desiderata for the Insane."

The paper drew attention to the Lunacy Com-
missioners' Blue-book, issued in June 1902, which
showed that insanity was on the increase. the
average annual increase of the rate-paid insane
in the County of London being about 500. The
Blue-book also showed that there was one insane
person to every 298 sane, whereas in 1859 the proportion was one to 536. It was their duty, therefore, to discover why there was no material advance in the recovery rate. Under the heading
of racial changes they noted that there was less
encouragement than formerly to elegible aliens
to settle in the country, and to infuse new blood
into the population. Most of the aliens were undesirable, often of the criminal type, and likely
to be detrimental to the future nerve stability of
the race.

In regard to heredity, Professor White pointed
out that the intermarriage of neurotics was all
too common, and should be discouraged, and, if
possible, prevented by statute. Late marriages
were more frequent than fifty years ago; and this
was not conducive to a healthy stock. The abuse
of alcohol was both a cause and a symptom of
insanity. Should not the Legislature enforce both
the maturity and the purity of all alcoholic drinks.

Another cause of insanity was to be found in
the marriage of weaklings, who would have
formerly died in infancy, but who now survived
to produce an unhealthy stock. In regard to environment changes of recent years, the population
was to-day urban rather than rural. Overcrowding
was common; and people breathed less pure air,
and had less outdoor exercise under the beneficent
action of the sun's rays than formerly. The stress
of life, too, was far greater; and late hours and
unnatural excitement must leave their marks upon
the race, as well as upon the individual.

The idea developed that even within the most advanced societies various kinds of repressed forces were subtly active. For the French doctor and social psychologist Gustave le Bon, the crowd itself had a mentality as atavistic and easily influenced as 'a woman, a savage or a child'.

GUSTAVE LE BON
The Crowd: A Study of the Popular Mind

(1896)

When studying the fundamental characteristics of a crowd we stated that it is guided almost exclusively by unconscious motives. Its acts are far more under the influence of the spinal cord than of the brain. In this respect a crowd is closely akin to quite primitive beings. The acts performed may be perfect so far as their execution is concerned, but as they are not directed by the brain, the individual conducts himself according as the exciting causes to which he is submitted may happen to decide. A crowd is at the mercy of all external exciting causes, and reflects their incessant variations. It is the slave of the impulses which it receives. The isolated individual may be submitted to the same exciting causes as the man in a crowd, but as his brain shows him the inadvisability of yielding to them, he refrains from yielding. This truth may be physiologically expressed by saying that the isolated individual possesses the capacity of dominating his reflex actions, while a crowd is devoid of this capacity.

The varying impulses which crowds obey may be, according to their exciting causes, generous or cruel, heroic or cowardly, but they will always be so imperious that the interest of the individual, even the interest of self-preservation, will not dominate them. The exciting causes that may act on crowds being so varied, and crowds always obeying them, crowds are in consequence extremely mobile. This explains how it is that we see them pass in a moment from the most bloodthirsty ferocity to the most extreme generosity and heroism. A crowd may easily enact the part of an executioner, but not less easily that of a martyr. It is crowds that have furnished the torrents of blood requisite for the triumph of every belief. It is not necessary to go back to the heroic ages to see what crowds are capable of in this latter direction.

They are never sparing of their life in an insurrection, and not long since a general,° becoming suddenly popular, might easily have found a hundred thousand men ready to sacrifice their lives for his cause had he demanded it.

Any display of premeditation by crowds is in consequence out of the question. They may be animated in succession by the most contrary sentiments, but they will always be under the influence of the exciting causes of the moment. They are like the leaves which a tempest whirls up and scatters in every direction and then allows to fall. When studying later on certain revolutionary crowds we shall give some examples of the variability of their sentiments.

This mobility of crowds renders them very difficult to govern, especially when a measure of public authority has fallen into their hands. Did not the necessities of everyday life constitute a sort of invisible regulator of existence, it would scarcely be possible for democracies to last. Still, though the wishes of crowds are frenzied they are not durable. Crowds are as incapable of willing as of thinking for any length of time.

A crowd is not merely impulsive and mobile. Like a savage, it is not prepared to admit that anything can come between its desire and the realization of its desire. It is the less capable of understanding such an intervention, in consequence of the feeling of irresistible power given it by its numerical strength. The notion of impossibility disappears for the individual in a crowd. An isolated individual knows well enough that alone he cannot set fire to a palace or loot a shop, and should he be tempted to do so, he will easily resist the temptation. Making part of a crowd, he is conscious of the power given him by number, and it is sufficient to suggest to him ideas of murder or pillage for him to yield immediately to temptation. An unexpected obstacle will be destroyed with frenzied rage. Did the human organism allow of the perpetuity of furious passion, it might be said that the normal condition of a crowd baulked in its wishes is just such a state of furious passion.

° General Boulanger.

. . . and the final pages of H. G. Wells's Island of Doctor Moreau *conjure le Bon's anxieties through the vision of the demented protagonist.*

H. G. WELLS
The Island of Doctor Moreau

(1896)

Though I do not expect that the terror of that island will ever altogether leave me, at most times it lies far in the back of my mind, a mere distant cloud, a memory and a faint distrust; but there are times when the little cloud spreads until it obscures the whole sky. Then I look about me at my fellow men. And I go in fear. I see faces keen and bright, others dull or dangerous, others unsteady, insincere; none that have the calm authority of a reasonable soul. I feel as though the animal was surging up through them; that presently the degradation of the Islanders will be played over again on a larger scale. I know this is an illusion, that these seeming men and women about me are indeed men and women, men and women for ever, perfectly reasonable creatures, full of human desires and tender solicitude, emancipated from instinct, and the slaves of no fantastic Law – beings altogether different from the Beast Folk. Yet I shrink from them, from their curious glances, their enquiries and assistance, and long to be away from them and alone.

For that reason I live near the broad free downland, and can escape thither when this shadow is over my soul; and very sweet is the empty downland then, under the wind-swept sky. When I lived in London the horror was wellnigh insupportable. I could not get away from men; their voices came through windows; locked doors were flimsy safeguards. I would go out into the streets to fight with my delusion, and prowling women would mew after me, furtive craving men glanced jealously at me, weary pale workers go coughing by me, with tired eyes and eager paces like wounded deer dripping blood, old people, bent and dull, pass murmuring to themselves, and all unheeding a ragged tail of gibing children. Then I would turn aside into some chapel, and even there, such was my disturbance, it seemed that the preacher gibbered Big Thinks even as the Ape Man had done; or into some library, and there the intent faces over the books seemed but patient creatures waiting for prey. Particularly nauseous were the blank expressionless faces of people in trains and omnibuses; they seemed no more my fellow creatures than dead bodies would be, so that I did not dare to travel unless I was assured of being alone. And even it seemed that I, too, was not a reasonable creature, but only an animal tormented with some strange disorder in its brain, that sent it to wander alone, like a sheep stricken with the gid.

These new techniques of mental manipulation led to a proliferation of anxieties about criminals endowed with powers over the unconscious. (From Ives scrapbook.)

BURGLARS WITH HYPNOTIC EYES.

" The burglar with the hypnotic eye" is, according to the New York correspondent of the " Telegraph," the latest product of that go-ahead country, America. At first, we are told, people scoffed at him as a fiction of the imagination, and they would have continued to reject him but for real learned college professors who came forward to declare that hypnotic power was not a monopoly of the righteous, and could, indeed, become a most dangerous asset of the criminal classes :

Professor Munsterburg, of Harvard, went so far as to declare his belief that a certain American criminal, now electrocuted, had not confessed to the murder of his own free will, but was in all probability innocent, and had been hypnotised into making a false confession. Only a few weeks ago it was alleged that another criminal on trial for his life at Chicago had the hypnotic eye, and used his power to such advantage that the jurymen who came under his influence quailed before him, and became mysteriously ill.

The latest instance comes from Cleveland, Ohio, to-day. The burglar, dressed in the height of fashion and gentle in manners and conversation, first appeared at the apartments of Mr. Arthur Croft on Sunday night, and represented himself to Mrs. Croft as a close friend of her husband. They sat on the verandah and talked for half an hour. He convinced Mrs. Croft that he really was a friend of her absent husband. The burglar returned last night and found Mrs. Croft again on the verandah. He asked for a drink of water, and when she returned with the glass she found him seated in the parlour. Mrs. Croft turned on the electric light, and noticed that the man had a most piercing eye, which gave her a peculiar feeling, so she told the police. Then the man arose, made a few passes, and she was dead to the world.

Mrs. McKinney, who occupied the adjoining apartments, saw the stranger quickly leave. Mrs. Croft, on regaining her senses, found that her jewels were gone and her drawers had been ransacked. She values the stolen jewellery at £800.

After all this it is disappointing to find that, although other hypnotic burglars are about, none has been captured; though that is scarcely to be wondered at, since the arresting officer must come within the influence of the hypnotic and arresting eye.

The fin-de-siècle's *most famous criminal, Jack the Ripper, came in the popular press to stand for the dark forces of the unconscious incarnate.*

'Another Murder – and More to Follow?'

Pall Mall Gazette (8 September 1888)

Something like a panic will be occasioned in London today by the announcement that another horrible murder has taken place in densely populated Whitechapel. This makes the fourth murder of the same kind, the perpetrator of which has succeeded in escaping the vigilance of the police. The triumphant success with which the metropolitan police have suppressed all political meetings in Trafalgar Square contrasts strangely with their absolute failure to prevent the most brutal kind of murder in Whitechapel. The Criminal Investigation Department under Mr Monro was so pre-occupied in tracking out the men suspected of meditating political crimes that the ordinary vulgar assassin has a free field in which to indulge his propensities. Whether or not this is the true explanation of the immunity which the Whitechapel murderer enjoys, the fact of that immunity is undoubted. Four poor women, miserable and wretched, have been murdered in the heart of a densely populated quarter, and not only murdered but mutilated in a peculiarly brutal fashion, and so far the police do not seem to have discovered a single clue to the perpetrator of the crimes.

There is some reason to hope that the latest in this grim and gory series of outrages will supply some evidence as to the identity of the murderer. The knife with which he disembowelled his unfortunate victim and a leathern apron were, it is said, found by the corpse. If so, these are the only traces left by this mysterious criminal. Dr Anderson, the new chief of the Detective Department, will now have an admirable opportunity of showing that wits sharpened by reflections upon the deeper problems of 'Human Destiny' and the millennium are quite capable of grappling with the mundane problems of the detection of crime. The fact that the police have been freely talking for a week past about a man nicknamed Leather Apron may have led the criminal to leave a leather apron near his victim in order to mislead. He certainly seems to have been capable of such an act of deliberate preparation. The murder perpetrated this morning shows no indication of hurry or of alarm. He seems to have first killed the woman by cutting her throat so deeply as almost to sever her head from her shoulders, then to have disembowelled her and then to have disposed of the viscera in a fashion recalling stories of Red Indian savagery. A man who was cool enough to do this, and who had time enough to do it, was not likely to leave his leather apron behind him and his knife apparently for no purpose but to serve as a clue. But be this as it may, if the police know of a ruffian who wears a leather apron in Whitechapel whom they have suspected of previous crimes, no time should be lost in ascertaining whether this leather apron, if it really exists, can be identified as his.

This renewed reminder of the potentialities of revolting barbarity which lie latent in man will administer a salutary shock to the complacent optimism which assumes that the progress of civilization has rendered unnecessary the bolts and bars, social, moral, and legal, which keep the Mr Hyde of humanity from assuming visible shape among us. There certainly seems to be a tolerably realistic impersonification of Mr Hyde at large in Whitechapel. The Savage of Civilization whom we are raising by the hundred thousand in our slums is quite as capable of bathing his hands in blood as any Sioux who ever scalped a foe. But we should not be surprised if the murderer in the present case should not turn out to be slum bred. The nature of the outrages and the calling of the victims suggests that we have to look out for a man who is animated by that mania of bloodthirsty cruelty which sometimes springs from the unbridled indulgence of the worst passions. We may have a plebeian Marquis de Sade at large in Whitechapel. If so, and if he is not promptly apprehended, we shall not have long to wait for another addition to the ghastly catalogue of murder.

There is some reason to hope that the sentiment of horror which the peculiar atrocity of the present crime excites even in the most callous will spur the police into a display of vigorous and intelligent activity. At present the disaffection in the force is so widespread that, unless we are strangely misinformed, the police are thinking more of the possibility of striking against a system which has become intolerable than of overexerting themselves in the detection of crime. As for the community at large, the panic will probably be confined to the area within which this midnight murderer confines his operations. If, however, a similar crime were now to be committed in the West End, there would be a panic, the like of which we have not seen in our time. From that, however, we shall probably be spared; but the public will be more or less uneasy as long as the Whitechapel murderer is left at large.

In the loose confederation of the avant-garde, the arts and philosophy, the fin-de-siècle also produced a counterculture which celebrated the unconscious as the revolt of the human mind against the repression of civilization, and a return of the repressed forces of nature.

H. P. BLAVATSKY
Studies in Occultism

Lucifer Magazine (1887–91)

Thousands of years ago the Phrygian Dactyls, the initiated priests, spoken of as the 'magicians and exorcists of sickness', healed diseases by magnetic processes. It was claimed that they had obtained these curative powers from the powerful breath of Cybele, the many-breasted goddess, the daughter of Coelus and Terra. Indeed, her genealogy and the myths attached to it show Cybele as the personification and type of the vital essence, whose source was located by the ancients between the Earth and the starry sky, and who was regarded as the very *fons vitae* of all that lives and breathes. The mountain air being placed nearer to that fount fortifies health and prolongs man's existence; hence, Cybele's life, as an infant, is shown in her myth as having been preserved on a mountain. This was before that *Magna* and *Bona Dea*, the prolific *Mater*, became transformed into Ceres–Demeter, the patroness of the Eleusinian Mysteries.

Animal magnetism (now called Suggestion and Hypnotism) was the principal agent in theurgic mysteries as also in the *Asclepieia* – the healing temples of Aesculapius, where the patients once admitted were treated, during the process of 'incubation', magnetically, during their sleep.

This creative and life-giving Force – denied and laughed at when named theurgic magic; accused for the last century as being principally based on superstition and fraud, whenever referred to as mesmerism – is now called Hypnotism, Charcotism, Suggestion, 'psychology' and what not.

The celebration of the irrational and atavistic was the driving power behind Nietzsche's vision of Ancient Greece in the Birth of Tragedy.

FRIEDRICH NIETZSCHE

The Birth of Tragedy: Out of the Spirit of Music

(1872)

From all corners of the ancient world – ignoring the modern world for the time being – from Rome to Babylon we can demonstrate the existence of Dionysiac festivals, which are at best related to the Greek festivals as the bearded satyr, deriving his name and attributes from the goat, is related to Dionysus himself. Almost universally, the centre of those festivals was an extravagant lack of sexual discipline, whose waves engulfed all the venerable rules of family life. The most savage beasts of nature were here unleashed, even that repellent mixture of lust and cruelty that I have always held to be a 'witch's brew'. It would seem that for some time, however, the Greeks were thoroughly secured and protected against the febrile excitements of these festivals, knowledge of which forced its way to the Greeks along every route of land and sea: the figure of Apollo rose up in all its pride and held out the Gorgon's head to the grotesque, barbaric Dionysiac, the most dangerous force it had to contend with. It was in Doric art that Apollo's majestically repudiating stance was immortalized.

This resistance became more questionable, even impossible, when similar impulses emerged from the deepest roots of Greek culture. Now all the Delphic god could do was to disarm his powerful opponent of his destructive weapon by effecting a timely reconciliation – the most important moment in the history of Greek religion. Wherever we look we can observe the transformations wrought by this event. It was the reconciliation of two adversaries, clearly defining the boundaries that they were henceforward to respect, and periodically exchanging gifts of honour. Fundamentally the chasm had not been bridged. But if we consider how Dionysiac power revealed itself under the terms of that peace accord, and establish a comparison with the Babylonian Sacaea and its throwback of man to the condition of the tiger and the ape, we will be able to understand the meaning of those new festivals of world redemption and days of transfiguration. It was here that nature was first given its artistic celebration, here that the breakdown of the *principium individuationis* became an artistic phenomenon. That terrible 'witch's brew' of lust and cruelty had now lost its potency, and only the peculiar blend and duality of emotions amongst the Dionysiac revellers recalls it, as medicines recall deadly poisons – the phenomenon that pain is experienced as joy, that jubilation tears tormented cries from the breast. At the moment of supreme joy we hear the scream of horror or the yearning lamentation for something irrevocably lost. Those Greek festivals reveal a sentimental trait in nature, as though she were bemoaning her fragmentation into individuals. The chanting and gestures of these revellers, with their dual inspiration, was something new and unheard of in the Homeric and Greek world; and Dionysiac music in particular induced feelings of awe and terror. Music was apparently already known as an Apolline art, but only because of its rhythm, as regular as the sound of waves crashing against the shore, the creative power of which was developed for the representation of Apolline states. The music of Apollo was Doric architecture transmuted into sounds, but only into suggestive sounds such as those of the cithara. Care was taken to ensure that the one element held to be non-Apolline was excluded, the very element of which Dionysiac music consisted – the overwhelming power of sound, the unified flow of melody and the utterly incomparable world of harmony. In the Dionysiac dithyramb, man's symbolic faculties are roused to their supreme intensity: a feeling never before experienced is struggling for expression – the destruction of the veil of Maya, Oneness as the source of form, of nature itself. The essence of nature was now to find symbolic expression. A new world of symbols was required, the whole of the symbolism of the body, not only the symbolism of the mouth, the eye, the word, but the rhythmic motion of all the limbs of the body in the complete gesture of the dance. Then all the other symbolic forces, the forces of music – rhythm, dynamics and harmony – would suddenly find impetuous expression.

The Great Sacrifice: The Russian artist and mystic Nicholas Roerich painted this backdrop for Stravinsky's *The Rite of Spring* in 1910. His stated intention was to conjure 'the awakening of the spirit of primeval man . . . the spirit of the prehistoric Slavs'. (Nicholas Roerich, *The Great Sacrifice*, 1910. Bolling Collection, Miami, Florida)

*In this climate of the rediscovery of the unconscious in art, Hans
Prinzhorn's collection of the Artistry of the Mentally Ill was widely seen
as significant. Here, Prinzhorn gives his account of what the art of the
insane has to teach us.*

HANS PRINZHORN
Artistry of the Mentally Ill: A Contribution to the Psychology and Psychopathology of Configuration

(1922)

The astonishing fact that the schizophrenic outlook and that
displayed in recent art can be described only by the same words immediately obliges us to state the differences as well. And that is not hard.
For the schizophrenic there is the fateful experience. The alienation
from the world of appearances is imposed on him as a gruesome,
inescapable lot against which he often struggles for some time until he
submits and slowly begins to feel at home in his autistic world, which
is enriched by his delusions. For the contemporary artist alienation
from the once familiar and courted reality may also result from an
overpowering experience, but at least it involves conscious and rational
decisions. It occurs because of painful self-analysis and because the
surmounted relationships to society become repulsive, and it is therefore
often mixed with doubts, a bad conscience and resentments. On the
other hand, it has a clear purpose, at least theoretically. By its nature
the liberation from the compulsion of external appearances should be
so complete that all configuration should deal only with pure psychic
qualities. Its source should be a completely autonomous personality
with ambitions of entering into a mystical union with the whole world.

The decline of the traditional outlook which gave rise to this extravagant, grandiose, often compulsively distorted attitude cannot be pursued
here. In any case it is not simply a concern of expressionism, as shortsighted people still hope even today. On the contrary, expressionism is
a symptom of the decline and an attempt to make the best of it. If
we ignore the confusion of artistic programmes and try to grasp the

motivating idea which produces ever greater exaltations, we find the same longing for inspired creation reported in primitives and known from the greatest periods of culture. That brings us to the weakness of our time – its tragedy and grimness. What we seem to lack is just that primary experience which precedes all knowledge and which alone produces inspired art. Instead, after all our extravagant wishing, after all the determined triumphs over ancient errors, we finally end up with intellectual substitutes.

If we are correct, then the passionate emotions with which sensitive artists react to our pictures become completely understandable. These works really emerged from autonomous personalities who carried out the mission of an anonymous force, who were independent of external reality, indebted to no one and sufficient solely unto themselves. The inborn primeval process of configuration ran its course far from the outside world, without plan but by necessity, like all natural processes.

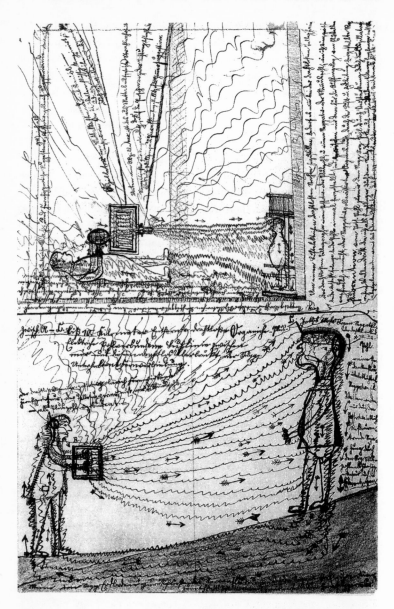

Jakob Mohr: The work of a certified lunatic. (From *Beyond Reason: Art and Psychosis, Works from the Prinzhorn Collection,* 1996.) (Courtesy of Prinzhorn-Sammlung der Psychiatrischen Universitätsklinik Heidelberg (Prinzhorn Collection))

The first manifesto of the Dada movement enthusiastically espouses the new dynamic in art.

dAdaIstiC ManIfestO!

(1916)

Art, in its execution and direction, is dependent upon the time in which it lives, and artists are creatures of their epoch. The highest art will be the one that presents in its contents of consciousness the thousand-fold problems of the time; to which one may note that this art allows itself to be tossed by the explosions of the last week, that it pieces together its parts again and again while being shoved by the day before. The best and most original artists will be those who hour by hour tear the tatters of their body out of the tumult of life's cataract, committed to the intellect of the age, bleeding from hands and hearts.

Did expressionism ever fulfil our expectations of this kind of art that is a confirmation of our most vital concerns?

No!No!No!

Did the expressionists fulfil our expectations of an art that burns the essence of life into our flesh?

No!No!No!

Under the pretence of interiorization the expressionists in literature and painting have made of themselves a generation that is still waiting today for literary- and art-historical veneration and that puts itself forward as a candidate for an honorable bourgeois recognition.

. . .

That sentimental resistance to an age that is no better and no worse, no more reactionary and no more revolutionary than any other age, that faded opposition that yearns for prayer and incense whenever it does not prefer to make its cardboard gun out of attic iambs – these are characteristics of a youth that never understood how to be young. Expressionism, discovered abroad, has become in Germany – as always happens – a fat idyll and the expectation of a good pension; it has nothing more to do with the struggles of active people. The signers of this manifesto have gathered under the battlecry

DADA!!!

for the propaganda of an art from which they expect the realization of new ideals. What exactly is DADAISM?

The word Dada symbolizes the primitive relationship to ambient reality; with dadaism a new reality achieves its majority. Life appears as a simultaneous confusion of noises, colours and mental rhythms that is absorbed cold-eyed into a dadaistic art with all the sensational screams and feverishness of its deviant everyday psyche and in its total, brutal reality.

. . .

The BRUITISTIC poem
shows a streetcar just as it is, the essence of the streetcar with the yawning of the pensioner Schulze and the scream of the brakes.

The SIMULTANEOUS poem
teaches the meaning of the jumbledness of all things, while Herr Schulze reads, the Balkan express crosses a bridge near Nisch, a pig bawls in the cellar at Nuttke the butcher's.

The STATIC poem
makes individuals of words, the woods with its tree tops, foresters' liverys and wild boars spit out of the three letters 'woods', maybe a small hotel even steps out, with the name Bellevue or Bella Vista. Dadaism leads to unheard of new possibilities and forms of expression in all the arts. It has made cubism into a dance on the stage; it has propagated the BRUITISTIC music of the futurists (whose purely Italian concerns it however doesn't wish to generalize) in all the countries of Europe. The word Dada points at the same time to the internationalism of the movement, which is bound to no borders, religions or professions. Dada is the international expression of all these offensives, peace congresses, ruckus at the vegetable market, suppers on the Esplenade, etc., etc. Dada seeks the use of

new materials in painting

Dada is a CLUB founded in Berlin that one can enter without taking on any responsibilities. Here everyone is chairman, and everyone can express an opinion on artistic matters. Dada is not a pretence for the ambition of a few belletrists (as our enemies would like to have you believe); Dada is a type of intellect that can reveal itself in every conversation so that one has to say: that one is a dadaist, this one is not; the Dada Club has members in every part of the world, in Honolulu as much as in New Orleans or Meseritz. To be a dadaist can mean, under certain circumstances, to be more of a businessman or politician than an artist – or to be an artist only by accident; to be a dadaist is to be thrown by all things, to be against all accretion of sediment, to sit down for a moment on a chair means that one has brought life in danger (Mr Wengs has already drawn the revolver out of his pocket). A fabric is torn when touched, one says yes to a life that wants to move higher through negation. To say yes – to say no; the mighty hocus-pocus of existence gives winds to the nerves of the true dadaist – he lies like this, he hunts like this, he cycles like this – half Pantagruel, half Franziskus and laughs and laughs. Down with the aesthetic-ethical attitude! Down with the bloodless abstraction of expressionism! Down with holier-than-thou theories of the literary fools! We are for dadaism in word and image, for the dadaistic happening in the world. To be against this manifesto is to be a dadaist!

Tristan Tzara. Franz Jung. George Grosz. Marcel Janco. Richard Hulsenbeck. Gerhard Preiss. Raoul Hausmann.

Others.

But there were voices, particularly in the British school of psychiatry, who found this celebration of the products of the unconscious both distasteful and dangerous.

SIR JAMES CRICHTON-BROWNE
The Doctor's After Thoughts

(1932)

PSYCHOANALYSIS
A Specimen with Comments

An invalid lady who had been a good performer on the violin, dreamed that the tuner had called to tune the piano. He was engaged in taking out a number of seeds from the inside of the piano.

Well, surely we may leave it at that as a dream reminiscence of a commonplace incident. But not at all. The psychoanalyst must be called in, and after an analysis which lasted one hour – Joseph was much more expeditious with the butler's and the baker's dreams – arrived at the interpretation thereof. He discovered what, in the occult jargon of the cult, is called symbolizations and determinations. The dreamer herself is representative of the piano; she had said the day before that she wanted to go piano for a bit. The desire 'to go piano' (represented symbolically by actually being a piano) is the first and most superficial wish-fulfilment of the dream. The tuner is a symbol of the analyst – one indeed that is apt enough, for there is an obvious analogy between the relation of a tuner of a piano and that of a psychoanalyst and his patient. The dream therefore contains a reference (as many dreams do) to the analytic situation itself. But why is the tuner (the analyst) removing seeds from the piano (the patient). Probably because they had dropped into it from a canary cage hanging over it. Not at all. 'With this question,' we are told, 'we come to the sexual elements, which are so seldom lacking in dreams' (a statement which most decent people will repudiate), 'for seed here as elsewhere refers to the biological processes of reproduction. But the association made it evident that there were three distinct meanings within this sphere: In the first place, seeds refer to certain sexual desires which, as the analyst was making her realize, she had all unknowingly harboured in her mind. The analyst she hoped would rid her of these, as it seemed to her, evil and unseemly desires. Hence the analyst was symbolically removing them.' But how did he do this? Did he extract them like a decayed tooth, or is he endowed with the power of plenary absolution, and is it the best way to remove evil and unseemly desires to stir them up and bring them from the depths of subconsciousness into the light of common day, from the unknown into the known, and is there not a risk that the analyst may be introducing evil and unruly desires into an entirely innocent mind?

'But there are two further wish-fulfilments of a cruder and more instinctive kind. The word seed can be metaphorically used for offspring, and the third meaning of the dream is that the analyst is acting as the patient's accoucheur at the birth of a child. Lest the reader should be astonished and disgusted, let him remember that Socrates, who with his motto "Know thyself", seems to have been in some way the forerunner of Freud.' But notwithstanding this perversion of the dictum of Socrates, whom Freud resembles as much as a toadstool does a British oak, the reader is astonished and disgusted by all this jargon and quest of the unclean, and feels sure that any right-minded father who found out that his daughter had been subjected for an hour to dream interpretation of this kind would kick the piano-tuner out of the house.

These sentiments are reflected in the denouement of du Maurier's Trilby, *where Svengali's manipulation of* Trilby *is finally exposed as sadistic victimization.*

GEORGE DU MAURIER
Trilby
(1894)

'**I** will tell you a secret.

'*There were two Trilbys.* There was the Trilby you knew, who could not sing one single note in tune. She was an angel of paradise. She is now! But she had no more idea of singing than I have of winning a steeple-chase at the croix de Berny. She could no more sing than a fiddle can play itself! She could never tell one tune from another – one note from the next. Do you remember how she tried to sing "Ben Bolt" that day when she first came to the studio in the Place St Anatole des Arts? It was droll, *hein? à se boucher les oreilles!* Well, that was Trilby, your Trilby! that was my Trilby too – and I loved her as one loves an only love, an only sister, an only child – a gentle martyr on earth, a blessed saint in heaven! And that Trilby was enough for *me!*

'And that was the Trilby that loved your brother, madame – oh! but with all the love that was in her! He did not know what he had lost, your brother! Her love, it was immense, like her voice, and just as full of celestial sweetness and sympathy! She told me everything! *ce pauvre Litrebili, ce qu'il a perdu!*

'But all at once – pr-r-r-out! presto! *augenblick!* . . . with one wave of his hand over her – with one look of his eye – with a word – Svengali could turn her into the other Trilby, *his* Trilby – and make her do whatever he liked . . . you might have run a red-hot needle into her and she would not have felt it . . .

'He had but to say "*Dors!*" and she suddenly became an unconscious Trilby of marble, who could produce wonderful sounds – just the sounds he wanted, and nothing else – and think his thoughts and wish his wishes – and love him at his bidding with a strange, unreal, factitious love . . . just his own love for himself turned inside out – *à l'envers* – and reflected back on him, as from a mirror . . . *un écho, un simulacre, quoi!*

pas autre chose! . . . It was not worth having! I was not even jealous!

'Well, that was the Trilby he taught how to sing – and – and I helped him, God of heaven forgive me! That Trilby was just a singing-machine – an organ to play upon – an instrument of music – a Stradivarius – a flexible flageolet of flesh and blood – a voice, and nothing more – just the unconscious voice that Svengali sang with – for it takes two to sing like La Svengali, monsieur – the one who has got the voice, and the one who knows what to do with it . . . So that when you heard her sing the "Nussbaum", the "Impromptu", you heard Svengali singing with her voice, just as you hear Joachim play a *chaconne* of Bach with his fiddle! . . . Herr Joachim's fiddle . . . what does it know of Sebastian Bach? and as for *chaconnes* . . . *il s'en moque pas mal, ce fameux violon*! . . .

'And *our* Trilby . . . what did she know of Schumann, Chopin? – nothing at all! She mocked herself not badly of Nussbaums and Impromptus . . . they would make her yawn to demantibulate her jaws! . . . When Svengali's Trilby was being taught to sing . . . when Svengali's Trilby was singing – or seemed to *you* as if she were singing – *our* Trilby had ceased to exist . . . *our* Trilby was fast asleep . . . in fact, *our* Trilby was *dead* . . .'

Svengali mesmerizing Trilby. (*Trilby*, 1894.) (Courtesy of Mary Evans Picture Library)

*Daniel Paul Schreber, presiding judge of the supreme court of Saxony,
suffered a complete nervous collapse in November 1893. His extraordinary* Memoirs of My Nervous Illness, *written ten years later, provided
the basis for Freud's analysis of the nature of paranoia.*

DANIEL PAUL SCHREBER
Memoirs of My Nervous Illness

(1903)

Other things that happened on my body were still more closely
connected with supernatural matters. It was mentioned in earlier chap-
ters that those rays (God's nerves) which were attracted, followed only
reluctantly, because it meant losing their own existence and therefore
went against their instinct of self-preservation. Therefore one continually
tried to stop the attraction, in other words to break free again from my
nerves. The only absolutely effective way of doing this would have been
to cure my nervous illness by procuring prolific sleep. But apparently
one could not decide to do this, or at least not systematically, because
it would have needed a self-denying sacrifice on the part of the rays
immediately concerned, for which they had neither the capacity nor
the necessary will-power.

All other conceivable methods were therefore tried in the course of
time, but from the nature of the matter they all proved thoroughly
unsuitable. Always the main idea behind them was to 'forsake' me, that
is to say abandon me; at the time I am now discussing it was thought
that this could be achieved by unmanning me and allowing my body to
be prostituted like that of a female harlot, sometimes also by killing me
and later by destroying my reason (making me demented).

But with regard to the efforts to unman me it was soon found that
the gradual filling of my body with nerves of voluptuousness (female
nerves) had exactly the reverse effect, because the resulting so-called
'soul-voluptuousness' in my body rather increased the power of attraction. Therefore *'scorpions'* were repeatedly put into my head, tiny
crab- or spider-like structures which were to carry out some work of
destruction in my head. These had the nature of souls and therefore
were *talking* beings; they were distinguished according to their place

of origin as 'Aryan', and 'Catholic' scorpions; the former were somewhat bigger and stronger. However, these scorpions regularly withdrew from my head without doing me harm, when they perceived the purity of my nerves and the holiness of my purpose – this was one of the innumerable triumphs which I have often experienced since then in a similar way. Just because the holiness of my purpose exerted too great a power of attraction on the souls, attempts were also made to falsify my mental individuality in all sorts of ways. 'Jesuits', that is to say departed souls of former Jesuits, repeatedly tried to put into my head a different 'determinant nerve', which was to change my awareness of my own identity; the inner table of my skull was lined with a different brain membrane° in order to extinguish my memory of my own ego. All this without any permanent effect. Finally attempts were made to blacken my nerves by miraculously placing the blackened nerves of other (deceased) human beings into my body, believing presumably that the blackness (impurity) of these nerves would be imparted to mine. Concerning these blackened nerves, I wish to mention a few names, the bearers of which were all said to have been in 'Flechsig's hell', which made me assume that Professor Flechsig must have some power of disposal over these nerves. Among them was a certain Bernhard Haase – his name was by coincidence identical with that of a distant relative of mine – a bad sort, who was supposed to have committed some crime, a murder or suchlike; further a certain R., a fellow student and member of my Students' Union, who had gone to America because he had not made good and had led a rather dissolute life, and as far as I know was killed there in the War of Independence in 1864 or 1865;† finally a certain Julius Emil Haase who, despite his blackened nerves, gave the impression of a very honourable person. Presumably at the time of the Frankfurt *attentat* he was a senior member of the Students' Union and then became a medical practitioner in Jena, if I heard correctly. Particularly

---

° As a layman in medicine I had also not heard of a brain membrane before, but was informed of this expression by the voices after I had appreciated (felt) this phenomenon myself.

† The above-mentioned R. is one of the instances from which I gather Professor Flechsig's powers as Governor of one of God's provinces must have stretched as far as America. The same seems to have applied to England; it was repeatedly stated that he had taken 'sixteen English rays' from their leader, an English Bishop, which were however only entrusted to him on the express condition that they were to be used solely in a war for the independence of Germany.

interesting was that the soul of this Julius Emil Haase was even still able to give me certain medical advice by virtue of its scientific experience during its life; I want to add here that up to a point the same applied to my father's soul. The presence of these blackened nerves in my body caused no lasting effect; they vanished in time without altering the condition of my nerves.

I could relate still more miraculous events from the time of my stay in Flechsig's Asylum. I could tell of happenings which make me believe that popular belief that *will-o'-the-wisps* are departed souls is true in many cases if not all; I could tell of *wandering clocks*, that is to say souls of departed heretics, said to have been preserved for centuries under glass in medieval cloisters (here too there is an undercurrent of something like a soul murder), who announced their survival by a vibration connected with an infinitely monotonous and doleful humming noise (I myself received this impression by way of nerve-contact), etc., etc. To avoid becoming too discursive I will now close my report about my experiences and memories of the time of my stay in Flechsig's Asylum.

Within the British tradition, too much introspection was seen as a retrograde, even dangerous, path. Thomas Clouston regarded the indulgence of paranoia as 'unsavoury' and degenerate.

T. S. CLOUSTON
Clinical Lectures on Mental Diseases

(1896)

It is exceedingly difficult to define paranoia as the term is used in Germany, and now largely also in America. As yet it is clear that different authors understand by it different things, but taking the sense of the majority of them, I think the following may be accepted as a short description of the condition. It always occurs in persons in whose brains there is the potentiality of mental or nervous disease through hereditary predisposition to the psychoses or the neuroses. It is, in fact, a strongly hereditary insanity. It evolves slowly without an acute first stage. It consists, in fact, of a slowly developed change from the normal mental state of the individual, and most commonly in the direction of elevated ideas and exaggerated self-importance. Sometimes the change is towards morbid suspicion and sensitiveness, this often going with the elevated ideas. Sometimes the sexual instincts are changed or perverted, constituting the 'sexual paranoiac' who has attracted such an amount of morbid attention in Germany. The conduct is always affected, but not necessarily at first taking the form of acutely insane action. Queernesses, oddities, impracticability, insensibility to the motives which ordinarily influence humanity – abnormal mental reaction – appear. The reasoning power cannot correct obviously mistaken conclusions, and cannot be trusted in regard to any subject. The hereditary social instincts and the gregariousness which seem to be the chief factor of the solidarity of human society are weakened, and gradually become perverted. Hereditary morality, probably the strongest ethical force, is weak in its power over conduct, or assumes perverted and diseased shapes. The instincts, appetites, and propensities are disturbed or perverted. The affective nature is always changed. No paranoiac loves his wife, or his brethren, or his friends in the right and normal way. His affectiveness takes strange and often a-social forms, so that instead of holding together and upholding the family and the state, it is disruptive in its effects. The moral sanctions and the affective drawings of the paranoiac do not tend towards social cohesion, but destruction. The man of the 'insane diathesis', as described by Maudsley, is a paranoiac in its early stage; later on he develops delusions, but not always fixed or organized delusions. He often commits crime, thinking it a virtue, as Guiteau did when he murdered President Garfield who had done him no harm whatever. Still later the paranoiac often sinks into mental enfeeblement, not of the complete kind, but often enough he lives out his life without thus mentally dying. King Louis II of Bavaria was a typical case of paranoia, all the symptoms of the disease being developed in exaggerated forms through his autocratic position and command of money, and brought out vividly through the 'fierce light that beats upon a throne'. In him there appeared to have been sexual perversion of the most abominable description. This unsavoury subject and all that relates to the pathological manifestations of the generative nisus have recently been very fully – far too fully, I take leave to say – treated by Krafft-Ebing and Schrenck-Notzing in Germany. In this country we rarely see such cases as are described in such repulsive detail by those two authors, and I think it is better we should not look too closely for them. The whole subject of paranoia is allied to the 'degeneracy' and the 'hysteria' which Max Nordau so vividly describes as influencing our present-day literature and art.

The American poet John Greenleaf Whittier vividly imagined the Orien-
tal ecstasies of the ancient Vedic soma *ritual before banishing this*
degenerate spectre in the second half of the poem, which became the
well-known hymn 'Dear Lord and Father of Mankind'.

JOHN GREENLEAF WHITTIER
'The Brewing of Soma'

(1873)

'These libations mixed with milk have been prepared for Indra;
offer Soma to the drinker of Soma.' – VASHISTA, Trans. by
MAX MULLER.

The faggots blazed, the cauldron's smoke
   Up through the green wood curled;
'Bring honey from the hollow oak,
Bring milky sap,' the brewers spoke,
   In the childhood of the world.

And brewed they well or brewed they ill,
   The priests thrust in their rods,
First tasted, and then drank their fill,
And shouted, with one voice and will,
   'Behold the drink of gods!'

They drank, and lo! in heart and brain
   A new, glad life began;
The grey of hair grew young again,
The sick man laughed away his pain,
   The cripple leaped and ran.

'Drink, mortals, what the gods have sent,
   Forget your long annoy.'
So sang the priests. From tent to tent
The Soma's sacred madness went,
   A storm of drunken joy.

Then knew each rapt inebriate
   A winged and glorious birth,
Soared upward, with strange joy elate,
Beat, with dazed head, Varuna's gate,
   And, sobered, sank to earth.

The land with Soma's praises rang,
   On Gihon's banks of shade
Its hymns the dusky maidens sang;
In joy of life or mortal pang
   All men to Soma prayed.

The morning twilight of the race
   Sends down these matin psalms:
And still with wondering eyes we trace
The simple prayers to Soma's grace,
   That Vedic verse embalms.

As in that child-world's early year,
   Each after age has striven
By music, incense, vigils drear,
And trance, to bring the skies more near,
   Or lift men up to heaven! –

Some fever of the blood and brain,
   Some self-exalting spell,
The scourger's keen delight of pain,
The Dervish dance, the Orphic strain,
   The wild-haired Bacchant's yell, –

The desert's hair-grown hermit sunk
   The saner brute below;
The naked Santon, hashish-drunk,
The cloister madness of the monk,
   The fakir's torture-show!

And yet the past comes round again
   And new doth old fulfil;
In sensual transports wild as vain

We brew in many a Christian fane
   The heathen Soma still!

Dear Lord and Father of mankind,
   Forgive our foolish ways!
Reclothe us in our rightful mind,
In purer lives thy service find,
   In deeper reverence, praise.

In simple trust like theirs who heard
   Beside the Syrian sea
The gracious calling of the Lord
Let us, like them, without a word,
   Rise up and follow thee.

O Sabbath rest by Galilee!
   O calm of hills above,
Where Jesus knelt to share with thee
The silence of eternity
   Interpreted by love!

With that deep hush subduing all
   Our words and works that drown
The tender whisper of thy call,
As noiseless let thy blessing fall
   As fell thy manna down.

Drop thy still dews of quietness,
   Till all our strivings cease;
Take from our souls the strain and stress,
And let our ordered lives confess
   The beauty of thy peace

Breathe through the heats of our desire
   Thy coolness and thy balm;
Let sense be dumb, let flesh retire;
Speak through the earthquake, wind and fire,
   O still, small voice of calm!

. . . and the Hungarian-born doctor, journalist and future Zionist Max Nordau, in his wide-ranging survey of the degenerate tendencies of the fin-de-siècle, was quick to categorize the contemporary fascination with the products of the unconscious as degenerate. Here, he dissects the figure he sees as its arch-manifestation, Nietzsche.

MAX NORDAU
Degeneration

(1892)

Not every aberrant person (*pervers*) is subject to impulsions. The perversion may be limited exclusively to the sphere of ideation, and get its satisfaction wholly in ideas. A subject thus affected never gets the notion of transforming his ideas into deeds. His derangement does not encroach upon the centres of will and movement, but carries on its fell work within the centres of ideation. We know forms of sexual perversion in which the sufferers never experience the impulse to seek satisfaction in acts, and who revel only in thought. This astonishing rupture of the natural connection between idea and movement, between thought and act, this detachment of the organs of will and movement from the organs of conception and judgement which they normally obey, is in itself a proof of deepest disorder throughout the machinery of thought. Incompetent critics eagerly point to the fact that many authors and artists live unexceptionable lives in complete contrast to their works, which may be immoral or contrary to nature, and deduce from this fact that it is unjustifiable to draw from his works conclusions as to the mental and moral Nature of their author. Those who talk in this manner do not even suspect that there are purely mental perversions which are quite as much a mental disease as the impulsions of the 'impulsivists'.

This is obviously the case with Nietzsche. His perversion is of a purely intellectual character, and has hardly ever impelled him to acts. Hence, in his mind there has been no conflict between instincts and the morality acquired by education. His explanation of conscience has quite another source than that assumed by Dr Türck. It is one of those perverted interpretations of a sensation by the consciousness perceiving it which are so frequently observed. Nietzsche remarks that with him ideas of a cruel kind are accompanied by feelings of pleasure – that they are, as mental therapeutics expresses it, 'voluptuously accentuated'. In consequence of this accompaniment of pleasure he has the inclination to conjure up sensually sensuous representations of that kind, and to dwell on them with enjoyment. Consciousness then seeks to give some sort of rational explanation of these experiences by assuming cruelty to be a powerful primordial instinct of man, that, since he may not actually commit cruel deeds, he may, at least, take pleasure in the representation of them, and that the rapturous lingering over representations of this kind, man calls his conscience. As I have shown above, it is Nietzsche's opinion that stings of conscience are not the consequence of evil deeds, but appear in men who have never committed any evil. Hence he obviously makes use of the word in a sense quite different from that of current usage, a sense peculiar to himself; he designates by it, simply his revelling in voluptuously accentuated representations of cruelty.

The alienist, however, is familiar with the perversion in which the invalid experiences voluptuous stimulation from acts or representations of a cruel nature. Science has a name for it. It is called Sadism. Sadism is the opposite form of sexual perversion to masochism. Nietzsche is a sufferer from Sadism in its most pronounced form, only with him it is confined to the intellectual sphere alone, and is satisfied by ideal debauchery. I do not wish to dwell too long on this repulsive subject, and will, therefore, quote only a few passages, showing that, in Nietzsche's thought, images of cruelty are without exception accompanied by ideas of a sensual character, and are italicized by him: 'The splendid beast ranging *in its lust* after prey and victory' (*Zur Genealogie der Moral* [1887], p. 21). 'The *feeling of content* at being able, without scruple, to wreak his power on a powerless being, the *voluptuousness de faire le mal pour le plaisir de le faire*, the *enjoyment* of vanquishing' (*Ibid.*, p. 51). 'Do your pleasure, ye wantons; roar for very *lust* and wickedness' (*Die fröhliche Wissenschaft* [1882], p. 226). 'The path to one's own heaven ever leads through the *voluptuousness* of one's own hell' (*Ibid.*, p. 249). 'How comes it that I have yet met no one . . . who knew morality as a problem, and this problem as his personal distress, torment, *voluptuousness*, passion?' (*Ibid.*, p. 264). 'Hitherto he has felt most at ease on earth at the sight of tragedies, bullfights and crucifixions; and when he invented hell, behold, that was his heaven on earth. When the great man cries aloud, the little man runs swiftly thither, and his tongue hangs out from his throat for very *lusting*' (*Also sprach Zarathustra* [1883–5], pt. iii., p. 96), etc. I beg the unprofessional reader particularly to observe the association of the words italicized with those expressing something evil. This association is neither accidental nor arbitrary. It is a psychical necessity, for in Nietzsche's consciousness no image of wickedness and crime can arise without exciting him sexually, and he is unable to experience any sexual stimulation without the immediate appearance in his consciousness of an image of some deed of violence and blood.

Hence the real source of Nietzsche's doctrine is his Sadism. And I will here make a general remark on which I do not desire to linger, but which I should like to recommend to the particular attention of the reader. In the success of unhealthy tendencies in art and literature, no quality of their authors has so large and determining a share as their sexual psychopathy. All persons of unbalanced minds – the neurasthenic, the hysteric, the degenerate, the insane – have the keenest scent for perversions of a sexual kind, and perceive them under all disguises. As a rule, indeed, they are ignorant of what it is in certain works and artists which pleases them, but investigation always reveals in the object of their predilection a veiled manifestation of some *Psychopathia sexualis*. The masochism of Wagner and Ibsen, the Skoptzism of Tolstoi, the erotomania (*folie amoureuse chaste*) of the Diabolists, the Decadents and of Nietzsche, unquestionably obtain for these authors and tendencies a large, and, at all events, the most sincere and fanatical fraction of their partisans. Works of a sexually psychopathic nature excite in abnormal subjects the corresponding perversion (till then slumbering and unconscious, perhaps also undeveloped, although present in the germ), and give them lively feelings of pleasure, which they, usually in good faith, regard as purely aesthetic or intellectual, whereas they are actually sexual. Only in the light of this explanation do the characteristic artistic tendencies of the abnormals, of which we have proof, become wholly intelligible. This confounding of aesthetic with sexual feelings is not surprising, for the spheres of these two feelings are not only contiguous, but, as has been proved elsewhere, are for the most part even coincident. At the base of all oddities of costume, especially that of women, there is hidden an unconscious speculation in something of a sexual-psychopathy, which finds incitation and attraction in the temporary fashion in dress. No professional person has yet viewed fashions from this standpoint. I may not here allow myself so broad a departure from my principal theme. The subject may, however, be most emphatically recommended to the consideration of experts. In the domain of fashions they will make the most remarkable psychiatrical discoveries.

Sadism (1900). Nordau saw the pathologies of sex and sadism as an underlying dynamic in the exploration of the unconscious. (From Serge Nazarieff, *Jeux de Dames Cruelles,* 1988.)

6

The Arrival of the Deviant: Sexology

The fin-de-siècle *human sciences sought to medicalize increasingly large areas of human behaviour, and their discoveries informed the laws governing 'abnormality'. One of the most sweeping changes was in the medical, psychiatric and legal descriptions of 'sexual deviance'. Instead of being a voluntary agent engaging in an illegal act (such as buggery), the sexual deviant was recast as a person in the grip of a medical condition. New expressions such as 'homosexual', 'sadism' and 'masochism' were coined, and the 'science' of sexology was born to study such types and to seek their security within hospitals. These developments on the one hand liberated 'deviant' sexual practices from moral and religious censure, but, on the other, imprisoned them within the new medical pathology.*

For early workers in the field, such as Krafft-Ebing, the appeal to medicine was an appeal to humanity and reason. His monumental compilation of case studies, Psychopathia Sexualis, *provided the underpinning for the new science of sexology.*

R. VON KRAFFT-EBING

Psychopathia Sexualis: With Especial Reference to Antipathic Sexual Instinct, A Medico-Forensic Study

(1886)

LUST-MURDER (LUST POTENTIATED AS CRUELTY,
MURDEROUS LUST EXTENDING TO ANTHROPOPHAGY)

The most horrible example, and one which most pointedly shows the connection between lust and a desire to kill, is the case of Andreas Bichel, which *Feuerbach* published in his 'Akteninässige Darstellung merkwürdiger Verbrechen'.

B. puellas stupratas necavit et dissecuit   With reference to one of his victims, at his examination he expressed himself as follows: 'I opened her breast and with a knife cut through the fleshy parts of the body. Then I arranged the body as a butcher does beef, and hacked it with an axe into pieces of a size to fit the hole which I had dug up in the mountain for burying it. I may say that while opening the body I was so greedy that I trembled, and could have cut out a piece and eaten it.'

Lombroso, too ('Geschlechtstrieb und Verbrechen in ihren gegenseitigen Beziehungen'. *'Goltdammer's* Archiv', Bd. xxx.), mentions cases falling in the same category. A certain Phillipe indulged in strangling prostitutes, post actum, and said: 'I am fond of women, but it is sport for me to strangle them after having enjoyed them.'

A certain Grassi (*Lombroso, op. cit.*, p. 12) was one night seized with sexual desire for a relative. Irritated by her remonstrance, he stabbed her several times in the abdomen with a knife, and also murdered her father and uncle who attempted to hold him back. Immediately thereafter he hastened to visit a prostitute in order to cool in her embrace his sexual passion. But this was not sufficient, for he then murdered his own father and slaughtered several oxen in the stable.

It cannot be doubted, after the foregoing, that a great number of so-called lust murders depend upon combined hyperaesthesia and paraesthesia sexualis. As a result of this perverse colouring of the feelings, further acts of bestiality with the corpse may result – e.g. cutting it up and wallowing in the intestines. The case of Bichel points to this possibility.

A modern example is that of Menesclou ('Annales d'hygiène publique'), who was examined by *Lasègue, Brouardel* and *Motet*, declared to be mentally sound, and executed.

Case 16.   A four-year-old girl was missing from her parents' home, 15th April 1880. On 16th April, Menesclou, one of the occupants of the house, was arrested. The forearm of the child was found in his pocket, and the head and entrails, in a half-charred condition, were taken from the stove. Other parts of the body were found in the water-closet. The genitals could not be found. M., when asked their whereabouts, became embarrassed. The circumstances, as well as an obscene poem found on his person, left no doubt that he had violated the child and then murdered her. M. expressed no remorse, asserting that his deed was an unhappy accident. His intelligence is limited. He presents no anatomical signs of degeneration; is somewhat deaf and scrofulous.

M., aged twenty; convulsions at the age of nine months. Later he suffered from disturbed sleep (enuresis nocturna); was nervous, and developed tardily and imperfectly. With puberty he became irritable, showed evil inclinations, was lazy, intractable, and in all trades proved to be of no use. He grew no better even in the House of Correction. He was made a marine, but there, too, he proved useless. When he returned home he stole from his parents, and spent his time in bad company. He did not run after women, but gave himself up passionately to masturbation, and occasionally indulged in sodomy with bitches. His mother suffered with *mania menstrualis periodica*. An uncle was insane, and another a drunkard. The examination of M.'s brain showed morbid changes of the frontal lobes, of the first and second temporal convolutions, and of a part of the occipital convolutions.

Case 17.   Alton, a clerk in England, goes out of town for a walk. He lures a child into a thicket, and returns after a time to his office, where he makes this entry in his notebook: 'Killed today a young girl; it was fine and hot.' The child was missed, searched for and found cut into pieces. Many parts, and among them the genitals, could not be found. A. did not show the slightest trace of emotion, and gave no explanation of the motive or circumstances of his horrible deed. He was a psychopathic individual, and occasionally subject to fits of depression with *taedium vitae*. His father had had an attack of acute mania. A near relative suffered from mania with homicidal impulses. A. was executed.

In such cases it may even happen that appetite for the flesh of the murdered victim arises, and in consequence of this perverse colouring of the idea, parts of the body may be eaten.

Havelock Ellis's Sexual Inversion *offered a perspective on 'deviant' sexual practices which both placed them in a biological context and questioned their 'degenerate' nature.*

HAVELOCK ELLIS
Sexual Inversion

(1897)

What is sexual inversion? Is it, as many would have us believe, an abominable acquired vice, to be stamped out by the prison? or is it, as a few assert, a beneficial variety of human emotion which should be tolerated or even fostered? Is it a diseased condition which qualifies its subject for the lunatic asylum? or is it a natural monstrosity, a human 'sport', the manifestations of which must be regulated when they become antisocial? There is probably an element of truth in more than one of these views. I am prepared to admit that very widely divergent views of sexual inversion are largely justified by the position and attitude of the investigator. It is natural that the police-official should find that his cases are largely mere examples of disgusting vice and crime. It is natural that the asylum superintendent should find that we are chiefly dealing with a form of insanity. It is equally natural that the sexual invert himself should find that he and his inverted friends are not so very unlike ordinary persons. We have to recognize the influence of professional and personal bias and the influence of environment, one investigator basing his conclusions on one class of cases, another on a quite different class of cases. Naturally, I have largely founded my own conclusions on my own cases. I believe, however, that my cases and my attitude toward them justify me in doing this with some confidence. I am not in the position of one who is pleading *pro domo*, nor of the police-official, nor even of the physician, for these persons have not come to me for treatment. I approach the matter as a psychologist who has ascertained certain definite facts, and who is founding his conclusions on those facts.

The first point which impresses me is that we must regard sexual inversion as largely a congenital phenomenon, or, to speak more accurately, as a phenomenon which is based on congenital conditions. This, I think, lies at the root of the right comprehension of the matter. There are at the present day two streams of tendency in the views regarding sexual inversion: one seeking to enlarge the sphere of the acquired (represented by Binet, – who, however, recognizes predisposition, – Schrenck-Notzing, and others), the other seeking to enlarge the sphere of the congenital (represented by Krafft-Ebing, Moll, Féré and others). There is, as usually happens, truth in both these views.

. . .

We can probably grasp the nature of the abnormality better if we reflect on the development of the sexes and on the latent organic bisexuality in each sex. At an early stage of development the sexes are indistinguishable, and throughout life the traces of this early community of sex remain. The hen fowl retains in a rudimentary form the spurs which are so large and formidable in her lord, and sometimes she develops a capacity to crow, or puts on male plumage. Among mammals the male possesses useless nipples, which occasionally even develop into breasts, and the female possesses a clitoris, which is merely a rudimentary penis, and may also develop. The sexually inverted person does not usually possess any gross exaggeration of these signs of community with the opposite sex. But, as we have seen, there are a considerable number of more subtle approximations to the opposite sex in inverted persons, both on the physical and the psychic side. Putting the matter in a purely speculative shape, it may be said that at conception the organism is provided with about 50 per cent of male germs and about 50 per cent of female germs, and that, as development proceeds, either the male or the female germs assume the upper hand, killing out those of the other sex, until in the maturely developed individual only a few aborted germs of the opposite sex are left. In the homosexual person, however, and in the psychosexual hermaphrodite, we may imagine that the process has not proceeded normally, on account of some peculiarity in the number or character of either the original male germs or female germs, or both, the result being that we have a person who is organically twisted into a shape that is more fitted for the exercise of the inverted than of the normal sexual impulse, or else equally fitted for both.

Thus in sexual inversion we have what may fairly be called a 'sport', or variation, one of those organic aberrations which we see throughout living nature, in plants and in animals.

It is not here asserted, as I would carefully point out, that an inverted sexual instinct, or organ for such instinct, is developed in early embryonic life; such a notion is rightly rejected as absurd. What we may reasonably regard as formed at an early stage of development is strictly a predisposition; that is to say, such a modification of the organism that it becomes more adapted than the normal or average organism to experience sexual attraction to the same sex. The sexual invert may thus be roughly compared to the congenital idiot, to the instinctive criminal, to the man of genius, who are all not strictly concordant with the usual biological variation (because this is of a less subtle character), but who become somewhat more intelligible to us if we bear in mind their affinity to variations.

. . .

A word may be said as to the connection between sexual inversion and degeneration. In France especially, since the days of Morel, the stigmata of degeneration are much spoken of. Sexual inversion is frequently regarded as one of them: i.e. as an episodic *syndrome* of a hereditary disease, taking its place beside other psychic stigmata, such as kleptomania and pyromania. Krafft-Ebing also so regards inversion. Strictly speaking, the invert is degenerate; he has fallen away from the genus. So is a colour-blind person. But Morel's conception of degenerescence has unfortunately been coarsened and vulgarized. As it now stands, we gain little or no information by being told that a person is a 'degenerate'. When we find a complexus of well-marked abnormalities, we are fairly justified in asserting that we have to deal with a condition of degeneration. Inversion is frequently found in such a condition. I have, indeed, already tried to suggest that a condition of diffused minor abnormality may be regarded as the basis of congenital inversion. In other words, inversion is bound up with a modification of the secondary sexual characters. But little is gained by calling these modifications 'stigmata of degeneration', a term which threatens to disappear from scientific terminology, to become a mere term of literary and journalistic abuse. So much may be said concerning a conception or a phrase of which far too much has been made in popular literature. At the best it remains vague and little fitted for scientific use.

. . . but Paul Möbius, German psychiatrist, neurologist and grandson of the inventor of the Möbius strip, stressed the links between sexual perversion, deviance and innate degeneracy.

P. J. MÖBIUS
'Gender and Illness'

(1903)

The present state of affairs is totally unsatisfactory in any case. In Germany the law threatens males indulging in mutual sexual acts, but it lets females go free. Created by our jurisdiction, the elastic concept (*Gummibegriff*) of 'acts resembling intercourse', is attended by great uncertainty. When you ask why we have Para. 175 of the *D.Str.G.B.* (the German Penal Code) you will be told the lawgiver has 'taken into account' the people's legal consciousness (*Rechtsbewusstsein*). I was given this answer by Supreme Court justices, but it is evident that in this way you also might justify the burning of witches and such. If you further consider that the vilest acts of sexual intercourse, especially the transmission of venereal disease, go unpunished, you shake your head. I am also of the opinion that the abolition of §175 is to be urgently desired as it mainly results in blackmail, often followed by suicide. In reason, only violence should be prohibited, which of course includes the abuse of underage persons. All sorts of acts one does not approve of exist where the law does not interfere. To repel what is offensive, to disapprove of what is indecent, are matters of public opinion. Pederasty is rightly despised and not to be excused, because there is no such thing as a drive to pederasty; it is always an infamous act, almost as infamous as the seduction of a young girl. But public opinion . . . must above all learn to distinguish between abnormal sexual trends that are an expression of degeneracy, and abnormal sex acts. The former must of course not be judged morally; they must be fought with the proper remedies and not reviled. The latter, the acts themselves, ought to be judged according to the danger they imply or the disgust they arouse, with special concern for the person who has so acted. Abnormal sex acts are performed both by mentally sick persons and by approximately sane ones . . . The answer is prevention, if possible . . . The degenerate person can in no way be transformed . . . That does not mean a physician cannot be helpful . . . on the contrary . . . Bromides . . . Trying to persuade a pervert to get married I consider a totally perverted effort . . . It is altogether undesirable for such people to procreate. On no account should one always talk them into believing that they are missing God knows what. The Catholic Church has shown that one can live content without wife and children provided one has a sufficient task to live for.

*J. A. Symonds, art historian, offered by contrast a courageous autobio-
graphical account of his own homosexuality.*

JOHN ADDINGTON SYMONDS
The Memoirs of John Addington Symonds

(written 1889–91; 1984)

It was my primary object when I began these autobiographical
notes to describe as accurately and candidly as I was able a type of
character, which I do not at all believe to be exceptional, but which for
various intelligible reasons has never yet been properly analysed. I
wanted to supply material for the ethical psychologist and the student
of mental pathology, by portraying a man of no mean talents, of no
abnormal depravity, whose life has been perplexed from first to last by
passion – natural, instinctive, healthy in his own particular case – but
morbid and abominable from the point of view of the society in which
he lives – persistent passion for the male sex.

(December 1891: This was written by me at Venice in May 1889. I had
not then studied the cases of sexual inversion recorded by Casper-Liman,
Ulrichs and Krafft-Ebing. Had I done so, I should not perhaps have
dealt with my personal experience so diffusely as I have done in this
chapter. What I wrote, I now leave as it stands. It forms a more direct
contribution to the psychology of sexual abnormality than if I were to
mix it up with the discussion of theories unknown to me at the time of
writing.).

. . .

I need not describe in detail the several stages by which this liaison
between myself and Angelo assumed its present form. At last he entered
my service as gondolier at fixed wages, with a certain allowance of food
and fuel. He took many journeys with me, and visited me at Davos. We
grew to understand each other and to conceal nothing. Everything I
learned about him made me forget the suspicions which had clouded
the beginning of our acquaintance, and closed my eyes to the anomaly
of a comradeship which retained so much of passion on my part and of

indulgence on his. I found him manly in the truest sense, with the manliness of a soldier and warm soft heart of an exceptionally kindly nature – proud and sensitive, wayward as a child, ungrudging in his service, willing and good-tempered, though somewhat indolent at the same time and subject to explosions of passion. He is truthful and sincere, frank in telling me what he thinks wrong about my conduct, attentive to my wants, perfect in his manners and behaviour – due allowance made for his madcap temperament, hoarse voice and wild impulsive freedom.

I can now look back with satisfaction on this intimacy. Though it began in folly and crime, according to the constitution of society, it has benefited him and proved a source of comfort and instruction to myself. Had it not been for my abnormal desire, I could never have learned to know and appreciate a human being so far removed from me in position, education, national quality and physique. I long thought it hopeless to lift him into something like prosperity – really because it took both of us so long to gain confidence in the stability of our respective intentions and to understand each other's character. At last, by constant regard on my side to his interests, by loyalty and growing affection on his side for me, the end has been attained. His father and brother have profited; for the one now plies his trade in greater comfort, and the other has a situation in the P & O service, which I got for him, and which enables him to marry. And all this good, good for both Angelo and myself, has its taproot in what at first was nothing better than a misdemeanour, punishable by the law and revolting to the majority of human beings. The situation is so anomalous that I still shudder when I think of it, knowing how impossible it is to bring forth good things out of evil, and how little I have done to eradicate my inborn insanity. Angelo's own theory about liaisons of this sort is that they do not signify, if they are monogamous and carefully protected by the prudence of both parties. Then they remain matters for the soul of each in sight of God – 'Our Lord above', as he says, pointing to the skies. On the other hand a man who goes from love to love – with Jack today and Tom tomorrow – sinks deep into the mire, loses respect and ends in degradation.

. . . and Magnus Hirschfeld stressed the healthy and normative aspects of homosexual love.

MAGNUS HIRSCHFELD
Sexual Anomalies: the Origins, Nature and Treatment of Sexual Disorders

(1905)

A careful investigation will show in all cases of genuine homosexuality that before a homosexual act has been engaged in the persons concerned have had a strong spiritual attraction for one another. This involuntary, erotically accentuated fixation of the senses as well as of the mind, is present long before its sexual character as such becomes conscious.

It might be argued that deep friendships between members of the same sex also occur in children who later develop into strictly heterosexual adults, and these friendships frequently persist even for a few years after puberty. They occur very frequently at schools, boarding schools and similar establishments, so frequently, indeed, that these friendships have been described as a physiological condition during the period of sexual indifference. But homosexual children differ from normal children not only as regards their general character and make-up, but also in their erotically tinged friendships. On the one hand, owing to the vague feeling *that their tendernesses have a deeper significance*, they are more self-conscious, reserved and particular, and, on the other hand, they are more intense and constant than their heterosexual comrades. Homosexual children are frequently the favourite objects of their school-fellows, who instinctively sense the feminine element in the homosexual boy and the virility in the homosexual girl. Above all, however, the homosexual activities of heterosexual children are of a more occasional character. After puberty the tendency is superseded by the increasing intensity of the child's love for the opposite sex, whereas in congenitally homosexual children the homosexual tendency at this period becomes stronger, and is finally directed toward the subject's own sex with the same yearning as the impulse of the heterosexual boy or girl is directed toward the opposite sex.

In the same way as heterosexual children between the ages of 15 and 20 sometimes contract firm friendships with members of their own sex, which gives the impression of entirely homosexual affects, homosexuals at this period of puberty also have heterosexual episodes, which do not appear to be due solely to the overwhelming power of suggestion exercised by the example of the grownups and romantic fiction, which always concerns love between men and women. The period referred to is a time of incomplete development, during which not only a clear physical differentiation is lacking, but the sexual impulse is also vague and groping, swinging this way and that, like a pendulum, until it fixes itself on a satisfactory sexual object either gradually or, through a great love affair, suddenly.

It is approximately at the age of 18 years, with slight deviations one way or another, that homosexual men and women, just like heterosexuals, develop that ideal eroticism that manifests itself in exaggerated admiration, serenades, love letters and love poems, with the sole difference that the object of this 'deification' is a member of the same sex.

Walt Whitman's poetry was a popular celebration of the polymorphous dimensions of love.

WALT WHITMAN
'Song of Myself'

Leaves of Grass (1855)

It is time to explain myself . . . . let us stand up.

What is known I strip away . . . . I launch all men and women forward with me into the unknown.

The clock indicates the moment . . . . but what does eternity indicate?

Eternity lies in bottomless reservoirs . . . . its buckets are rising for ever and ever,
They pour and they pour and they exhale away.

We have thus far exhausted trillions of winters and summers;
There are trillions ahead, and trillions ahead of them.

Births have brought us richness and variety,
And other births will bring us richness and variety.

I do not call one greater and one smaller,
That which fills its period and place is equal to any.

Were mankind murderous or jealous upon you my brother or my sister?
I am sorry for you . . . . they are not murderous or jealous upon me;
All has been gentle with me . . . . I keep no account with lamentation;
What have I to do with lamentation?

I am an acme of things accomplished, and I an encloser of
   things to be.

My feet strike an apex of the apices of the stairs,
On every step bunches of ages, and larger bunches between the
   steps,
All below duly travelled – and still I mount and mount.

Rise after rise bow the phantoms behind me,
Afar down I see the huge first Nothing, the vapour from the
   nostrils of death,
I know I was even there . . . . I waited unseen and always,
And slept while God carried me through the lethargic mist,
And took my time . . . . and took no hurt from the foetid
   carbon.

Long I was hugged close . . . . long and long.
Immense have been the preparations for me,
Faithful and friendly the arms that have helped me.

Cycles ferried my cradle, rowing and rowing like cheerful
   boatmen;
For room to me stars kept aside in their own rings,
They sent influences to look after what was to hold me.

Before I was born out of my mother generations guided me,
My embryo has never been torpid . . . . nothing could overlay it;
For it the nebula cohered to an orb . . . . the long slow strata
   piled to rest it on . . . . vast vegetables gave it sustenance,
Monstrous sauroids transported it in their mouths and
   deposited it with care.

All forces have been steadily employed to complete and delight
   me,
Now I stand on this spot with my soul.

. . . while Oscar Wilde offered a darker view of a love which contained the seeds of its own destruction.

OSCAR WILDE
'The Ballad of Reading Gaol'

(1898)

He did not wear his scarlet coat,
   For blood and wine are red,
And blood and wine were on his hands
   When they found him with the dead,
The poor dead woman whom he loved,
   And murdered in her bed.

He walked amongst the Trial Men
   In a suit of shabby grey;
A cricket cap was on his head,
   And his step seemed light and gay;
But I never saw a man who looked
   So wistfully at the day.

I never saw a man who looked
   With such a wistful eye
Upon that little tent of blue
   Which prisoners call the sky,
And at every drifting cloud that went
   With sails of silver by.

I walked, with other souls in pain,
   Within another ring,
And was wondering if the man had done
   A great or little thing,
When a voice behind me whispered low,
   'That fellow's got to swing.'

Dear Christ! the very prison walls
   Suddenly seemed to reel,
And the sky above my head became
   Like a casque of scorching steel;
And, though I was a soul in pain,
   My pain I could not feel.

I only knew what hunted thought
   Quickened his step, and why
He looked upon the garish day
   With such a wistful eye;
The man had killed the thing he loved,
   And so he had to die.

Yet each man kills the thing he loves,
   By each let this be heard,
Some do it with a bitter look,
   Some with a flattering word.
The coward does it with a kiss,
   The brave man with a sword!

Some kill their love when they are young,
   And some when they are old;
Some strangle with the hands of Lust,
   Some with the hands of Gold:
The kindest use a knife, because
   The dead so soon grow cold.

Some love too little, some too long,
   Some sell, and others buy;
Some do the deed with many tears,
   And some without a sigh:
For each man kills the thing he loves,
   Yet each man does not die.

He does not die a death of shame
   On a day of dark disgrace,
Nor have a noose about his neck,
   Nor a cloth upon his face,

Nor drop feet foremost through the floor
  Into an empty space.

He does not sit with silent men
  Who watch him night and day;
Who watch him when he tries to weep,
  And when he tries to pray;
Who watch him lest himself should rob
  The prison of its prey.

He does not wake at dawn to see
  Dread figures throng his room,
The shivering Chaplain robed in white,
  The Sheriff stern with gloom,
And the Governor all in shiny black,
  With the yellow face of Doom.

. . .

In Reading gaol by Reading town
  There is a pit of shame,
And in it lies a wretched man
  Eaten by teeth of flame,
In a burning winding-sheet he lies,
  And his grave has got no name.

And there, till Christ call forth the dead,
  In silence let him lie:
No need to waste the foolish tear,
  Or heave the windy sigh:
The man had killed the thing he loved,
  And so he had to die.

And all men kill the thing they love,
  By all let this be heard,
Some do it with a bitter look,
  Some with a flattering word,
The coward does it with a kiss,
  The brave man with a sword!

Despite the growing recognition of homosexual love as a moral choice, Wilde's final appeal, in his letter to the Home Secretary from prison, is to the medical account of disease in the face of which the sufferer is powerless.

OSCAR WILDE
Letter to the Home Secretary

(written 1896)

To the Home Secretary

2 *July 1896*   *H.M. Prison Reading*
To the Right Honourable Her Majesty's Principal Secretary of State for the Home Department.

The Petition of the above-named prisoner humbly sheweth that he does not desire to attempt to palliate in any way the terrible offences of which he was rightly found guilty, but to point out that such offences are forms of sexual madness and are recognized as such not merely by modern pathological science but by much modern legislation, notably in France, Austria and Italy, where the laws affecting these misdemeanours have been repealed, on the ground that they are diseases to be cured by a physician, rather than crimes to be punished by a judge. In the works of eminent men of science such as Lombroso and Nordau, to take merely two instances out of many, this is specially insisted on with references to the intimate connection between madness and the literary and artistic temperament, Professor Nordau in his book on 'Degenerescence' published in 1894 having devoted an entire chapter to the petitioner as a specially typical example of this fatal law.

The petitioner is now keenly conscious of the fact that while the three years preceding his arrest were from the intellectual point of view the most brilliant years of his life (four plays from his pen having been produced on the stage with immense success, and played not merely in England, America and Australia, but in almost every European capital, and many books that excited much interest at home and abroad having been published), still that during the entire time he was suffering from the most horrible form of erotomania, which made him forget his wife and children, his high social position in London and Paris, his European distinction as an artist, the honour of his name and family, his very humanity itself, and left him the helpless prey of the most revolting passions, and of a gang of people who for their own profit ministered to them, and then drove him to his hideous ruin.

It is under the ceaseless apprehension lest this insanity, that displayed itself in monstrous sexual perversion before, may now extend to the entire nature in intellect, that the petitioner writes this appeal which he earnestly entreats may be at once considered.

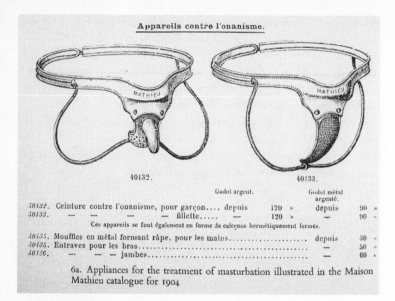

Appareils contre l'onanisme.

40132.

Godet argent.

40133.

Godet métal
argenté.

40132. Ceinture contre l'onanisme, pour garçon.... depuis   120 »   depuis   90 »
40133.   —   —   —   fillette.....   —   120 »   —   90 »
        Ces appareils se font également en forme de caleçons hermétiquement fermés.
40134. Moufles en métal formant râpe, pour les mains.................... depuis 30 »
40135. Entraves pour les bras...   —   50 »
40136.   —   —   —   jambes...   —   60 »

6a. Appliances for the treatment of masturbation illustrated in the Maison Mathieu catalogue for 1904

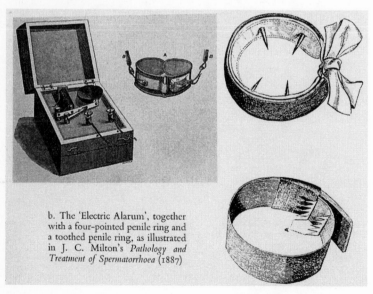

b. The 'Electric Alarum', together with a four-pointed penile ring and a toothed penile ring, as illustrated in J. C. Milton's *Pathology and Treatment of Spermatorrhoea* (1887)

Anti-masturbation devices: The new science of sexology associated masturbation with a range of deviant behaviour from criminality to madness. (Courtesy of the Wellcome Institute Library, London)

Along with sexual deviance, another contentious problem for the sexologists was syphilis. With its periods of latency, the uncertain nature of its transmission and its resistance to treatment, it had become a spectre which threatened the fabric of society itself through its involuntary introduction into marriage and childbirth. Alfred Fournier, the French doctor and venereologist, was the first to give an account of its hereditary transmission.

ALFRED FOURNIER
Syphilis & Marriage
(1881)

Now, when husbands, so sure of themselves, when men of the profession, all repeat to you to satiety, 'No, I affirm to you that I have had nothing in the way of a symptom since my marriage. I have had no indication, either upon the penis, the mouth or elsewhere, not the least erosion, the slightest pain, the least redness, capable of infecting my wife'; when such assertions are made to you, under such guarantees, and when these assertions are identically reproduced, not only in a few cases, but in a crowd of cases of the same description; when a fact so inexplicable, so extraordinary as it appears, becomes not the exception but an almost habitual rule under such conditions, the fact must be accepted, and we must depart from our otherwise legitimate incredulity, and say, 'So be it! Here is a woman who, on the one hand, has syphilis without *having shown a primary lesion*; on the other, has been infected by her husband *without this husband having had any contagious symptom*. What then is the mystery?'

I say, What then is the mystery? Well, Gentlemen, here is the key: it is, that this woman who has become syphilitic without a primary lesion, without chancre, and become diseased by contact with a husband exempt since his marriage from all contagious lesion – it is, I say, that this woman is PREGNANT, and she is infected by conception.

. . .

Truly, Gentlemen, we answer in the affirmative, such without doubt is the origin of this syphilis in the cases here in question. The wife-mother, infected in this manner, that is to say become syphilitic without primary symptoms, and become so by contact with a husband long since freed from all exterior indications, is a patient, who contracts syphilis, not from her husband, but *from her child*.

This is not then syphilis transmitted by contagion in the usual manner, as cases run; it is syphilis conceived *in utero*, conveyed by the child while in the mother's womb, communicated to the mother by the infant; it is this, in one word, that we call SYPHILIS BY CONCEPTION.

I should depart from my subject were I now to approach the clinical side of this syphilis by conception, so different from ordinary syphilis, both in its origin and in its primordial evolution. But it is necessary that you should not have any doubt as to its real existence; and it is with this end in view that I will add the following considerations: –

1st, In the first place, if one should reject this pathogenesis of the transmission of infection to the mother by the foetus, in the class of cases now occupying our attention, the syphilis of young married women, who, on the one hand, never present the primary symptom of chancre, and who, on the other hand, receive, or appear to receive, the contagion from a husband who is apparently healthy – this syphilis, I say, would remain absolutely incomprehensible, absolutely inexplicable.

And I again repeat to you that cases of this nature are too numerous, too defined, for one to oppose to them the argument of not proven; for one to dream of interpreting them by material errors of observation. They impress themselves on you in practice, and we must accept them as so many facts, however much we may discuss them in theory.

. . .

The peculiarity of hereditary syphilis, you know, is its appearance at once by general symptoms, that is, without any primary period; in a word, exempt from those two symptoms which constitute the fatal and necessary *début* of all syphilis contracted in the usual way, the chancre and the primitive adenopathy, symptomatic of it.

Well, it is exactly the same in syphilis by conception. It also presents neither the chancre nor the bubo among its symptoms. It also begins at once, by manifestations of a general kind, and this departure from the great laws which rule syphilis in its usual forms, certainly finds its reason in the special mode in which contamination here takes place.

The spectre of syphilis, all but unmentionable, was daringly summoned at the climax of Henrik Ibsen's play Ghosts, *which the* Daily Telegraph *described as 'a loathsome sore unbandaged'.*

HENRIK IBSEN
Ghosts

(1881)

O SVALD: This disease that I've inherited – [*he points to his forehead and goes on very softly*] – is seated here.

MRS ALVING [*almost speechless*]: Osvald! No, no!

OSVALD: Don't scream, I couldn't bear it. Yes, it sits here and waits. And it may break out any day – any minute.

MRS ALVING: But that's terrible . . . !

OSVALD: Now keep quiet. That's how things are with me.

MRS ALVING [*starting up*]: It isn't true, Osvald. It's not possible – it *can't* be!

OSVALD: I had one attack when I was abroad. It was soon over; but when I found out how it had been, I began to be haunted by this ghastly fear, and I hurried home to you as quickly as I could.

MRS ALVING: Then this is the fear –

OSVALD: Yes, you see, it's so unspeakably loathsome . . . Oh, if only it had been an ordinary fatal illness . . . because I'm not afraid to die, although I'd like to live as long as I can.

MRS ALVING: Yes, Osvald, you must.

OSVALD: But this is so horribly loathsome. To become like a helpless child again; to have to be fed; to have to – Oh, I can't speak of it!

MRS ALVING: My child will have his mother to look after him.

OSVALD [*springing up*]: No, never! That's just what I don't want. [*Simply*] I daren't think that perhaps I might linger on like that for years – until I'm old and grey. And perhaps you might die before me. [*He sits in Mrs Alving's chair.*] Because the doctor told me it might not be fatal at once. He called it a kind of softening of the brain, or something of the sort. [*With a wan smile*] I think it sounds such a nice expression; it always makes me think of cherry-coloured velvet curtains – something soft to stroke.

MRS ALVING [*screaming*]: Osvald!

An allegorical image of syphilis by Richard Cooper from 1910. (Courtesy of the Wellcome Institute Library, London.)

The mode of transmission of syphilis necessitated a 'marital advice culture', the principles of which are here proposed by Fournier to the medical profession.

ALFRED FOURNIER
Syphilis & Marriage

(1881)

It will happen to you, Gentlemen, more than once, in the course of your practice, to be consulted by a patient (known or unknown to you) with a preoccupied, almost an anxious air, who will probably address you somewhat in the following manner: –

Doctor, I have come to consult you on the question of my marriage; now, I have not always been straitlaced, particularly in my younger days, and, what is worse, I have not always been fortunate; in fact, I formally contracted syphilis. I exhibited such and such symptoms, and was treated in such and such a manner. Now the matter becomes serious, and I come to you to see if I am sufficiently cured, and to ask you the momentous question, Can I, without danger to my future wife, without danger to my possible progeny, consummate the marriage upon which I have risked my happiness? Will you then fully examine and question me, and give me your verdict?

Now, Gentlemen, when such a question is asked of you, you cannot think of it too seriously, or treat it with too much gravity.

Upon your reply hang the most serious, the most sacred interests, and those most dear to the heart of every right-minded man, as also they are the most varied and the most numerous. The reply that you are about to give, involves you, on your part, in a responsibility which I cannot designate otherwise than *overwhelming*. And I do not think I exaggerate in saying that in the many serious questions which a medical man has to solve, few present phases, on the one part so grave, and on the other part so complex, so difficult, or so delicate, as this one now before us. Judge then of this matter, and see what may be the consequence of an error on your part in such a situation.

Suppose then, that a physician should speak lightly in a case of this kind, and as it were pledge himself to one or the other of the two sole errors, possible in such circumstances, to what deplorable results would he not lead his patients?

...

A man who enters upon marriage with syphilitic antecedents may become dangerous to his wife.

This is evident, and need not in truth be discussed. It is manifest that a healthy young girl who unites herself to a syphilitic man, may become the victim of the same disease. Common sense admits it *a priori*, and it is undoubtedly confirmed by experience.

In fact, and how many times have we not seen – and who has not seen – cases of this kind? A young girl, in perfect health, marries a man who has had syphilis in the days of his bachelorhood. Some months later syphilitic symptoms appear; this evidently by the means, and by the means only, of her husband.

This syphilis of young married people – let us say it incidentally, since the occasion presents itself – is sufficiently frequent, even more frequent than one dares to suppose. You will find the proof of this in the numerous observations collected in different works, as also in the following statistics, which I myself have collected: – In a total of 572 syphilitic women, who have come to me in my private practice, I find not less than 81 who have contracted syphilis *from their husbands in the early days of marriage.* This list is sufficiently eloquent of itself to need any comment.

Let, then, families be more attentive to the health of proposed sons-in-law; let them be careful to protect their daughters against men of light, cynical or indifferent character, to whom it is a matter of little care whether or not they import disease into their homes.

Thus this fact is patent: young married women frequently receive syphilis from their husbands.

This culture of marital advice was diffused beyond the medical world into romantic novels such as Sarah Grand's The Heavenly Twins. *In an interview, Grand insisted: 'I hope that we shall soon see the marriage of certain men made a criminal offence.'*

SARAH GRAND
The Heavenly Twins

(1893)

'*I* do,' said Evadne decidedly. 'I would stop the imposition, approved of custom, connived at by parents, made possible by the state of ignorance in which we are carefully kept – the imposition upon a girl's innocence and inexperience of a disreputable man for a husband.'

Mrs Orton Beg was startled by this bold assertion, which was so unprecedented in her experience that for a moment she could not utter a word; and when she did speak she avoided a direct reply, because she thought any discussion on the subject of marriage, except from the sentimental point of view, was indelicate.

'But tell me your position exactly,' she begged – 'what you did next: why you are here!'

'I went by the night mail North,' Evadne answered, 'and saw them. They were very kind. They told me everything. I can't repeat the details; they disgust me.'

'No, pray don't!' Mrs Orton Beg exclaimed hastily. She had no mind for anything unsavoury.

'They had been abroad, you know,' Evadne pursued; 'Otherwise I should have heard from them as soon as the engagement was announced. They hoped to be in time, however. They had no idea the marriage would take place so soon.'

Mrs Orton Beg reflected for a little, and then she asked in evident trepidation, for she had more than a suspicion of what the reply would be: 'And what are you going to do?'

'Decline to live with him,' Evadne answered.

This was what Mrs Orton Beg had begun to suspect, but there is often an element of surprise in the confirmation of our shrewdest suspicions, and now she sat upright, leant forward, and looked at her niece aghast. 'What?' she demanded.

'I shall decline to live with him,' Evadne repeated with emphasis.

Mrs Orton Beg slowly resumed her reclining position, acting as one does who has heard the worst, and realizes that there is nothing to be done but to recover from the shock.

'I thought you loved him,' she ventured, after a prolonged pause.

'Yes, so did I,' Evadne answered, frowning – 'but I was mistaken. It was a mere affair of the senses, to be put off by the first circumstance calculated to cause a revulsion of feeling by lowering him in my estimation – a thing so slight that, after reading the letter, as we drove to the station – even so soon! I could see him as he is. I noticed at once – but it was for the first time – I noticed that, although his face is handsome, the expression of it is not noble at all.' She shuddered as at the sight of something repulsive. 'You see,' she explained, 'my taste is cultivated to so fine an extent, I require something extremely well-flavoured for the dish which is to be the *pièce de résistance* of my life-feast. My appetite is delicate, it requires to be tempted, and a husband of that kind, a moral leper' – she broke off with a gesture, spreading her hands, palms outward, as if she would fain put some horrid idea far from her. 'Besides, marrying a man like that, allowing him an assured position in society, is countenancing vice, and' – she glanced round apprehensively, then added in a fearful whisper – '*helping to spread it.*'

Mrs Orton Beg knew in her head that reason and right were on Evadne's side, but she felt in her heart the full force of the custom and prejudice that would be against her, and shrank appalled by the thought of what the cruel struggle to come must be if Evadne persisted in her determination. In view of this, she sat up in her chair once more energetically, prepared to do her best to dissuade her; but then again she relapsed, giving in to a doubt of her own capacity to advise in such an emergency, accompanied by a sudden and involuntary feeling of respect for Evadne's principles, however peculiar and unprecedented they might be, and for the strength of character which had enabled her so far to act upon them. 'You must obey your own conscience, Evadne,' was what she found herself saying at last. 'I will help you to do that. I would rather not influence you. You may be right. I cannot be sure – and yet – I don't agree with you. For I know if I could have my husband back with me, I would welcome him, even if he were – a leper.' Evadne compressed her lips in steady disapproval. 'I should think only of his future. I should forgive the past.'

'That is the mistake you good women all make,' said Evadne. 'You set a detestably bad example. So long as women like you will forgive anything, men will do anything. You have it in your power to set up a high standard of excellence for men to reach in order to have the privilege of associating with you. There is this quality in men, that they will have the best of everything; and if the best wives are only to be obtained by being worthy of them, they will strive to become so. As it is, however, why should they? Instead of punishing them for their depravity, you encourage them in it by overlooking it; and besides,' she added, 'you must know that there is no past in the matter of vice. The consequences become hereditary, and continue from generation to generation.'

Again Mrs Orton Beg felt herself checked.

'Where did you hear all this, Evadne!' she asked.

'I never heard it. I read – and I thought,' she answered. 'But I am only now beginning to understand,' she added. 'I suppose moral axioms are always the outcome of pained reflection. Knowledge cries to us in vain as a rule before experience has taken the sharp edge off our egotism – by experience, I mean the addition of some personal feeling to our knowledge.'

'I don't understand you in the least, Evadne,' Mrs Orton Beg replied.

'Your husband was a good man,' Evadne answered indirectly. 'You have never thought about what a woman ought to do who has married a bad one – in an emergency like mine, that is. You think I should act as women have been always advised to act in such cases, that I should sacrifice myself to save that one man's soul. I take a different view of it. I see that the world is not a bit the better for centuries of self-sacrifice on the woman's part and therefore I think it is time we tried a more effectual plan. And I propose now to sacrifice the man instead of the woman.'

Mrs Orton Beg was silent.

'Have you nothing to say to me, auntie?' Evadne asked at last, caressingly.

'I do not like to hear you talk so, Evadne. Every word you say seems to banish something – something from this room – something from my life to which I cling. I think it is my faith in love – and loving. You may be right, but yet – the consequences! the struggle, if we must resist! It is best to submit. It is better not to know.'

'It is easier to submit – yes; it is disagreeable to know,' Evadne translated.

There was another pause, then Mrs Orton Beg broke out: 'Don't make me think about it. Surely I have suffered enough? Disagreeable to know! It is torture. If I ever let myself dwell on the horrible depravity that goes on unchecked, the depravity which you say we women license by ignoring it when we should face and unmask it, I should go out of my mind. I do know – we all know; how can we live and not know? But we don't think about it – we can't – we daren't.'

. . .

Major Colquhoun looked depressed.

'Yes,' Mrs Frayling protested, shaking her head. 'She says her husband must be a Christlike man. She says men have agreed to accept Christ as an example of what a man should be, and asserts that therefore they must feel in themselves that they *could* live up to his standard if they chose.'

'There now!' Mr Frayling exclaimed triumphantly. 'That is just what I said. A Christlike man, indeed! What absurdity will women want next? I don't know what to advise, Colquhoun. I really don't.'

'Can't you *order* her?' Mrs Frayling suggested.

'Order her! How can *I* order her? She belongs to Major Colquhoun now,' he retorted irritably, but with a fine conservative regard for the rights of property.

'And this is the way she keeps her vow of obedience,' Major Colquhoun muttered.

'Oh, but you see – the poor misguided child considers that she made the vow under a misapprehension,' Mrs Frayling explained, her maternal instinct acting on the defensive when her offspring's integrity was attacked, and making the position clear to her. 'Don't you think, dear,' – to her husband – 'that if you asked the bishop, he would talk to her.'

'The bishop!' Mr Frayling ejaculated with infinite scorn. '*I* know what women are when they go off like this. Once they set up opinions of their own, there's *no* talking to them. Why, haven't they gone to the stake for their opinions? She wouldn't obey the whole bench of bishops in her present frame of mind; and, if they condescended to talk to her,

they would only confirm her belief in her own powers. She would glory
to find herself opposing what she calls her opinions to theirs.'

'Oh, the child is mad!' Mrs Frayling wailed. 'I've said it all along.
She's quite mad.'

'Is there any insanity in the family?' Major Colquhoun asked, looking
up suspiciously.

'None, none whatever,' Mr Frayling hastened to assure him. 'There
has never been a case. In fact, the women on both sides have always
been celebrated for good sense and exceptional abilities – *for* women,
of course; and several of the men have distinguished themselves, as you
know.'

'That does not alter *my* opinion in the least!' Mrs Frayling put in.
'Evadne must be mad.'

'She's worse, I think,' Major Colquhoun exclaimed in a tone of deep
disgust. 'She's worse than mad. She's clever. You can do something with
a mad woman; you can lock her up; but a clever woman's the devil. And
I'd never have thought it of her,' he added regretfully. 'Such a nice
quiet little thing as she seemed, with hardly a word to say for herself.
You wouldn't have imagined that she knew what "views" are, let alone
having any of her own. But that is just the way with women. There's no
being up to them.'

'That is true,' said Mr Frayling.

'Well, I don't know where she got them,' Mrs Frayling protested, 'for
I am sure *I* haven't any. But she seems to know so much about –
everything!' she declared, glancing at the letter. 'At *her* age I knew
nothing!'

'I can vouch for that!' her husband exclaimed. He was one of those
men who oppose the education of women might and main, and then
jeer at them for knowing nothing. He was very particular about the
human race when it was likely to suffer by an injurious indulgence on
the part of women, but when it was a question of extra port wine for
himself, he never considered the tortures of gout he might be entailing
upon his own hapless descendants. However, there was an excuse for
him on this occasion, for it is not every day that an irritated man has an
opportunity of railing at his wife's incapacity and the inconvenient
intelligence of his daughter both in one breath. 'But how has Evadne
obtained all this mischievous information? I cannot think how she could
have obtained it!' he ejaculated, knitting his brows at his wife in a
suspicious way, as he always did when this importunate thought recurred

to him. In such ordinary everyday matters as the management of his estate, and his other duties as a county gentleman, and also in solid comprehension of the political situation of the period, he was by no means wanting; but his mind simply circled round and round this business of Evadne's like a helpless swimmer in a whirlpool, able to keep afloat, but with nothing to take hold of. The risk of sending the mind of an elderly gentleman of settled prejudices spinning 'down the ringing grooves of change' at such a rate is considerable.

7

Love's Coming of Age:
The New Woman

The growth of sexology and questions of the evolution of society both coincided with and contributed to the change of the position of women during the fin-de-siècle: *this was so dramatic that it led the Jewish author and satirist Karl Kraus to refer to the new twentieth century as 'the vaginal century'.*

The nineteenth century had seen the development of the view that sexual differences were rooted in biology, and the essential need of women was a settled domestic sphere to ensure healthy offspring for civilized ascendancy. Darwin, in his Descent of Man, *puts this view in historical terms – male sexual selection had always been one of the motors of human evolution, and male superiority was a biological inevitability.*

CHARLES DARWIN
The Descent of Man and Selection in Relation to Sex

(1871)

The chief distinction in the intellectual powers of the two sexes is shewn by man's attaining to a higher eminence in whatever he takes up, than can woman – whether requiring deep thought, reason or imagination, or merely the use of the senses and hands . . . Partly through sexual selection – that is through the contest of rival males, and partly through natural selection – that is from success in the general struggle for life . . . as in both cases the struggle will have been during maturity, the characters gained will have been transmitted more fully to the male than to the female offspring . . . Thus man has ultimately become superior to woman.

Man is more powerful in body and mind than woman and in the savage state he keeps her in a far more abject state of bondage than does the male of any other animal; therefore it is not surprising that he should have gained the power of selection . . .

The expectations of women which this view generated are portrayed in acid detail by H. G. Wells in The Wife of Sir Isaac Harman, *one of the first of his 'feminist novels'.*

H. G. WELLS
The Wife of Sir Isaac Harman

(1913)

His interpretations of the relationship of marriage were simple and strict. A woman, he knew, had to be wooed to be won, but when she was won, she was won. He did not understand wooing after that was settled. There was the bargain and her surrender. He, on his side, had to keep her, dress her, be kind to her, give her the appearances of pride and authority, and in return he had his rights and his privileges and undefined powers of control. That, you know, by the existing rules is the reality of marriage, where there are no settlements and no private property of the wife's. That is to say, it is the reality of marriage in ninety-nine cases out of the hundred. And it would have shocked Sir Isaac extremely, and, as a matter of fact, it did shock him, for any one to suggest the slightest revision of so entirely advantageous an arrangement. He was confident of his good intentions, and resolved to the best of his ability to make his wife the happiest of living creatures, subject only to reasonable acquiescences and general good behaviour.

Never before had he cared for anything so much as he did for her – not even for the International Bread and Cake Stores. He gloated upon her. She distracted him from business. He resolved from the outset to surround her with every luxury and permit her no desire that he had not already anticipated. Even her mother and Georgina, whom he thought extremely unnecessary persons, were frequent visitors to his house. His solicitude for her was so great that she found it difficult even to see her doctor except in his presence. And he bought her a pearl necklace that cost six hundred pounds. He was, in fact, one of those complete husbands who grow rare in these decadent days.

. . .

The same exceptional aptitude of Sir Isaac for detailed administration that had relieved his wife from the need of furnishing and arranging a home, made the birth of her children and the organization of her nursery an almost detached affair for her. Sir Isaac went about in a preoccupied way, whistling between his teeth and planning with expert advice the equipment of an ideal nursery, and her mother and his mother became as it were, voluminous clouds of uncommunicative wisdom and precaution. In addition, the conversation of Miss Crump, the extremely skilled and costly nurse, who arrived a full Advent before the child, fresh from the birth of a viscount, did much to generalize whatever had remained individual of this thing that was happening. With so much intelligence focused, there seemed to Lady Harman no particular reason why she should not do her best to think as little as possible about the impending affair, which meant for her, she now understood quite clearly, more and more discomfort, culminating in an agony. The summer promised to be warm, and Sir Isaac took a furnished house for the great event in the hills behind Torquay. The maternal instinct is not a magic thing, it has to be evoked and developed, and I decline to believe it is indicative of any peculiar unwomanliness in Lady Harman that when at last she beheld her newly-born daughter in the hands of the experts, she moaned druggishly, 'Oh! please take it away. Oh! Take it – away. Anywhere – anywhere.'

It was very red and wrinkled and aged-looking and, except when it opened its mouth to cry, extraordinarily like its father. This resemblance disappeared – along with a crop of darkish red hair – in the course of a day or two, but it left a lurking dislike to its proximity in her mind long after it had become an entirely infantile and engaging baby.

Later, Sir Isaac watches with incomprehension and dismay as his wife begins to assume the role of the New Woman.

It would be like counting the bacteria to an infection to trace how ideas of insubordination came drifting into Sir Isaac's paradise. The epidemic is in the air. There is no Tempter nowadays, no definite apple. The disturbing force has grown subtler, blows in now like a draught, creeps and gathers like the dust – a disseminated serpent. Sir Isaac brought home this young, beautiful and rather crumpled and astonished Eve, and by all his standards he was entitled to be happy ever afterwards. He knew of one danger, but against that he was very watchful. Never once, for six long years, did she have a private duologue with another male. But Mudie and Sir Jesse Boot sent parcels to the house unchecked, the newspaper drifted in not even censored; the nurses who guided Ellen through the essential incidents of a feminine career talked of something called a 'movement'. And there was Georgina . . .

The thing they wanted they called the Vote, but that demand so hollow, so eyeless, had all the terrifying effect of a mask. Behind that mask was a formless, invincible discontent with the lot of womanhood. It wanted – it was not clear what it wanted, but whatever it wanted, all the domestic instincts of mankind were against admitting there was anything it could want. That remarkable agitation had already worked up to the thunderous pitch, there had been demonstrations at public meetings, scenes in the Ladies' Gallery and something like rioting in Parliament Square, before ever it occurred to Sir Isaac that this was a disturbance that touched his home. He had supposed suffragettes were ladies of all too certain an age, with red noses and spectacles and a masculine style of costume, who wished to be hugged by policemen. He said as much rather knowingly and wickedly to Charterson. He could not understand any woman not coveting the privileges of Lady Harman. And then one day, while Georgina and her mother were visiting them, as he was looking over the letters at the breakfast table, according to his custom before giving them out, he discovered two identical newspaper packets addressed to his wife and his sister-in-law, and upon them were these words, printed very plainly, 'Votes for Women'.

*The 'New Woman' became a cultural icon, complete with her stage props
of bicycles, cigarettes, short hair and vociferous political agitation. One
of her most definitive portrayals was in Grant Allen's novel* The Woman
Who Did.

GRANT ALLEN
The Woman Who Did

(1895)

'Yes, I've made up my mind,' Herminia answered with a faint
tremor in her maidenly voice, but with hardly a trace now of a traitorous
blush where no blush was needed. 'I've made up my mind, Alan; and
from all we had said and talked over together, I thought you, at least,
would sympathize with my resolve.'

She spoke with a gentle tinge of regret, nay, almost of disillusion.
The bare suggestion of that regret stung Alan to the quick. He felt it
was shame to him that he could not rise at once to the height of her
splendid self-renunciation. 'You mistake me, dearest,' he answered,
petting her hand in his own (and she allowed him to pet it). 'It wasn't
for myself or for the world I hesitated. My thought was for you. You
are very young yet. You say you have counted the cost. I wonder if you
have. I wonder if you realize it.'

'Only too well,' Herminia replied, in a very earnest mood. 'I have
wrought it all out in my mind beforehand, covenanted with my soul
that for women's sake I would be a free woman. Alan, whoever would
be free must himself strike the blow. I know what you will say – what
every man would say to the woman he loved under similar circumstances
– "Why should *you* be the victim? Why should *you* be the martyr? Bask
in the sun yourself. Leave this doom to some other." But, Alan, I can't.
I feel *I* must face it. Unless one woman begins, there will be no
beginning.' She lifted his hand in her own, and fondled it in her turn
with caressing tenderness. 'Think how easy it would be for me, dear
friend,' she cried, with a catch in her voice, 'to do as other women do;
to accept the *honourable marriage* you offer me, as other women would
call it; to be false to my sex, a traitor to my convictions; to sell my kind
for a mess of pottage – a name and a home; or even for thirty pieces of

silver – to be some rich man's wife – as other women have sold it. But, Alan, I can't. My conscience won't let me. I know what marriage is – from what vile slavery it has sprung; on what unseen horrors for my sister women it is reared and buttressed; by what unholy sacrifices it is sustained and made possible. I know it has a history. I know its past: I know its present: and I can't embrace it. I can't be untrue to my most sacred beliefs. I can't pander to the malignant thing, just because a man who loves me would be pleased by my giving way, and would kiss me and fondle me for it. And I love you to fondle me. But I must keep my proper place, the freedom which I have gained for myself by such arduous efforts. I have said to you already, "So far as my will goes, I am yours; take me and do as you choose with me." That much I can yield, as every good woman should yield it to the man she loves, to the man who loves her. But more than that – no. It would be treason to my sex. Not my life, not my future, not my individuality, not my freedom.'

*One of the thinkers who integrated the New Woman most fully into his
view of a future society was the homosexual socialist Edward Carpenter.
In his view, the freedom of women was a necessary condition of a healthy
society.*

EDWARD CARPENTER
Love's Coming-of-Age

(1896)

It has not escaped the attention of thinkers on these subjects
that the rise of Women into freedom and larger social life here alluded
to – and already indeed indicated by the march of events – is likely to
have a profound influence on the future of our race. It is pointed out
that among most of the higher animals, and indeed among many of the
early races of mankind, the males have been selected by the females
on account of their prowess or superior strength or beauty, and this has
led to the evolution in the males and in the race at large of a type which
(in a dim and unconscious manner) was the ideal of the female. But as
soon as in the history of mankind the property-love set in, and woman
became the chattel of man, this action ceased.

. . .

With the return of woman to freedom the ideal of the female may again
resume its sway. It is possible indeed that the more dignified and serious
attitude of women towards sex may give to sexual selection when
exercised by them a nobler influence than when exercised by the males.
Anyhow it is not difficult to see that women really free would never
countenance for their mates the many mean and unclean types of men
who today seem to have things all their own way, nor consent to have
children by such men; nor is it difficult to imagine that the feminine
influence might thus sway to the evolution of a more manly and dignified
race than has been disclosed in these last days of commercial civilization!
The Modern Woman with her clubs, her debates, her politics, her
freedom of action and costume, is forming a public opinion of her own
at an amazing rate; and seems to be preparing to 'spank' and even

thump the Middle-class Man in real earnest! What exactly evolution may be preparing for us, we do not know, but apparently some lively sparring matches between the sexes.

. . .

If it should turn out that a certain fraction of the feminine sex should for one reason or another not devote itself to the work of maternity, still the influence of this section would react on the others to render their notion of motherhood far more dignified than before. There is not much doubt that in the future this most important of human labours will be carried on with a degree of conscious intelligence hitherto unknown, and such as will raise it from the fulfilment of a mere instinct to the completion of a splendid social purpose. To save the souls of children as well as their bodies, to raise heroic as well as prosperous citizens, will surely be the desire and the work of the mothers of our race.

. . .

At the last, and after centuries of misunderstanding and association of triviality and superficiality with the female sex, it will perhaps dawn upon the world that the truth really lies in an opposite direction – that, in a sense, there is something more deep-lying fundamental and primitive in the woman nature than in that of the man; that instead of being the over-sensitive hysterical creature that civilization has too often made her, she is essentially of calm large and acceptive even though emotional temperament. 'Her shape arises,' says Walt Whitman,

> She less guarded than ever, yet more guarded than ever,
> The gross and soil'd she moves among do not make her gross and
>   soil'd,
> She knows the thoughts as she passes, nothing is concealed from her,
> She is none the less considerate or friendly therefor,
> She is the best belov'd, it is without exception; she has no reason to
>   fear, and she does not fear.

The Greek goddesses look down and across the ages to the very outposts beyond civilization; and already from far America, Australasia,

Africa, Norway, Russia, as even in our midst from those who have crossed the border-line of all class and caste, glance forth the features of a grander type – fearless and untamed – the primal merging into the future Woman; who, combining broad sense with sensibility, the passion for Nature with the love of Man, and commanding indeed the details of life, yet risen out of localism and convention, will help us to undo the bands of death which encircle the present society, and open the doors to a new and a wider life.

Stereotypes of the New Woman. 'The New Woman, German Style' –
a sexless, driven intellectual . . . (A. Oberlander, *Graphic* 1882.) (Courtesy of Mary Evans Picture Library)

. . . and a graphically contrasting image of the sexualized, sensual predator. (Erotic lithograph: Franz von Bayros.)

In the view of the radical feminist Frances Swiney, woman was not simply man's equal – man is, rather, a form of arrested development en route to womanhood. (From Ives scrapbook.)

THE ULTIMATE DESTINY OF MAN
IS TO BECOME A WOMAN!

IN the *Westminster Review* for April the indomitable Mrs. Swiney pursues her triumphant way, demonstrating (1) that man is but undeveloped woman, (2) that he is the product of starvation, and (3) that when the millennium arrives he will disappear by absorption into the victorious female, who will alone survive. Is it not written in " The Sayings of Jesus," " When that which is perfect is come, then that which is imperfect shall be done away ; and ' the two shall be one, the male as the female.' " ?

MAN BUT AN IMPERFECT WOMAN.

Mrs. Swiney exults in believing that the old superstition is dying which ascribed to the male the gift of life. Science now recognises the male factor as of secondary biological importance :—

The male was primarily short-lived, puny, feeble, undeveloped, dependent and parasitic. What is more, its appearance, even among the higher species and where it has developed to great complexity of organic function, is directly attributable to a defective state of malnutrition in the maternal organism.

The latest word of modern research is that " adverse circumstances, especially of nutrition, but also including age and the like, tend to the production of males, the reverse conditions favouring females."

HIS ASCENT TO WOMANHOOD.

Man, being thus the product of starvation, is temporary and will pass. The process of evolution will gradually evolve him into a woman :—

As man approaches the industrial age, of which the highly evolved instincts of the bee and the ant are the precursors, we cannot but recognise that the characteristics of humanity are becoming the same in the men and women of the higher civilisation. Height, bearing, vigour of muscle, equality of brain power, decrease of hairiness, assimilate the boy and the girl.

The male begins to develop certain rudimentary organs hitherto entirely feminine, thus proving the oneness of the constructive creative elements in the male and female organisms, and the ultimate goal intended by natural evolution. In extreme cases in the lower species, the male develops in a certain period, generally of two or three years, entirely into the female ; such is the case among those curious animals, the *Ostracoda* and *Cirripedia*. There is no known case where the female, through atrophy of her distinctive organs, degenerates into a male.

THE FEMINISING OF THE MALE.

In some species so great and fundamental is the change wrought, that actually the male becomes more feminised than the female, develops stronger maternal traits and constructive habits.

See, for instance, the case of many of the fish tribe, where the smaller male, after fertilisation, takes sole charge of the ova. Among the sticklebacks the male forms the nest, keeps jealous guard over the eggs therein deposited, and protects the young when hatched, while the female lives the life of a free-lance.

Among birds the bower-bird devotes weeks of loving labour in preparing a fit habitation for his prospective mate, and when he is safely ensconced therein, assiduously replenishes and variegates the æsthetic adornments of the nuptial chamber and its approaches.

The male ostrich broods over the eggs with a greater devotion than his inconsequent partner. And thus characteristics normally functional in the feminine organism have been transmitted to the male in so great a degree as to overcome his normal katabolic tendency.

The contrasting view was also – and more frequently – offered to newspaper readers. (From Ives scrapbook.)

SCIENCE PROVES WOMAN INFERIOR.

Many Arguments Put Forward by Objectors Answered.

"NO FEMALE GENIUS."

By CHARLES H. HEYDEMANN, Ph.D.

In his article published in *The Daily Mirror* yesterday on the question whether women are equal to men. Dr. Heydemann pointed out that the result of frequent experiments had been to show that women are inferior to men in the senses of smell, taste, and sight and hearing. This is the reason, he contends, that piano tuners, tea and wine tasters, and great dressmakers are men. Woman may be able to assimilate knowledge quickly, but this assimilation faculty is sponge-like and "turns out knowledge like Birmingham buttons." In the following instalment of his article Dr. Heydemann answers objections to his argument.

One remembers the story of how Sydney Smith was appealed to by a witless bore : "But we all row in the same boat, Canon," and his retort : "Yes, but not with the same skulls ! "

The vast majority of the objections one currently hears against the inferiority of women possess the same sentimental character. Sentiment says, "I hope," but science says, "I know."

The misty sentimentalism of "A Mere Woman " asks "Why is it that the skulls of lunatics are notoriously larger than those of sane persons?" This fact, which she "notoriously" quotes, is, however, contrary to scientific experience. The condition known as hydrocephalus (water on the brain) may produce distention of the head, but I have never heard this condition distinctively applied to the insane.

JUMPING TO CONCLUSIONS.

In fact, all experience points in the opposite direction. Below a certain size and weight we get microcephaly, and idiocy generally goes with these. There have, of course, been some remarkably powerful minds accompanied by exceptionally small heads (Shelley, Descartes, Foscolo, Donizetti, and Schumann), but what people forget is that science deals with the results of averages, taken from all races and from all times.

Nobody denies that Miss Pankhurst, who wants a vote, is superior to Hodge, who has one. Individually, yes ; collectively, no !

This habit of hastily jumping to conclusions is that of the tripper to Boulogne, who, having seen a Normandy fishing-girl with red hair, wrote home on a picture-postcard, "All the French women have red hair." And he was a man !

"The skull of the stupid hippopotamus is larger than that of the fox-terrier." Does a "Mere Woman " know that skulls are (normally) proportionate to total bulk? That the average weight of brain, taking 10,000 as the unit of total bulk, is 1.8 with fishes, 7.6 with reptiles, 42.2 with birds, 53.8 with mammals, 277.8 with man? The size of the skull is not the whole argument, but it is one part of it.

BRAIN AS HOTEL.

One can compare a large brain to an hotel with many rooms, in which numerous people can be accommodated. The rooms may be unoccupied, of course, while a small boarding-house is full up. But not with the same class of people.

When we find (according to the celebrated French anthropologist, Professor Broca) the poets Schiller and Byron, great men like Cromwell and Napoleon, having abnormally large skulls, we are justified in considering a large head an advantage.

As for the argument (put forward by " F. L. D.") that woman was always put down formerly, and received little education, there is considerably less truth in this than is generally supposed.

At the highest, the Periclean era of Greek civilisation, women such as Aspasia were highly cultured, and followed the schooling of the philosophers. Sappho, Hypatia, and many others prove the existence of a cultured class of women, to whom the religion of antiquity had given a position of unqualified honour.

"LONG SKIRTS, SHORT SENSES."

Two thousand years B.C. woman was more free and honoured in Egypt than she is to-day. She was the mistress of the house. She inherited equally with her brothers, and had full control of her property. She could go where she liked and speak with whom she liked.

She could bring actions and plead in the courts. She practised the art of medicine. She had authority in the temples. As queen (or the Amazons, Queen of Sheba) she was frequently the highest in the land.

In later times, Boadicea, Heloise, Elizabeth, Lady Jane Grey are familiar examples of high consideration and erudition.

And, with all that, they have not produced one great artist, philosopher, author, musician, inventor, etc., and yet the difficulties they had to encounter were not greater than those of many a genius who has fought his way up through poverty from the lower classes to the higher. The poorer classes produce no female genius. "Long skirts, short senses," says the German proverb.

Lastly, as I have already pointed out, the assimilative faculties (that of learning things) are always predominant where the associative faculties (those which create) are missing. Spencer points this out. Woman is a creature who doesn't reason, and pokes the fire from the top.

The medical and psychiatric mainstream had many objections to the idea that women could potentially adopt male roles in society.

'The "Can" and "Shall" of Woman-Culture'

Lancet (1886)

The female is undoubtedly from a developmental point of view an animal in which the evolutionary process has been arrested or, more accurately speaking, diverted from the general to the particular, for special reproductive purposes, before the culminating point could be reached . . . The point to perceive is that the differentiation of sex is not in the nature of superiority or inferiority as regards the animal organism, but one of special fitness and therefore there are certain plus or minus qualities connected with sex which are the natural concomitants of the differentiation, but do not constitute disabilities . . . We do not doubt that in a certain number of generations women, if cultured as men are cultured, might be developed in all respects to the same proportion as men in respect to brain or muscle or both; but we contend that if this were accomplished they would be *monstrous*. A masculine race of women would be as abnormal as an effeminate race of men and in process of time the instinct of nature would assert itself so that womanly women would feel the same contempt for masculinity in their sex as manly men feel for effeminacy in theirs; and when this instinct asserted itself there would commence, involuntarily and uncontrollably, a reversion to the normal type.

For the Austrian philosopher Otto Weininger, the 'liberation' of the female was a project which had been tried and found wanting throughout history, and was fundamentally misconceived.

OTTO WEININGER
Sex & Character

(1903)

Amongst human beings the state of the case is as follows: There exist all sorts of intermediate conditions between male and female – sexual transitional forms. In physical inquiries an 'ideal gas' is assumed, that is to say, a gas, the behaviour of which follows the law of Boyle-Guy-Lussac exactly, although, in fact, no such gas exists, and laws are deduced from this so that the deviations from the ideal laws may be established in the case of actually existing gases. In the same fashion we may suppose the existence of an ideal man, M, and of an ideal woman, W, as sexual types, although these types do not actually exist. Such types not only can be constructed, but must be constructed. As in art so in science, the real purpose is to reach the type, the Platonic Idea. The science of physics investigates the behaviour of bodies that are absolutely rigid or absolutely elastic, in the full knowledge that neither the one nor the other actually exists. The intermediate conditions actually existing between the two absolute states of matter serve merely as a starting-point for investigation of the 'types' and in the practical application of the theory are treated as mixtures and exhaustively analysed. So also there exist only the intermediate stages between absolute males and females, the absolute conditions never presenting themselves.

. . .

A woman's demand for emancipation and her qualification for it are in direct proportion to the amount of maleness in her. The idea of emancipation, however, is many-sided, and its indefiniteness is increased by its association with many practical customs which have nothing to do with the theory of emancipation. By the term emancipation of a woman, I imply neither her mastery at home nor her subjection of her husband. I have not in mind the courage which enables her to go freely by night or by day unaccompanied in public places, or the disregard of social rules which prohibit bachelor women from receiving visits from men, or discussing or listening to discussions of sexual matters. I exclude from my view the desire for economic independence, the becoming fit for positions in technical schools, universities and conservatoires or teachers' institutes. And there may be many other similar movements associated with the word emancipation which I do not intend to deal with. Emancipation, as I mean to discuss it, is not the wish for an outward equality with man, but what is of real importance in the woman question, the deep-seated craving to acquire man's character, to attain his mental and moral freedom, to reach his real interests and his creative power. I maintain that the real female element has neither the desire nor the capacity for emancipation in this sense. All those who are striving for this real emancipation, all women who are truly famous and are of conspicuous mental ability, to the first glance of an expert reveal some of the anatomical characters of the male, some external bodily resemblance to a man. Those so-called 'women' who have been held up to admiration in the past and present, by the advocates of woman's rights, as examples of what women can do, have almost invariably been what I have described as sexually intermediate forms.

. . .

If we now look at the question of emancipation from the point of view of hygiene (not morality) there is no doubt as to the harm in it. The undesirability of emancipation lies in the excitement and agitation involved. It induces women who have no real original capacity but undoubted imitative powers to attempt to study or write, from various motives, such as vanity or the desire to attract admirers. Whilst it cannot be denied that there are a good many women with a real craving for emancipation and for higher education, these set the fashion and are followed by a host of others who get up a ridiculous agitation to convince themselves of the reality of their views. And many otherwise estimable and worthy wives use the cry to assert themselves against their husbands, whilst daughters take it as a method of rebelling against maternal authority. The practical outcome of the whole matter would be as follows; it being remembered that the issues are too mutable for the establishment of uniform rules or laws. Let there be the freest scope given to, and the fewest hindrances put in the way of all women with masculine dispositions who feel a psychical necessity to devote themselves to masculine occupations and are physically fit to undertake them. But the idea of making an emancipation party, of aiming at a social revolution, must be abandoned. Away with the whole 'woman's movement', with its unnaturalness and artificiality and its fundamental errors.

. . .

Women were first allowed on the stage in the sixteenth century, and actresses date from that time. 'At that period it was admitted that women were just as capable as men of embodying the highest possible artistic ideals.' It was the period when panegyrics on the female sex were rife; Sir Thomas More claimed for it full equality with the male sex, and Agrippa von Nettesheim goes so far as to represent women as superior to men! And yet this was all lost for the fair sex, and the whole question sank into the oblivion from which the nineteenth century recalled it.

Is it not very remarkable, that the agitation for the emancipation of women seems to repeat itself at certain intervals in the world's history, and lasts for a definite period?

. . .

A complete obliteration will be the fate of any emancipation movement which attempts to place the whole sex in a new relation to society, and to see in man its perpetual oppressor. A corps of Amazons might be formed, but as time went on the material for the corps would cease to occur. The history of the woman movement during the Renaissance and its complete disappearance contains a lesson for the advocates of women's rights. Real intellectual freedom cannot be attained by an agitated mass; it must be fought for by the individual. Who is the enemy? What are the retarding influences?

The greatest, the one enemy of the emancipation of women is woman herself.

8
Mondo Exotica:
The New Frontiers

Another force for dynamic change in the fin-de-siècle *was the fall-out from the programme of exploration and colonialism which had been avidly pursued throughout the century. As the empty spaces on the globe began to fill up, the remaining frontiers came to be seen with an elegiac romanticism; and, conversely, as the people from the far frontiers came to make their presence felt in the cities of Europe and America, anxieties about contamination from alien cultures came to mirror the fears about the repressed and unconscious forces of humanity.*

The fin-de-siècle *was also the pioneer era in the Wild West, and the open spaces of America came to stand both for the virgin perfection of nature and for the atavistic impulses which the frontier life presented to the modern observer. Isabella Bird, the pioneering English travel writer and archetypal New Woman abroad, gives us both these impressions.*

ISABELLA BIRD
A Lady's Life in the Rocky Mountains

(1879)

A very pretty mare, hobbled, was feeding; a collie dog barked at us, and among the scrub, not far from the track, there was a rude, black log cabin, as rough as it could be to be a shelter at all, with smoke coming out of the roof and window. We diverged towards it; it mattered not that it was the home, or rather den, of a notorious 'ruffian' and 'desperado'. One of my companions had disappeared hours before, the remaining one was a town-bred youth. I longed to speak to someone who loved the mountains. I called the hut a *den* – it looked like the den of a wild beast. The big dog lay outside it in a threatening attitude and growled. The mud roof was covered with lynx, beaver and other furs laid out to dry, beaver paws were pinned out on the logs, a part of the carcass of a deer hung at one end of the cabin, a skinned beaver lay in front of a heap of peltry just within the door, and antlers of deer, old horseshoes, and offal of many animals, lay about the den.

Roused by the growling of the dog, his owner came out, a broad, thickset man, about the middle height, with an old cap on his head, and wearing a grey hunting suit much the worse for wear (almost falling to pieces, in fact), a digger's scarf knotted round his waist, a knife in his belt and 'a bosom friend', a revolver, sticking out of the breast pocket of his coat; his feet, which were very small, were bare, except for some dilapidated moccasins made of horse hide. The marvel was how his clothes hung together, and on him. The scarf round his waist must have had something to do with it. His face was remarkable. He is a man about forty-five, and must have been strikingly handsome. He has large grey-blue eyes, deeply set, with well-marked eyebrows, a handsome aquiline nose, and a very handsome mouth. His face was smooth shaven except for a dense moustache and imperial. Tawny hair, in thin uncared-for curls, fell from under his hunter's cap and over his collar. One eye was entirely gone, and the loss made one side of the face repulsive, while the other might have been modelled in marble. 'Desperado' was written in large letters all over him. I almost repented of having sought his acquaintance. His first impulse was to swear at the dog, but on seeing a lady he contented himself with kicking him, and coming to me he raised his cap, showing as he did so a magnificently formed brow and head, and in a cultured tone of voice asked if there were anything he could do for me? I asked for some water, and he brought some in a battered tin, gracefully apologizing for not having anything more presentable. We entered into conversation, and as he spoke I forgot both his reputation and appearance, for his manner was that of a chivalrous gentleman, his accent refined and his language easy and elegant. I enquired about some beavers' paws which were drying, and in a moment they hung on the horn of my saddle. *Apropos* of the wild animals of the region, he told me that the loss of his eye was owing to a recent encounter with a grizzly bear, which, after giving him a death hug, tearing him all over, breaking his arm and scratching out his eye, had left him for dead. As we rode away, for the sun was sinking, he said, courteously, 'You are not an American. I know from your voice that you are a countrywoman of mine. I hope you will allow me the pleasure of calling on you.'°

This man, known through the Territories and beyond them as 'Rocky Mountain Jim', or, more briefly, as 'Mountain Jim', is one of the famous scouts of the Plains, and is the original of some daring portraits in fiction concerning Indian Frontier warfare. So far as I have at present heard, he is a man for whom there is now no room, for the time for blows and blood in this part of Colorado is past, and the fame of many daring exploits is sullied by crimes which are not easily forgiven here. He now

° Of this unhappy man, who was shot nine months later within two miles of his cabin, I write in the subsequent letters only as he appeared to me. His life, without doubt, was deeply stained with crimes and vices, and his reputation for ruffianism was a deserved one. But in my intercourse with him I saw more of his nobler instincts than of the darker parts of his character, which, unfortunately for himself and others, showed itself in its worst colours at the time of his tragic end. It was not until after I left Colorado, not indeed until after his death, that I heard of the worst points of his character.

has a 'squatter's claim', but makes his living as a trapper, and is a complete child of the mountains. Of his genius and chivalry to women there does not appear to be any doubt; but he is a desperate character, and is subject to 'ugly fits', when people think it best to avoid him. It is here regarded as an evil that he has located himself at the mouth of the only entrance to the park, for he is dangerous with his pistols, and it would be safer if he were not here. His besetting sin is indicated in the verdict pronounced on him by my host: 'When he's sober Jim's a perfect gentleman; but when he's had liquor he's the most awful ruffian in Colorado.'

The presence of unspoilt natural beauty was regarded as a canonical element in healthy American life. Emerson's thoughts from the 1830s cast a long shadow and were very influential.

RALPH WALDO EMERSON
Nature

(1836)

To speak truly, few adult persons can see nature. Most persons do not see the sun. At least they have a very superficial seeing. The sun illuminates only the eye of the man, but shines into the eye and the heart of the child. The lover of nature is he whose inward and outward senses are still truly adjusted to each other; who has retained the spirit of infancy even into the era of manhood. His intercourse with heaven and earth becomes part of his daily food. In the presence of nature a wild delight runs through the man, in spite of real sorrows. Nature says, – he is my creature, and maugre all his impertinent griefs, he shall be glad with me. Not the sun or the summer alone, but every hour and season yields its tribute of delight; for every hour and change corresponds to and authorizes a different state of the mind, from breathless noon to grimmest midnight. Nature is a setting that fits equally well a comic or a mourning piece. In good health, the air is a cordial of incredible virtue. Crossing a bare common, in snow puddles, at twilight, under a clouded sky, without having in my thoughts any occurrence of special good fortune, I have enjoyed a perfect exhilaration. I am glad to the brink of fear. In the woods, too, a man casts off his years, as the snake his slough, and at what period soever of life is always a child. In the woods is perpetual youth. Within these plantations of God, a decorum and sanctity reign, a perennial festival is dressed, and the guest sees not how he should tire of them in a thousand years. In the woods, we return to reason and faith. There I feel that nothing can befall me in life, – no disgrace, no calamity (leaving me my eyes), which nature cannot repair. Standing on the bare ground, – my head bathed by the blithe air and uplifted into infinite space, – all mean egotism vanishes. I become a transparent eyeball; I am nothing; I see all; the currents of the Universal Being circulate through me; I am part or parcel of God. The name of the nearest friend sounds then foreign and accidental: to be brothers, to be acquaintances, master or servant, is then a trifle and a disturbance. I am the lover of uncontained and immortal beauty. In the wilderness, I find something more dear and connate than in streets or villages. In the tranquil landscape, and especially in the distant line of the horizon, man beholds somewhat as beautiful as his own nature.

The greatest delight which the fields and woods minister is the suggestion of an occult relation between man and the vegetable. I am not alone and unacknowledged. They nod to me, and I to them. The waving of the boughs in the storm is new to me and old. It takes me by surprise, and yet is not unknown. Its effect is like that of a higher thought or a better emotion coming over me, when I deemed I was thinking justly or doing right.

Yet it is certain that the power to produce this delight does not reside in nature, but in man, or in a harmony of both.

. . . but, at the same time, the empty wastes of the American West could be terrifying to modern eyes. In his account of his travels across the West, Robert Louis Stevenson paints a much bleaker picture, both of the land and its native inhabitants.

ROBERT LOUIS STEVENSON
The Amateur Emigrant from the Clyde to Sandy Hook

(1895)

THE DESERT OF WYOMING

To cross such a plain is to grow homesick for the mountains. I longed for the Black Hills of Wyoming, which I knew we were soon to enter, like an ice-bound whaler for the spring. Alas! and it was a worse country than the other. All Sunday and Monday we travelled through these sad mountains, or over the main ridge of the Rockies, which is a fair match to them for misery of aspect. Hour after hour it was the same unhomely and unkindly world about our onward path; tumbled boulders, cliffs that drearily imitate the shape of monuments and fortifications – how drearily, how tamely, none can tell who has not seen them; not a tree, not a patch of sward, not one shapely or commanding mountain form; sagebrush, eternal sagebrush; over all, the same weariful and gloomy colouring, greys warming into brown, greys darkening towards black; and for sole sign of life, here and there a few fleeing antelopes; here and there, but at incredible intervals, a creek running in a cañon. The plains have a grandeur of their own; but here there is nothing but a contorted smallness. Except for the air, which was light and stimulating, there was not one good circumstance in that God-forsaken land.

I had been suffering in my health a good deal all the way; and at last, whether I was exhausted by my complaint or poisoned in some wayside eating-house, the evening we left Laramie, I fell sick outright. That was a night which I shall not readily forget. The lamps did not go out; each made a faint shining in its own neighbourhood, and the shadows were confounded together in the long, hollow box of the car. The sleepers lay in uneasy attitudes; here two chums alongside, flat upon their backs like dead folk; there a man sprawling on the floor, with his face upon his arm; there another half-seated with his head and shoulders on the bench. The most passive were continually and roughly shaken by the movement of the train; others stirred, turned or stretched out their arms like children; it was surprising how many groaned and murmured in their sleep; and as I passed to and fro, stepping across the prostrate, and caught now a snore, now a gasp, now a half-formed word, it gave me a measure of the worthlessness of rest in that unresting vehicle. Although it was chill, I was obliged to open my window, for the degradation of the air soon became intolerable to one who was awake and using the full supply of life. Outside, in a glimmering night, I saw the black, amorphous hills shoot by unweariedly into our wake. They that long for morning have never longed for it more earnestly than I.

And yet when day came, it was to shine upon the same broken and unsightly quarter of the world. Mile upon mile, and not a tree, a bird, or a river. Only down the long, sterile cañons, the train shot hooting and awoke the resting echo. That train was the one piece of life in all the deadly land; it was the one actor, the one spectacle fit to be observed in this paralysis of man and nature. And when I think how the railroad had been pushed through this unwatered wilderness and haunt of savage tribes, and now will bear an emigrant for some twelve pounds from the Atlantic to the Golden Gates; how at each stage of the construction, roaring, impromptu cities, full of gold and lust and death, sprang up and then died away again, and are now but wayside stations in the desert; how in these uncouth places pigtailed Chinese pirates worked side by side with border ruffians and broken men from Europe, talking together in a mixed dialect, mostly oaths, gambling, drinking, quarrelling and murdering like wolves; how the plumed hereditary lord of all America heard, in this last fastness, the scream of the 'bad medicine-wagon' charioting his foes; and then when I go on to remember that all this epical turmoil was conducted by gentlemen in frock coats, and with a view to nothing more extraordinary than a fortune and a subsequent visit to Paris, it seems to me, I own, as if this railway were the one typical achievement of the age in which we live, as if it brought together into one plot all the ends of the world and all the degrees of social rank, and offered to some great writer the busiest, the most extended and the most varied subject for an enduring literary work. If it be romance, if it be contrast, if it be heroism that we require, what was Troy town to this? But, alas! it is not these things that are necessary – it is only Homer.

Here also we are grateful to the train, as to some god who conducts us swiftly through these shades and by so many hidden perils. Thirst, hunger, the sleight and ferocity of Indians are all no more feared, so lightly do we skim these horrible lands; as the gull, who wings safely through the hurricane and past the shark. Yet we should not be forgetful of these hardships of the past; and to keep the balance true, since I have complained of the trifling discomforts of my journey, perhaps more than was enough, let me add an original document. It was not written by Homer, but by a boy of eleven, long since dead, and is dated only twenty years ago. I shall punctuate, to make things clearer, but not change the spelling.

'My dear sister Mary, – I am afraid you will go nearly crazy when you read my letter. If Jerry' (the writer's eldest brother) 'has not written to you before now, you will be surprised to heare that we are in California, and that poor Thomas' (another brother, of fifteen) 'is dead. We started from —— in July, with plenty of provisions and too yoke oxen. We went along very well till we got within six or seven hundred miles of California, when the Indians attacked us. We found places where they had killed the emigrants. We had one passenger with us, too guns, and one revolver; so we ran all the lead We had into bullets (and) hung the guns up in the wagon so that we could get at them in a minit. It was about two o'clock in the afternoon; droave the cattel a little way; when a prairie chicken alited a little way from the wagon.

'Jerry took out one of the guns to shoot it, and told Tom to drive the oxen. Tom and I drove the oxen, and Jerry and the passenger went on. Then, after a little, I left Tom and caught up with Jerry and the other man. Jerry stopped for Tom to come up; me and the man went on and sit down by a little stream. In a few minutes, we heard some noise; then three shots (they all struck poor Tom, I suppose); then they gave the war hoop, and as many as twenty of the red skins came down upon us. The three that shot Tom was hid by the side of the road in the bushes.

'I thought the Tom and Jerry were shot; so I told the other man that Tom and Jerry were dead, and that we had better try to escape, if possible. I had no shoes on; having a sore foot, I thought I would not put them on. The man and me run down the road, but We was soon stopt by an Indian on a pony. We then turend the other way, and run up the side of the Mountain, and hid behind some cedar *trees, and stayed there till dark. The Indians hunted all over after us, and verry close to us, so close that we could hear there tomyhawks Jingle. At dark the man and me started on, I stubing my toes against sticks and stones. We traveld on all night; and next morning, Just as it was getting gray, we saw something in the shape of a man. It layed Down in the grass. We went up to it, and it was Jerry. He thought we ware Indians. You can imagine how glad he was to see me. He thought we was all dead but him, and we thought him and Tom was dead. He had the gun that he took out of the wagon to shoot the prairie Chicken; all he had was the load that was in it.*

'We traveld on till about eight o'clock, We caught up with one wagon with too men in it. We had traveld with them before one day; we stopt and they Drove on; we knew that they was ahead of us, unless they had been killed to. My feet was so sore when we caught up with them that I had to ride; I could not step. We traveld on for too days, when the men that owned the cattle said they would (could) not drive them another inch. We unyoked the oxen; we had about seventy pounds of flour; we took it out and divided it into four packs. Each of the men took about 18 pounds apiece and a blanket. I carried a little bacon, dried meat, and little quilt; I had in all about twelve pounds. We had one pint of flour a day for our alloyance. Sometimes we made soup of it; sometimes we (made) pancakes; and sometimes mixed it up with cold water and eat it that way. We traveld twelve or fourteen days. The time came at last when we should have to reach some place or starve. We saw fresh horse and cattle tracks. The morning come, we scraped all the flour out of the sack, mixed it up, and baked it into bread, and made some soup, and eat everything we had. We traveld on all day without anything to eat, and that evening we Caught up with a sheep train of eight wagons. We traveld with them till we arrived at the settlements; and know I am safe in California, and got to good home, and going to school.

'Jerry is working in ——. It is a good country. You can get from 50 to 60.75 Dollars for cooking. Tell me all about the affairs in the States, and how all the folks get along.'

And so ends this artless narrative. The little man was at school again, God bless him! while his brother lay scalped upon the deserts.

It was also becoming apparent that the ports, slums and ghettos of modern cities offered a dark reflection of this 'savagery'. In his account of living incognito in London's East End, the American novelist Jack London observes a 'jungle' as savage as anything from the frontier.

JACK LONDON
The People of the Abyss

(1903)

Late last night I walked along Commercial Street from Spitalfields to Whitechapel, and still continuing south, down Leman Street to the docks. And as I walked I smiled at the East End papers, which, filled with civic pride, boastfully proclaim that there is nothing the matter with the East End as a living place for men and women.

It is rather hard to tell a tithe of what I saw. Much of it is untellable. But in a general way I may say that I saw a nightmare, a fearful slime that quickened the pavement with life, a mess of unmentionable obscenity that put into eclipse the 'nightly horror' of Piccadilly and the Strand. It was a menagerie of garmented bipeds that looked something like humans and more like beasts, and to complete the picture, brass-buttoned keepers kept order among them when they snarled too fiercely.

I was glad the keepers were there, for I did not have on my 'seafaring' clothes, and I was what is called a 'mark' for the creatures of prey that prowled up and down. At times, between keepers, these males looked at me sharply, hungrily, gutter-wolves that they were, and I was afraid of their hands, of their naked hands, as one may be afraid of the paws of a gorilla. They reminded me of gorillas. Their bodies were small, ill-shaped and squat. There were no swelling muscles, no abundant thews and wide-spreading shoulders. They exhibited, rather, an elemental economy of nature, such as the cave-men must have exhibited. But there was strength in those meagre bodies, the ferocious, primordial strength to clutch and gripe and tear and rend. When they spring upon their human prey they are known even to bend the victim backward and double its body till the back is broken. They possess neither conscience nor sentiment, and they will kill for a half-sovereign, without fear or favour, if they are given but half a chance. They are a new species, a breed of city savages. The streets and houses, alleys and courts, are their hunting grounds. As valley and mountain are to the natural savage, street and building are valley and mountain to them. The slum is their jungle, and they live and prey in the jungle.

The dear soft people of the golden theatres and wonder-mansions of the West End do not see these creatures, do not dream that they exist. But they are here, alive, very much alive in their jungle. And woe the day, when England is fighting in her last trench, and her able-bodied men are on the firing line! For on that day they will crawl out of their dens and lairs, and the people of the West End will see them, as the dear soft aristocrats of Feudal France saw them and asked one another, 'Whence came they?' 'Are they men?'

But they were not the only beasts that ranged the menagerie. They were only here and there, lurking in dark courts and passing like grey shadows along the walls; but the women from whose rotten loins they spring were everywhere. They whined insolently, and in maudlin tones begged me for pennies, and worse. They held carouse in every boozing ken, slatternly, unkempt, bleary-eyed, and tousled, leering and gibbering, overspilling with foulness and corruption, and, gone in debauch, sprawling across benches and bars, unspeakably repulsive, fearful to look upon.

And there were others, strange weird faces and forms and twisted monstrosities that shouldered me on every side, inconceivable types of sodden ugliness, the wrecks of society, the perambulating carcasses, the living deaths – women, blasted by disease and drink till their shame brought not tuppence in the open mart; and men, in fantastic rags, wrenched by hardship and exposure out of all semblance of men, their faces in a perpetual writhe of pain, grinning idiotically, shambling like apes, dying with every step they took and each breath they drew.

Fin-de-siècle *London did indeed have some strange denizens. The acrobat and circus impresario The Great Farini lived in the East End with his 'menagerie' of human curiosities, including Krao the Human Monkey, who became his closest friend and companion.*

A. H. KEANE
'Krao, the "Human Monkey"'

Nature (1883)

Through the courtesy of Mr Farini, I have had a private interview with this curious little waif, which he is now exhibiting at the Royal Aquarium, Westminster, and for which he claims the distinction of being the long-sought-for 'missing link' between man and the Anthropoid apes. Krao certainly presents some abnormal peculiarities, but they are scarcely of a sufficiently pronounced type to justify the claim. She is, in fact, a distinctly human child, apparently about seven years old, endowed with an average share of intelligence, and possessing the faculty of articulate speech. Since her arrival about ten weeks ago in London, she has acquired several English words, which she uses intelligently, and not merely parrot-fashion, as has been stated. Thus, on my suddenly producing my watch at the interview, she was attracted by the glitter, and cried out *c'ock, c'ock*, that is, *clock, clock!* This showed considerable powers of generalization, accompanied by a somewhat defective articulation, and it appears that her phonetic system does not yet embrace the liquids *l* and *r*. But in this and other respects her education is progressing favourably, and she has already so far adapted herself to civilized ways, that the mere threat to be sent back to her own people is always sufficient to suppress any symptoms of unruly conduct.

Physically Krao presents several peculiar features. The head and low forehead are covered down to the bushy eyebrows with the deep black, lank and lustreless hair, characteristic of the Mongoloid races. The whole body is also overgrown with a far less dense coating of soft, black hair about a quarter of an inch long, but nowhere close enough to conceal the colour of the skin, which may be described as of a dark olive-brown shade. The nose is extremely short and low, with excessively broad nostrils, merging in the full, pouched cheeks, into which she appears to have the habit of stuffing her food, monkey-fashion. Like those of the anthropoids her feet are also prehensile, and the hands so flexible that they bend quite back over the wrists. The thumb also doubles completely back, and of the four fingers, all the top joints bend at pleasure independently inwards. Prognathism seems to be very slightly developed, and the beautiful round black eyes are very large and perfectly horizontal. Hence the expression is on the whole far from unpleasing, and not nearly so ape-like as that of many Negritos, and especially of the Javanese 'Ardi', figured by me in NATURE, vol. xxiii. p. 200. But it should be mentioned that when in a pet, Krao's lips are said to protrude so far as to give her 'quite a chimpanzee look'.

Apart from her history one might feel disposed to regard this specimen merely as a 'sport' or *lusus naturae*, possessed rather of a pathological than of a strictly anthropological interest. Certainly isolated cases of hairy persons, and even of hairy families, are not unknown to science. Several were figured in a recent number of the Berlin *Zeitschrift für Ethnologie*, and, if I remember, both Crawfurd ('Journal of an Embassy to Ava') and Col. Yule ('Mission to the Count of Ava') speak of a hairy family resident for two or three generations at the Burmese capital. This family is reported to have come originally from the interior of the Lao country, and in the same region we are now told that little Krao and her parents, also hairy people, were found last year by the well-known eastern explorer, Mr Carl Bock. Soon after their capture, the father appears to have died of cholera, while the mother was detained at Bangkok by the Siamese Government, so that Krao alone could be brought to England. But before his death a photograph of the father was taken by Mr Bock, who describes him as 'completely covered with a thick hairy coat, exactly like that of the anthropoid apes. On his face not only had he a heavy, bushy beard and whiskers, similar in every respect to the hairy family at the court of the King of Burmah, who also came from the same region as that in which Krao and her father were found; but every part was thoroughly enveloped in hair. The long arms and the rounded stomach also proclaimed his close alliance to the monkey-form, while his power of speech and his intelligence were so far developed that before his death he was able to utter a few words in Malay.'

Assuming the accuracy of these statements, and of this description, little Krao, of course, at once acquires exceptional scientific importance. She would at all events be a living proof of the presence of a hairy race in Further India, a region at present mainly occupied by almost hairless Mongoloid peoples. From these races the large straight eyes would also detach the Krao type, and point to a possible connection with the hairy, straight-eyed Aino tribes still surviving in Yesso and Sakhalin, and formerly widely diffused over Japan and the opposite mainland.

It was against this background that Conan Doyle introduced one of his most memorable creations, the Andaman Island pigmy living with a vengeful ex-colonial convict among the wharves of the East End.

SIR ARTHUR CONAN DOYLE
'The Sign of Four'

(1890)

At our hail the man in the stern sprang up from the deck and shook his two clenched fists at us, cursing the while in a high, cracked voice. He was a good-sized, powerful man, and as he stood poising himself with legs astride, I could see that, from the thigh downwards, there was but a wooden stump upon the right side. At the sound of his strident, angry cries, there was a movement in the huddled bundle upon the deck. It straightened itself into a little black man – the smallest I have ever seen – with a great, misshapen head and a shock of tangled dishevelled hair. Holmes had already drawn his revolver, and I whipped out mine at the sight of this savage, distorted creature. He was wrapped in some sort of a dark ulster or blanket, which left only his face exposed; but that face was enough to give a man a sleepless night. Never have I seen features so deeply marked with all bestiality and cruelty. His small eyes glowed and burned with a sombre light, and his thick lips were writhed back from his teeth, which grinned and chattered at us with half-animal fury.

'Fire if he raises his hand,' said Holmes quietly.

We were within a boat's-length by this time, and almost within touch of our quarry. I can see the two of them now as they stood: the white man with his legs far apart, shrieking out curses, and the unhallowed dwarf with his hideous face, and his strong, yellow teeth gnashing at us in the light of our lantern.

It was well that we had so clear a view of him. Even as we looked he plucked out from under his covering a short, round piece of wood, like a school-ruler, and clapped it to his lips. Our pistols rang out together. He whirled round, threw up his arms and, with a kind of choking cough, fell sideways into the stream. I caught one glimpse of his venomous, menacing eyes amid the white swirl of the waters. At the same moment the wooden-legged man threw himself upon the rudder and put it hard down, so that his boat made straight in for the southern bank, while we shot past her stern, only clearing her by a few feet. We were round after her in an instant, but she was already nearly at the bank. It was a wild and desolate place, where the moon glimmered upon a wide expanse of marsh-land, with pools of stagnant water and beds of decaying vegetation. The launch, with a dull thud, ran up upon the mud-bank, with her bow in the air and her stern flush with the water. The fugitive sprang out, but his stump instantly sank its whole length into the sodden soil. In vain he struggled and writhed. Not one step could he possibly take either forwards or backwards. He yelled in impotent rage, and kicked frantically into the mud with his other foot; but his struggles only bored his wooden pin the deeper into the sticky bank. When we brought our launch alongside he was so firmly anchored that it was only by throwing the end of a rope over his shoulders that we were able to haul him out, and, to drag him, like some evil fish over our side. The two Smiths, father and son, sat sullenly in their launch, but came aboard meekly enough when commanded. The *Aurora* herself we hauled off and made fast to our stern. A solid iron chest of Indian workmanship stood upon the deck. This, there could be no question, was the same that had contained the ill-omened treasure of the Sholtos. There was no key, but it was of considerable weight, so we transferred it carefully to our own little cabin. As we steamed slowly upstream again, we flashed our searchlight in every direction, but there was no sign of the Islander. Somewhere in the dark ooze at the bottom of the Thames lie the bones of that strange visitor to our shores.

The most conspicuous 'alien' presence in London's East End was the Chinese community, a population living mostly in Limehouse and Poplar. Chinese culture and civilization was a subject of intense curiosity, interest and, accordingly, anxiety. Here is Isabella Bird's assessment from her earlier trip to the Yangtze.

ISABELLA BIRD
The Yangtze Valley and Beyond

(1899)

Western civilization finds itself confronted . . . by a people at once grossly material and grossly superstitious, swayed at once by the hazy speculations and unintelligible metaphysic which in Chinese Buddhism have allied themselves with the most extravagant and childish superstitions, and by the daemonism of Taoism, while over both tower the lofty ethics and profound agnosticism of Confucius. It finds a classical literature universally held in profound reverence, in which, according to all testimony, there is not a thought which could sully the purest mind, and an idolatry puerile, superstitious and free from grand conceptions, but in which bloody sacrifices and the deification of vice have never had a part, or immoral rites a place.

The human product of Chinese civilization, religion and government is to me the greatest of all enigmas, and so he remains to those who know him best. At once conservative and adaptable, the most local of peasants in his attachments, and the most cosmopolitan and successful of emigrants – sober, industrious, thrifty, orderly, peaceable, indifferent to personal comfort, possessing great physical vitality, cheerful, contented, persevering – his filial piety, tenacity, resourcefulness, power of combination and respect for law and literature, place him in the van of Asiatic nations.

The Chinese constitute an order by themselves, and their individuality cannot be read in the light of that of any other nation. The aspirations and modes of thinking by which we are ruled do not direct their aims. They are keen and alert, but unwilling to strike out new lines, and slow to be influenced in any matters. Their trading instincts are phenomenal. They are born bargainers, and would hardly think half an hour wasted if through chaffering they gained an advantage of half a *cash*, a coin forty of which are about one penny. They are suspicious, cunning, and corrupt; but it is needless to run through the established formula of their vices. Among the things which they lack are CONSCIENCE, and such an enlightened public opinion as shall sustain right and condemn wrong.

Matthew Arnold has said that Greece perished for want of attention to conduct, and that the revelation which rules the world is the 'pre-eminence of righteousness'. It may be that the western powers are not giving the Middle Kingdom a very desirable object-lesson.

On the whole, as I hope to show to some extent in the following pages, throughout the Yangtze valley, from the great cities of Hangchow and Hankow to the trading cities of SZE-CHUAN, the traveller receives very definite impressions of the completeness of Chinese social and commercial organization, the skill and carefulness of cultivation, the clever adaptation of means to ends – the existence of provincial patriotism, or, perhaps, more truly, of local public spirit, of the general prosperity and of the backbone, power of combination, resourcefulness and independence possessed by the race. It is not an effete or decaying people which we shall have to meet in serious competition when it shall have learned our sciences and some of our methods of manufacturing industry. Indeed, it is not improbable that chemistry, for instance, might be eagerly adapted by so ingenious a race to the perpetration of new and hitherto unthought-of frauds! But if the extraordinary energy, adaptability and industry of the Chinese may be regarded from one point of view as the 'Yellow Peril', surely looked at from another they constitute the Yellow Hope, and it may be possible that an empire genuinely Christianized, but not denationalized, may yet be the dominant power in Eastern Asia.

The Chinese are ignorant and superstitious beyond belief, but on the whole, with all their faults, I doubt whether any other Oriental race runs so straight.

. . . but the presence of the Chinese in London was more disturbing.
The fear of an alien race in the heart of Empire grew sharply, the new
xenophobia emphatically expressed in Dickens's Edwin Drood, *which*
uses the classic image of insidious Chinese influence, the 'opium den'.

CHARLES DICKENS
The Mystery of Edwin Drood

(1870)

An ancient English Cathedral town? How can the ancient
English Cathedral town be here! The well-known massive grey square
tower of its old Cathedral? How can that be here! There is no spike of
rusty iron in the air, between the eye and it, from any point of the real
prospect. What IS the spike that intervenes, and who has set it up?
Maybe, it is set up by the Sultan's orders for the impaling of a horde of
Turkish robbers, one by one. It is so, for cymbals clash, and the Sultan
goes by to his palace in long procession. Ten thousand scimitars flash
in the sunlight, and thrice ten thousand dancing-girls strew flowers.
Then, follow white elephants caparisoned in countless gorgeous colours,
and infinite in number and attendants. Still, the Cathedral tower rises
in the background, where it cannot be, and still no writhing figure is on
the grim spike. Stay! Is the spike so low a thing as the rusty spike on
the top of a post of an old bedstead that has tumbled all awry? Some
vague period of drowsy laughter must be devoted to the consideration
of this possibility.

Shaking from head to foot, the man whose scattered consciousness
has thus fantastically pieced itself together, at length rises, supports his
trembling frame upon his arms, and looks around. He is in the meanest
and closest of small rooms. Through the ragged window-curtain, the
light of early day steals in from a miserable court. He lies, dressed,
across a large unseemly bed, upon a bedstead that has indeed given
way under the weight upon it. Lying, also dressed and also across the
bed, not longwise, are a Chinaman, a Lascar and a haggard woman.
The two first are in a sleep or stupor; the last is blowing at a kind of
pipe, to kindle it. And as she blows, and shading it with her lean hand,

concentrates its red spark of light, it serves in the dim morning as a lamp to show him what he sees of her.

'Another?' says this woman, in a querulous, rattling whisper. 'Have another?'

He looks about him, with his hand to his forehead.

'Ye've smoked as many as five since ye come in at midnight,' the woman goes on, as she chronically complains. 'Poor me, poor me, my head is so bad. Them two come in after ye. Ah, poor me, the business is slack, is slack! Few Chinamen about the Docks, and fewer Lascars, and no ships coming in, these say! Here's another ready for ye, deary. Ye'll remember like a good soul, won't ye, that the market price is dreffle high just now? More nor three shillings and sixpence for a thimbleful! And ye'll remember that nobody but me (and Jack Chinaman t'other side the court; but he can't do it as well as me) has the true secret of mixing it? Ye'll pay up according, deary, won't ye?'

She blows at the pipe as she speaks, and, occasionally bubbling at it, inhales much of its contents.

'O me, O me, my lungs is weak, my lungs is bad! It's nearly ready for ye, deary. Ah, poor me, poor me, my poor hand shakes like to drop off! I see ye coming-to, and I ses to my poor self, "I'll have another ready for him, and he'll bear in mind the market price of opium, and pay according." O my poor head! I makes my pipes of old penny ink-bottles, ye see, deary – this is one – and I fits in a mouthpiece, this way, and I takes my mixter out of this thimble with this little horn spoon; and so I fills, deary. Ah, my poor nerves! I got Heavens-hard drunk for sixteen year afore I took to this; but this don't hurt me, not to speak of. And it takes away the hunger as well as wittles, deary.'

She hands him the nearly-emptied pipe, and sinks back, turning over on her face.

He rises unsteadily from the bed, lays the pipe upon the hearthstone, draws back the ragged curtain, and looks with repugnance at his three companions. He notices that the woman has opium-smoked herself into a strange likeness of the Chinaman. His form of cheek, eye, and temple, and his colour, are repeated in her. Said Chinaman convulsively wrestles with one of his many Gods, or Devils, perhaps, and snarls horribly. The Lascar laughs and dribbles at the mouth. The hostess is still.

The fear of the Chinese found its ultimate popular expression in Sax Rohmer's personification of the Yellow Peril, Fu Manchu.

SAX ROHMER
The Mystery of Doctor Fu Manchu

(1913)

The cab moved off with a metallic jerk, and I turned and looked back through the little window in the rear.

'Some one has got into another cab. It is following ours, I think.'

Nayland Smith lay back and laughed unmirthfully.

'Petrie,' he said, 'if I escape alive from this business I shall know that I bear a charmed life . . .'

I made no reply, as he pulled out the dilapidated pouch and filled his pipe.

'You have asked me to explain matters,' he continued, 'and I will do so to the best of my ability. You no doubt wonder why a servant of the British Government, lately stationed in Burma, suddenly appears in London in the character of a detective. I am here, Petrie – and I bear credentials from the very highest sources – because, quite by accident, I came upon a clue. Following it up, in the ordinary course of routine, I obtained evidence of the existence and malignant activity of a certain man. At the present stage of the case I should not be justified in terming him the emissary of an Eastern Power, but I may say that representations are shortly to be made to that Power's ambassador in London.'

He paused, and glanced back towards the pursuing cab.

'There is little to fear until we arrive home,' he said calmly. 'Afterwards there is much. To continue. This man, whether a fanatic, or a duly appointed agent, is, unquestionably, the most malign and formidable personality existing in the known world today. He is a linguist who speaks with almost equal facility in any of the civilized languages, and in most of the barbaric. He is an adept in all the arts and sciences which a great university could teach him. He also is an adept in certain obscure arts and sciences which *no* university of today can teach. He has the brains of any three men of genius. Petrie, he is a mental giant.'

'You amaze me!' I said.

'As to his mission among men. Why did M. Jules Furneaux fall dead in a Paris opera-house? Because of heart failure? No! Because his last speech had shown that he held the key to the secret of Tongking. What became of the Grand Duke Stanislaus? Elopement? Suicide? Nothing of the kind. He alone was fully alive to Russia's growing peril. He alone knew the truth about Mongolia. Why was Sir Crichton Davey murdered? Because, had the work he was engaged upon ever seen the light, it would have shown him to be the only living Englishman who understood the importance of the Tibetan frontiers. I say to you solemnly, Petrie, that these are but a few. Is there a man who would arouse the West to a sense of the awakening of the East, who would teach the deaf to hear, the blind to see, that the millions only await their leader? He will die. And this is only one phase of the devilish campaign. The others I can merely surmise.'

'But, Smith, this is almost incredible! What perverted genius controls this awful secret movement?'

'Imagine a person, tall, lean and feline, high-shouldered, with a brow like Shakespeare and a face like Satan, a close-shaven skull and long, magnetic eyes of the true cat-green. Invest him with all the cruel cunning of an entire Eastern race, accumulated in one giant intellect, with all the resources of science past and present, with all the resources, if you will, of a wealthy government – which, however, already has denied all knowledge of his existence. Imagine that awful being, and you have a mental picture of Dr Fu-Manchu, the yellow peril incarnate in one man.'

The 'Yellow Peril' – a Chinese secret society. (From D. O. Wirdhaeff,
Je sais tout, 1905.) (Courtesy of Mary Evans Picture Library)

MARIANI WINE

MARIANI WINE Quickly Restores **HEALTH, STRENGTH, ENERGY & VITALITY.**

MARIANI WINE FORTIFIES, STRENGTHENS, STIMULATES & REFRESHES THE BODY & BRAIN.

HASTENS CONVALESCENCE
especially after
INFLUENZA.

His Holiness THE POPE
writes that he has fully appreciated the beneficent effects of this Tonic Wine and has forwarded to Mr. Mariani as a token of his gratitude a gold medal bearing his august effigy.

MARIANI WINE

is delivered free to all parts of the United Kingdom by WILCOX & CO., 83, Mortimer Street, London, W., price 4/- per Single Bottle, 22 6 half-dozen, 45/- dozen, and is sold by Chemists and Stores.

Mariani wine: Along with opium, other 'alien' stimulants from foreign cultures were becoming increasingly popular in the cities of the *fin-de-siècle*. The cocaine-based Mariani Wine, declared in the *British Medical Journal* to be a 'very useful nervine stimulant', was endorsed by public figures including Ibsen, H. G. Wells, Jules Verne, the Kings of Greece and Spain, Thomas Edison, President McKinley and, as here, the Pope. (From *Graphic*, 1899.)

The secret society of anarchists appeared with increasing frequency in
fiction. In Joseph Conrad's The Secret Agent, *anarchists plan an attack*
on the Royal Observatory at Greenwich.

JOSEPH CONRAD
The Secret Agent: A Simple Tale

(1907)

'This is what you should try for. An attempt upon a crowned head
or on a president is sensational enough in a way, but not so much as it
used to be. It has entered into the general conception of the existence
of all chiefs of state. It's almost conventional – especially since so many
presidents have been assassinated. Now let us take an outrage upon –
say, a church. Horrible enough at first sight, no doubt, and yet not so
effective as a person of an ordinary mind might think. No matter how
revolutionary and anarchist in inception, there would be fools enough
to give such an outrage the character of a religious manifestation. And
that would detract from the especial alarming significance we wish to
give to the act. A murderous attempt on a restaurant or a theatre would
suffer in the same way from the suggestion of non-political passion; the
exasperation of a hungry man, an act of social revenge. All this is used
up; it is no longer instructive as an object lesson in revolutionary
anarchism. Every newspaper has ready made phrases to explain such
manifestations away. I am about to give you the philosophy of bomb
throwing from my point of view; from the point of view you pretend to
have been serving for the last eleven years. I will try not to talk above
your head. The sensibilities of the class you are attacking are soon
blunted. Property seems to them an indestructible thing. You can't
count upon their emotions either of pity or fear for very long. A bomb
outrage to have any influence on public opinion now must go beyond
the intention of vengeance or terrorism. It must be purely destructive.
It must be that, and only that, beyond the faintest suspicion of any other
object. You anarchists should make it clear that you are perfectly
determined to make a clean sweep of the whole social creation. But
how to get that appallingly absurd notion into the heads of the middle
classes so that there should be no mistake? That's the question. By

directing your blows at something outside the ordinary passions of humanity is the answer. Of course, there is art. A bomb in the National Gallery would make some noise. But it would not be serious enough. Art has never been their fetish. It's like breaking a few back windows in a man's house; whereas, if you want to make him really sit up, you must try at least to raise the roof. There would be some screaming of course, but from whom? Artists – art critics and such like – people of no account. Nobody minds what they say. But there is learning – science. Any imbecile that has got an income believes in that. He does not know why, but he believes it matters somehow. It is the sacrosanct fetish. All the damned professors are radicals at heart. Let them know that their great panjandrum has got to go, too, to make room for the Future of the Proletariat. A howl from all these intellectual idiots is bound to help forward the labours of the Milan Conference. They will be writing to the papers. Their indignation would be above suspicion, no material interests being openly at stake, and it will alarm every selfishness of the class which should be impressed. They believe that in some mysterious way science is at the source of their material prosperity. They do. And the absurd ferocity of such a demonstration will affect them more profoundly than the mangling of a whole street – or theatre – full of their own kind. To that last they can always say: "Oh! it's mere class hate." But what is one to say to an act of destructive ferocity so absurd as to be incomprehensible, inexplicable, almost unthinkable; in fact, mad? Madness alone is truly terrifying, inasmuch as you cannot placate it either by threats, persuasion or bribes. Moreover, I am a civilized man. I would never dream of directing you to organize a mere butchery, even if I expected the best results from it. But I wouldn't expect from a butchery the result I want. Murder is always with us. It is almost an institution. The demonstration must be against learning – science. But not every science will do. The attack must have all the shocking senselessness of gratuitous blasphemy. Since bombs are your means of expression, it would be really telling if one could throw a bomb into pure mathematics. But that is impossible. I have been trying to educate you; I have expounded to you the higher philosophy of your usefulness, and suggested to you some serviceable arguments. The practical application of my teaching interests *you* mostly. But from the moment I have undertaken to interview you I have also given some attention to the practical aspect of the question. What do you think of having a go at astronomy?'

For sometime already Mr Verloc's immobility by the side of the armchair resembled a state of collapsed coma – a sort of passive insensibility interrupted by slight convulsive starts, such as may be observed in the domestic dog having a nightmare on the hearthrug. And it was in an uneasy, doglike growl that he repeated the word:

'Astronomy.'

The new internationalism led to a pervasive fear not merely of immi-
gration, but of international secret societies working for the downfall of
the imperial status quo. This was reflected in the Aliens Act of 1904,
passed on the strength of this Royal Commission report.

Report of the Royal Commission on Alien Immigration

(1903)

In respect of many of these Alien Immigrants it is alleged –
  (1) That on their arrival they are (a) in an impoverished and destitute condition (b) deficient in cleanliness and practice insanitary habits (c) being subject to no medical examination on embarkation or arrival are liable to infectious diseases
  (2) That amongst them are criminals, anarchists, prostitutes and persons of bad character, in number beyond the ordinary percentage of the native population

. . .

(4) That on their arrival in this country they congregate as dwellers in certain districts, principally in the East End of London and especially in the Borough of Stepney and that when they so settle they become a compact, non-assimilating community

. . .

(8) That the unskilled Aliens on their arrival in this country set them-selves to learn the easier portions of different trades, that during such probationary periods they produce work for a very low remuneration and when by degrees they become skilled workers they are willing to accept a lower rate of wage than that demanded by the native workmen, who have by this cause been driven to some extent out of certain trades
(9) In addition to these allegations it was complained in respect to immigrants of the Jewish faith (a) that they do not assimilate and

intermarry with the native race and so remain a solid and distinct colony and (b) that their existence in large number in certain areas gravely interferes with the observance of the Christian Sunday.

. . .

There was general agreement in designating as 'undesirables'

(1) Criminals other than political
(2) Anarchists and other persons of notoriously bad character
(3) Prostitutes and persons living on the proceeds of prostitution
(4) Persons affected by infection or contagious diseases
(5) Lunatics or idiots

Anarchist bomb in the French Chamber of Deputies. The international anarchist organization became a potent folk-devil of the *fin-de-siècle*. (From *Petit Journal*, 1893.) (Courtesy of the Mary Evans Picture Library)

The developing genre of the international espionage thriller occasionally cast secret societies in the glamorous light of post-imperial freedom-fighters. In George Griffith's Angel of the Revolution, *the protagonist, Richard Arnold, has his design for a military airship rejected by the British government, and finds himself co-opted into the Brotherhood of international 'Nihilists, Anarchists and Socialists'.*

GEORGE GRIFFITH
The Angel of the Revolution: A Tale of the Coming Terror

(1893)

As soon as Arnold's eyes got accustomed to the light, he saw that he was in a large, lofty room with panelled walls adorned with a number of fine paintings. As he looked at these his gaze was fascinated by them, even more than by the strange company which was assembled round the long table that occupied the middle of the room.

Though they were all manifestly the products of the highest form of art, their subjects were dreary and repulsive beyond description. There was a horrible realism about them which reminded him irresistibly of the awful collection of pictorial horrors in the Musée Wiertz, in Brussels – those works of the brilliant but unhappy genius who was driven into insanity by the sheer exuberance of his own morbid imagination.

Here was a long line of men and women in chains staggering across a wilderness of snow that melted away into the horizon without a break. Beside them rode Cossacks armed with long whips that they used on men and women alike when their fainting limbs gave way beneath them, and they were like to fall by the wayside to seek the welcome rest that only death could give them.

There was a picture of a woman naked to the waist, and tied up to a triangle in a prison yard, being flogged by a soldier with willow wands, while a group of officers stood by, apparently greatly interested in the performance. Another painting showed a poor wretch being knouted to death in the market-place of a Russian town, and yet another showed a young and beautiful woman in a prison cell with her face distorted by the horrible leer of madness, and her little white hands clawing nervously at her long dishevelled hair.

Arnold stood for several minutes fascinated by the hideous realism of the pictures, and burning with rage and shame at the thought that they were all too terribly true to life, when he was startled out of his reverie by the same voice that had called them from the dark room saying to him in English –

'Well, Richard Arnold, what do you think of our little picture gallery? The paintings are good in themselves, but it may make them more interesting to you if you know that they are all faithful reproductions of scenes that have really taken place within the limits of the so-called civilized and Christian world. There are some here in this room now who have suffered the torments depicted on those canvases, and who could tell of worse horrors than even they portray. We should like to know what you think of our paintings?'

Arnold glanced towards the table in search of Colston, but he had vanished. Around the long table sat fourteen masked and shrouded forms that were absolutely indistinguishable one from the other. He could not even tell whether they were men or women, so closely were their forms and faces concealed. Seeing that he was left to his own discretion, he laid the case containing the model, which he had so far kept under his arm, down on the floor, and, facing the strange assembly, said as steadily as he could –

'My own reading tells me that they are only too true to the dreadful reality. I think that the civilized and Christian Society which permits such crimes to be committed against humanity, when it has the power to stop them by force of arms, is neither truly civilized nor truly Christian.'

. . .

'We are glad to see that your sentiments are so far in accord with our own, for that fact will make our negotiations all the easier.

'As you are aware, you are now in the Inner Circle of the Terrorists. Yonder empty chair at the head of the table is that of our Chief, who, though not with us in person, is ever present as a guiding influence in our councils. We act as he directs, and it was from him that we received news of you and your marvellous invention. It is also by his direction that you have been invited here tonight with an object that you are already aware of'

. . .

'I must first know as exactly as possible what the work of the Brotherhood is.'

'Under the circumstances there is no objection to your knowing that. In the first place, that which is known to the outside world as the Terror is an international secret society underlying and directing the operations of the various bodies known as Nihilists, Anarchists, Socialists – in fact, all those organizations which have for their object the reform or destruction, by peaceful or violent means, of Society as it is at present constituted.

'Its influence reaches beyond these into the various trade unions and political clubs, the moving spirits of which are all members of our Outer Circle. On the other side of Society we have agents and adherents in all the Courts of Europe, all the diplomatic bodies, and all the parliamentary assemblies throughout the world.

'We believe that Society as at present constituted is hopeless for any good thing. All kinds of nameless brutalities are practised without reproof in the names of law and order, and commercial economics. On one side human life is a splendid fabric of cloth of gold embroidered with priceless gems, and on the other it is a mass of filthy, festering rags, swarming with vermin.

'We think that such a Society – a Society which permits considerably more than the half of humanity to be sunk in poverty and misery while a very small portion of it fools away its life in perfectly ridiculous luxury – does not deserve to exist, and ought to be destroyed.

'We also know that sooner or later it will destroy itself, as every similar Society has done before it.

. . .

'That is a rough, brief outline of the policy of the Brotherhood, which we are going to ask you tonight to join. Of course, in the eyes of the world we are only a set of fiends, whose sole object is the destruction of Society, and the inauguration of a state of universal anarchy. That, however, has no concern for us. What is called popular opinion is merely manufactured by the Press according to order, and does not count in serious concerns. What I have described to you are the true objects of the Brotherhood; and now it remains for you to say, yes or no, whether you will devote yourself and your invention to carrying them out or not.'

For two or three minutes after the masked spokesman of the Inner Circle had ceased speaking, there was absolute silence in the room. The calmly spoken words which deliberately sketched out the ruin of a civilization and the establishment of a new order of things made a deep impression on Arnold's mind. He saw clearly that he was standing at the parting of the ways, and facing the most tremendous crisis that could occur in the life of a human being.

It was only natural that he should look back, as he did, to the life from which a single step would now part him for ever, without the possibility of going back. He knew that if he once put his hands to the plough, and looked back, death, swift and inevitable, would be the penalty of his wavering. This, however, he had already weighed and decided.

Most of what he had heard had found an echo in his own convictions. Moreover, the life that he had left had no charms for him, while to be one of the chief factors in a world-revolution was a destiny worthy both of himself and his invention.

. . .

Arnold bowed his acquiescence, and the spokesman took a piece of paper from the table and read aloud –

'I, Richard Arnold, sign this paper in the full knowledge that in doing so I devote myself absolutely for the rest of my life to the service of the Brotherhood of Freedom, known to the world as the Terrorists. As long as I live its ends shall be my ends, and no human considerations shall weigh with me where those ends are concerned. I will take life without mercy, and yield my own without hesitation at its bidding. I will break all other laws to obey those which it obeys, and if I disobey these I shall expect death as the just penalty of my perjury.'

As he finished reading the oath, he handed the paper to Arnold, saying as he did so –

'There are no theatrical formalities to be gone through. Simply sign the paper and give it back to me, or else tear it up and go in peace.'

Arnold read it through slowly, and then glanced round the table. He saw the eyes of the silent figures sitting about him shining at him through the holes in their masks. He laid the paper down on the table in front of him, dipped a pen in an inkstand that stood near, and signed the oath in a firm, unfaltering hand. Then – committed for ever, for good or evil, to the new life that he had adopted – he gave the paper back again.

The President took it and read it, and then passed it to the mask on his right hand. It went from one to the other round the table, each one reading it before passing it on, until it got back to the President. When it reached him he rose from his seat, and, going to the fireplace, dropped it into the flames, and watched it until it was consumed to ashes. Then, crossing the room to where Arnold was sitting, he removed his mask with one hand, and held the other out to him in greeting, saying as he did so –

'Welcome to the Brotherhood! Thrice welcome! for your coming has brought the day of redemption nearer!'

9
Before Armageddon:
Rumours of Total War

Beyond the fears of international anarchism, socialism and nihilism lurked the spectre of war: a war the like of which had never been seen before. Technological development offered the prospect of war fought with ironclad tanks and airships, between nations unprecedently industrialized and militarized. The nation most feared was the recently formed Germany who, it was believed, had both the capacity and the will to fight a 'total war', a war to end civilization.

GUSTAVE LE BON
The Psychology of the Great War
(1916)

Among the characteristics which are most prevalent in the German mentality may be mentioned brutality, lack of good-breeding and an entire absence of the chivalrous spirit, all of which traits exist among the educated classes no less than among the common people. These fundamental qualities of the Teutonic mind are more clearly revealed by the notebooks which have been taken from prisoners of all classes since the war began than by any books which have been written on the subject. A Colonel who has translated several of these documents, says: –

'I hope that the enormous mass of German correspondence which has come into our possession will one day be published. We have letters from men of the middle classes, from workmen, merchants, professors and artists, and in them are revealed the secret thoughts of all classes, callings and grades of social environment.

'Conflagrations kindled in cold blood are described in them, artistic instincts are represented as satisfied by the sight of accumulated and wanton ruin, and the idiotic cruelties of enraged beer-drinkers are laid bare. They show us the gluttony of pillagers delighted to surfeit themselves free of cost, and the filthy sadism of violators of children. We witness the pedantic cruelty of men who massacre in cold blood and seek in the *philosophy of war* a justification for useless slaughter; and our very eyes behold the torturers of women and old men, wretches who find the reward of battle in the sack of a conquered village. This is how they look in uniform; this is how we officers and soldiers see the whole German nation.'

Under the title *Pensées d'un lieutenant allemand*, the *Temps* has published a pamphlet whose author preaches slaughter, pillage, incendiarism, and also the violation of women, that the chosen race may increase and multiply, and who hopes that the struggle may go on 'over mountains of the dead and across oceans of tears'. He says: –

'Ought civilization to erect its temples upon mountains of the dead, across oceans of tears and on the agony of the dying? Yes, it ought. If a nation has the right to dominate, its power to conquer is the supreme moral law, before which the conquered must bow. Woe to the vanquished!'

. . .

The influences which we have been describing in the preceding paragraphs, and which have held their own, unyielding and austere, under Prussia's heavy hand, have produced similar changes in all the manifestations of the Teutonic mentality, have destroyed the individual mind of the German by degrees, and have transformed it into a collective mind.

The mental unification of a nation has never been carried to such an extent. As I have said before, it has impressed every one who has had occasion during the war to inspect German prisoners of every social class; and all those who have had personal experience agree with the following remarks, which I quote from a correspondent of the *Gazette de Lausanne*: –

'I could never have believed that the psychological unification of the masses could have been so completely attained. There is something about it which makes one ask whether it is admirable or deplorable. One would say that a single brain thinks inside all those thousands of heads. I do not know whether it is a phenomenon of mental contagion, or the result of a strict education directed exclusively to purposes of war. But while their sensibilities are different, their intellects are diverse, and their methods of expression various, their personality appears to have vanished. There are no longer any individuals in Germany. There is nothing but a nation, a social organism, whose brain is the all-powerful State.'

The inhumanity of 'total war' is vividly conjured in Zola's La Débâcle.

ÉMILE ZOLA
The Débâcle

(1892)

Suddenly there was a furious scrimmage, with stampings and slippings, muffled oaths and snorts. Sambuc and the two others had fallen upon Goliath, and in spite of their number they could not immediately master the giant, whose strength was increased by danger. In the darkness there could be heard crackings of bones and the panting of men grappling. Fortunately the revolver had fallen on to the floor. A voice, Cabasse's, gasped: 'The ropes! The ropes!' and Ducat passed to Sambuc the bundle of ropes they had taken the precaution of bringing with them. There followed a long, savage operation involving kicks and punches; the legs tied first, then the arms tied to the sides, then the whole body tied up by feel, depending on the man's jerking struggles, with such a riot of turns and knots that the man was enveloped in a sort of net, some of the meshes of which cut into his flesh. He never stopped shouting and Ducat's voice went on saying: 'Shut your jaw!' The cries stopped. Cabasse had roughly tied an old blue handkerchief over his mouth. Then they regained their breath and carried him like a bale into the kitchen, where they laid him out on the big table beside the candle.

'The Prussian shit!' swore Sambuc, mopping his brow. 'He didn't half give us some trouble! I say, Silvine, light another candle, will you, so as we can take a good look at the bleeding swine!'

Silvine was standing there with her big eyes staring in her pale face. She didn't say a word, but lit a candle and put it on the other side of Goliath, who could be seen lit up as though between two church candles. At that moment their eyes met, and his desperately implored her, for he was terrified, but she showed no sign of understanding, and stepped backwards to the dresser and stood there cold and immovable.

. . .

Sambuc had opened the table drawer and taken out a big kitchen knife, the one they used for slicing the bacon.

'All right, as you're a pig I'm going to bleed you like a pig.'

He took his time, and discussed with Cabasse and Ducat the way to do the butchering job properly. There was even a dispute because Cabasse said that in his part of the world, in Provence, pigs were bled head down, while Ducat protested, outraged, considering this method barbarous and inconvenient.

'Move him to the edge of the table over the tub so as not to make a mess.'

They moved him over, and Sambuc proceeded calmly and neatly. With a single cut of the big knife he slit the throat across. The blood from the severed carotid poured out at once into the tub with a little noise like falling water. He had taken care with the cut and only a few drops pumped out with the heartbeats. Although this made death slower, there were no struggles visible, for the ropes were strong and the body remained quite motionless. Not a single jerk or gasp. The only way the march of death could be followed was on the face, a mask distorted by terror, from which the blood was receding drop by drop as the skin lost its colour and went white as a sheet. The eyes also emptied themselves. They dimmed and then went out.

'I say, Silvine, we shall have to have a sponge, though.'

She did not respond, but seemed rooted to the floor, and her arms had closed instinctively over her breast like a collar of iron. She was watching. Then she suddenly realized that Charlot was there, clinging to her skirt. He must have woken up and managed to open the doors, and nobody had seen him tiptoe in, like the inquisitive child he was. How long had he been there, half hidden behind his mother? He was watching, too. With his big blue eyes, under his mop of yellow hair, he was looking at the blood running down, the little red trickle slowly filling the tub. Perhaps it amused him. Had he not understood at first? Was he suddenly touched by the wind of horror, did he have an instinctive consciousness of the abomination he was witnessing? Anyhow, he suddenly screamed in panic:

'Oh Mummy, Mummy! I'm frightened, take me away!'

It shook Silvine to the depths of her being. It was too much, and something gave way within her, horror at last got the better of the strength and excitement of the obsession that had kept her going for two days. The woman in her came back, she burst into tears and desperately picked up Charlot and hugged him to her breast. In terror she rushed madly away with him, unable to hear or see any more, with no other desire but to lose herself anywhere in the first hole she could find.

It was at that moment that Jean made up his mind to open the door of his room gently. Although he never bothered about the sounds in the house, he was surprised this time by the comings and goings and loud voices he heard. And so it was into his quiet room that Silvine tumbled sobbing and shaken in such a paroxysm of distress that at first he could not make any sense out of the disconnected words she muttered through clenched teeth. She kept repeating the same gesture, as though she were thrusting aside an atrocious vision. But at length he did understand, and he also pieced together the story of the ambush, the mother standing by, the child clinging to her skirt, the face of the father with his throat cut and life-blood ebbing away; it froze him, and the heart of this peasant and soldier was rent with anguish. Oh war, abominable war, that turned all these poor people into wild beasts, sowed dreadful hatreds, the son splashed with his father's blood, perpetuating national hatred and doomed to grow up in time to execrate his father's family, whom some day perhaps he would go and exterminate! Murderous seed sown to produce appalling harvests!

Silvine collapsed on to a chair, wildly kissing Charlot who was crying on her breast, and she repeated on and on the same sentence, the cry of her bleeding heart.

'Oh my poor child, they'll never call you a Prussian again! . . . Oh my poor child, they'll never call you a Prussian again!'

German children: An image of a German nation dedicated to military conquest. (*Glückliche Kinderzeit*, late nineteenth century.) (Courtesy of Mary Evans Picture Library)

The war of the future: Among Nikola Tesla's promised inventions was a total war machine, a proto-Star Wars defence system which would protect the nation which developed it with force-fields and long-distance rays. (Courtesy of Gernsback Publications, Inc., New York)

In the face of this threat, the potential of the British population to furnish an adequate fighting force came under severe scrutiny. The evidence supplied by the Boer War was highly discouraging: a century of industrialization, it was feared, had left the nation with a high proportion of the male working class unfit for combat.

Memorandum Prepared by Surgeon-General Sir William Taylor

(1904)

1. A deep interest has been aroused, both in the lay and medical press, by the writings of Sir Frederick Maurice and others, who have brought into prominence certain observations pointing to the fact that there is an alarming proportion of the young men of this country, more especially among the urban population, who are unfit for military service on account of defective physique.

The questions naturally arise as to whether this impeachment of the national health has a solid foundation in fact, and as to whether the condition is true of the population as a whole, or only of a certain section of it. The teaching of public health statistics would appear to show that progressive improvement of the national health has steadily followed the improved conditions of life which have been brought about by the advance of sanitary knowledge and its practical application. It has also been pointed out that athletic records are constantly being broken for all sorts of feats of strength, agility and endurance, facts which would seem to indicate that the physique of the well-to-do classes, at least, is improving rather than deteriorating. It is nevertheless true, and the fact is a disturbing and disquieting one, that a very large proportion of the men who offer themselves for enlistment in the Army are found to be physically unfit for military service.

2. In an article on the National Health, which appeared in a recent number of the *Contemporary Review*, Sir Frederick Maurice states that, according to the best estimate he had been able to arrive at, it has been for many years the case that out of every five men who wished to enlist, and primarily offer themselves for enlistment, you will find that

by the end of two years' service there are only two men remaining in the Army as effective soldiers. Of the men who offer themselves, some are rejected by the recruiting sergeant or recruiting officer, some by the examining medical officer, and some, though enlisted, are found after three months to be unlikely to develop into effective soldiers and are summarily discharged. According to General Maurice's experience, at the end of two years not more than 40 per cent of the men who wished to become soldiers will be found serving; or, in other words, 60 per cent of the men offering themselves are physically unfit to serve as soldiers. He points out that it is no good talking of conscription or of any form of compulsory service if we already have five men offering themselves for every two men who are fit for the work; no one has suggested that we should increase our Army in the proportion of two to five, i.e. make it two-and-a-half times as large as it is now. He then goes on to say that no nation was ever yet for any long time great and free, when the army it put in the field no longer represented its own virility and manhood.

The Boer War threw up alarming stories of unfitness and degenerate behaviour. (From Ives scrapbook.)

"MAD DRUNK" WITH CORDITE.

TERRIBLE HABIT OF SOLDIERS IN SOUTH AFRICA.

The South African war and the weariness of life on the "illimitable veldt" are responsible for the discovery of a new and extraordinary form of intoxication.

Some British soldiers discovered that by eating cordite they could get all the excitement of the most powerful narcotic—and all the terrible after-effects, too. Cordite consists roughly of about 58 parts of nitroglycerine, 37 parts gun cotton, and five-parts of mineral jelly.

Each cartridge contains 60 cylindrical strands of cordite, and when Major Jennings, D.S.O., learned that the men were eating these (says the "British Medical Journal") he experimented on himself by sucking a strand. He found that it tasted sweet, pleasant, and pungent, but it resulted in giving him the most racking, splitting headache he ever had in his life, and it lasted for 36 hours.

Dissolved in tea, cordite produces an almost immediately exhilarating effect "inciting to almost demoniacal actions." If many persons have partaken of the beverage all begin talking at once, each seemingly anxious to inform the other of everything that has happened to him since his birth.

This condition is followed by heavy sleep and stupor, lasting five to twelve hours, according to the quantity taken. To awaken the subject it is often necessary to slap his face, punch or shake him, and awakening is accompanied by severe dull, boring headache, muscular twitchings, and protrusion of the eyes.

It is as an addition to beer that cordite appears to produce its worst effects. It then excites a quarrelsome, destructive mania in an otherwise peacefully disposed individual, and produces immediate intoxication in a man who can commonly consume as much as four or five pints of beer without exhibiting a trace of having done so. If taken in quantity insufficient to produce sleep it makes him not only quarrelsome, but brings out the worst traits in his character.

A possible clue to the inception of this habit is given by the fact that a large number of the men seem to have used cordite as a means of lighting pipes in default of matches.

Hawkish 'tales from the future', such as Chesney's Battle of Dorking, *insisted that a war for which Britain was unprepared could lead to a calamity of historic proportions.*

G. T. CHESNEY
'The Battle of Dorking'

Blackwood's Magazine (1871)

You ask me to tell you, my grandchildren, something about my own share in the great events that happened fifty years ago. 'Tis sad work turning back to that bitter page in our history, but you may perhaps take profit in your new homes from the lesson it teaches. For us in England it came too late. And yet we had plenty of warnings, if we had only made use of them. The danger did not come on us unawares. It burst on us suddenly, 'tis true; but its coming was foreshadowed plainly enough to open our eyes, if we had not been wilfully blind. We English have only ourselves to blame for the humiliation which has been brought on the land. Venerable old age! Dishonourable old age, I say, when it followed a manhood dishonoured as ours has been. I declare, even now, though fifty years have passed, I can hardly look a young man in the face when I think I am one of those in whose youth happened this degradation of Old England – one of those who betrayed the trust handed down to us unstained by our forefathers.

. . .

And yet, if ever a nation had a plain warning, we had. If we were the greatest trading country, our neighbours were the leading military power in Europe.

. . .

There was a Radical section of the House, . . . whose votes had to be secured by conciliation, and which blindly demanded a reduction of armaments as the price of allegiance. This party always decried military establishments as part of a fixed policy for reducing the influence of the

Crown and the aristocracy. They could not understand that the times had altogether changed, that the Crown had really no power, and that the Government merely existed at the pleasure of the House of Commons, and that even Parliament-rule was beginning to give way to mob-law. At any rate, the Ministry, baffled on all sides, gave up by degrees all the strong points of a scheme which they were not heartily in earnest about. It was not that there was any lack of money, if only it had been spent in the right way. The army cost enough, and more than enough, to give us a proper defence, and there were armed men of sorts in plenty and to spare, if only they had been decently organized. It was in organization and forethought that we fell short, because our rulers did not heartily believe in the need for preparation. The fleet and the Channel, they said, were sufficient protection. So army reform was put off to some more convenient season, and the militia and volunteers were left untrained as before, because to call them out for drill would 'interfere with the industry of the country'. We could have given up some of the industry of those days, forsooth, and yet be busier than we are now. But why tell you a tale you have so often heard already? The nation, although uneasy, was misled by the false security its leaders professed to feel; the warning given by the disasters that overtook France was allowed to pass by unheeded. We would not even be at the trouble of putting our arsenals in a safe place, or of guarding the capital against a surprise, although the cost of doing so would not have been so much as missed from the national wealth. The French trusted in their army and its great reputation, we in our fleet; and in each case the result of this blind confidence was disaster, such as our forefathers in their hardest struggles could not have even imagined.

Baden-Powell's scout movement was a direct response to these clarion calls, an emergency programme to raise the nation's level of fitness.

ROBERT BADEN-POWELL
Scouting for Boys

(1908)

One aim of the Boy Scouts scheme is to revive amongst us, if possible, some of the rules of the knights of old, which did so much for the moral tone of our race, just as the Bushido of the ancient Samurai Knights has done and is still doing for Japan. Unfortunately, chivalry with us has, to a large extent, been allowed to die out, whereas in Japan it is taught to the children, so that it becomes with them a practice of their life, and it is also taught to children in Germany and Switzerland with the best results. Our effort is not so much to discipline the boys as to teach them to discipline themselves . . . You patrol leaders and scouts are therefore very like the knights and retainers, especially if you keep your honour ever before you in the first place, and do your best to help other people who are in trouble or want assistance. Your motto is 'Be Prepared' to do this and the motto of the knights was a similar one, 'Be Always Ready'.

*The 'Fight For Right' movement, launched by Colonel Younghusband
with this letter to the* Daily Telegraph, *was an extension of Baden-
Powell's ideas into the mainstream of adult life. One of its morale-boosting
contributions was to set part of William Blake's poem* Milton *to music,
under the title* Jerusalem.

FRANCIS YOUNGHUSBAND
'The Fight For Right'

Daily Telegraph (1915)

TO THE EDITOR OF 'THE DAILY TELEGRAPH.'

SIR – Fundamentally – in the last resort – all depends upon spirit.
Organization is only a means for bringing spirit into effect. A machine is
the means we employ for utilizing energy. It is the steam in the engine
and the spirit in the national organization that is the important thing.

Shells are necessary, but these are useless without the energy in the
gun to propel them. Guns are required, but the man behind the gun is
more important than the gun. Millions of men are wanted, but their
value is in their spirit, and in the spirit of the nation which sends them
and upholds them.

It is the spirit that matters. And the spirit of the nation should be the
affair of its spiritual leaders.

Especially in the present war is attention to the spirit called for. As
the Prime Minister says, it is a spiritual conflict – a conflict between the
German spirit and the spirit which animates us. The future of the world
is at stake. If the Germans win, the German spirit will dominate human
affairs for ages to come. German necessity will know no law. Belgiums
will be trampled on; Lusitanias will be submarined. All who oppose will
be either poisoned or, with liquid fire, scorched off the earth. No
considerations of honour, of humanity, or of anything else will stand in
the way. 'Woe to the vanquished,' the Kaiser has said. The German will
and German 'Kultur' alone will be permitted.

What we are fighting for is that German necessity shall know law –
the law of Right – and, what is more, shall obey it. We are fighting that
the rights of Serbia, Belgium, and every other State, small or great,

shall be respected. We are fighting that the ordinary human rights of defenceless women and children and of unarmed civilians shall be preserved. We are engaged in a spiritual conflict – a holy war – the Fight for Right.

This fight we have to win. But to win those of us who are able must stir the spirit of the people, summon up all the spiritual forces of the nation, collect those energies together and direct them on to the one great end we have in view – the maintenance of human right.

And not merely quantity of spiritual energy is required, but quality also. The Germans have unsurpassed organization and immense spirit behind it. But the quality of their spirit is gross. It is the spirit of the beast, not of the man. Ours must be different, and our finest spirits must refine it till it is of the best. And, fortunately, the finest is also the strongest and most enduring.

MEETINGS ON SUNDAYS

Now it is in the assembling of ourselves together for some high purpose that spiritual energy is generated. There human touch is felt, elbow to elbow and heart to heart; and something higher emerges than the individuals in isolation possess. There, too, the multitude has the opportunity of being influenced by the best, and the best have a chance of making their influence felt. And for assemblings for so sacred a purpose as maintaining the right what more fitting occasions than those offered by our Sundays could be found?

What I would urge, then, is that on Sundays meetings should be held (at times not interfering with the usual church services) on ground common to the whole community – in the open air, the town hall, or other public building – and that the spiritual nature of this conflict be impressed upon the people. And these meetings might be addressed by laymen as well as by ministers; by women as well as by men; by members of the congregation as well as by occupants of the platform. The whole idea would be to make the call felt by each and to let the spirit come out where and when it will that it may communicate itself to others.

Every means – music, speech, song, the recital of the great words of others, the examples of men and women of to-day – should be used to arouse the spirit of the people, and appeal be made to their highest and not to their lowest sentiments – not to self-interest, fear, hate, revenge, but to self-sacrifice and that devotion to country and to kind which gives up all that the world may be a better place for those who follow after.

And that something practical might eventuate, those who are willing to offer themselves for service to their country might be asked to present themselves at the close of the meeting, and they might then be directed by competent advisers to where their own particular services might be used with fullest effect. Recruits – and free and willing recruits – for every department of the country's service would then come forward, and every single one would have felt the great call on him and his spirit rising to the call. He would ever after feel an abhorrence of all that hindered his answering it to the full, and he would be possessed of a determination to do his best in his own little line to carry the great cause forward till the Fight for Right is won. – I am, Sir, your obedient servant,

FRANCIS YOUNGHUSBAND,
3, Buckingham-gate, S.W., Aug. 2.

The destruction of Britain by military invasion was the subject of ever more vivid and gruesome fantasies.

WILLIAM LE QUEX
The Great War in England in 1897

(1893)

LOOTING IN THE SUBURBS!

While famished men crept into Hyde Park and Kensington Gardens and there expired under the trees of absolute hunger, and starving women with babes at their breasts sank upon doorsteps and died, the more robust Londoners had, on hearing of the enemy's march on the metropolis, gone south to augment the second line of defence. For several weeks huge barricades had been thrown up in the principal roads approaching London from the south. The strongest of these were opposite the Convalescent Home on Kingston Hill, in Coombe Lane close to Raynes Park Station, in the Morden Road at Merton Abbey, opposite Lynwood in the Tooting Road; while nearer London, on the same road, there was a strong one with machine guns on the crest of Balham Hill, and another in Clapham Road. At Streatham Hill, about one hundred yards from the hospital, earthworks had been thrown up, and several guns brought into position; while at Beulah Hill, Norwood, opposite the Post Office at Upper Sydenham, at the Half Moon at Herne Hill, and in many of the roads between Honor Oak and Denmark Hill, barricades had been constructed and banked up with bags and baskets filled with earth.

. . .

LONDON BOMBARDED

The Hand of the Destroyer had reached England's mighty metropolis. The lurid scene was appalling.

In the stormy sky the red glare from hundreds of burning buildings grew brighter, and in every quarter flames leaped up and black smoke curled slowly away in increasing volume.

The people were unaware of the events that had occurred in Surrey that day. Exhausted, emaciated and ashen pale, the hungry people had endured every torture. Panic-stricken, they rushed hither and thither in thousands up and down the principal thoroughfares, and as they tore headlong away in this *sauve qui peut* to the northern suburbs, the weaker fell and were trodden under foot.

Men fought for their wives and families, dragging them away out of the range of the enemy's fire, which apparently did not extend beyond the line formed by the Hackney Road, City Road, Pentonville Road, Euston Road and Westbourne Park. But in that terrible rush to escape many delicate ladies were crushed to death, and numbers of others, with their children, sank exhausted, and perished beneath the feet of fleeing millions.

. . .

Time after time shells whistled above and fell with a crash and explosion, some in the centre of the road, tearing up the paving, and others striking the clubs in Pall Mall, blowing out many of those noble time-mellowed walls. The portico of the Athenaeum had been torn away like pasteboard, the rear premises of the War Office had been pulverized, and the Carlton, Reform and United Service Clubs suffered terrible damage. Two shells striking the Junior Carlton crashed through the roof, and exploding almost simultaneously, brought down an enormous heap of masonry, which fell across the roadway, making an effectual barricade; while at the same moment shells began to fall thickly in Grosvenor Place and Belgrave Square, igniting many houses, and killing some of those who remained in their homes petrified by fear.

Up Regent Street shells were sweeping with frightful effect. The Café Monico and the whole block of buildings surrounding it was burning, and the flames leaping high, presented a magnificent though appalling spectacle. The front of the London Pavilion had been partially blown away, and of the two uniform rows of shops forming the Quadrant many had been wrecked. From Air Street to Oxford Circus, and along Piccadilly to Knightsbridge, there fell a perfect hail of shells and bullets. Devonshire House had been wrecked, and the Burlington Arcade destroyed. The thin pointed spire of St James's Church had fallen, every

window in the Albany was shattered, several houses in Grosvenor Place
had suffered considerably, and a shell that struck the southern side of
St George's Hospital had ignited it, and now at 2 a.m., in the midst of
this awful scene of destruction and disaster, the helpless sick were being
removed into the open streets, where bullets whistled about them and
fragments of explosive shells whizzed past.

As the night wore on London trembled and fell. Once Mistress of
the World, she was now, alas! sinking under the iron hand of the invader.
Upon her there poured a rain of deadly missiles that caused appalling
slaughter and desolation. The newly introduced long-range guns, and
the terrific power of the explosives with which the French shells were
charged, added to the horrors of the bombardment; for although the
batteries were so far away as to be out of sight, yet the unfortunate
people, overtaken by their doom, were torn limb from limb by the
bursting bombs.

Over the roads lay men of London, poor and rich, weltering in their
blood, their lower limbs shattered or blown completely away. With
wide-open haggard eyes, in their death agony they gazed around at the
burning buildings, at the falling débris, and upward at the brilliantly-
illumined sky. With their last breath they gasped prayers for those they
loved, and sank to the grave, hapless victims of Babylon's downfall.

Plans for a Channel Tunnel were extensively mooted throughout the 1890s. One of the main objections to the tunnel was, as in this image from 1905, that it would be a target for German attack. (From D. O. Wirdhaeff, *Je sais tout,* 1905.) (Courtesy of Mary Evans Picture Library)

Behind this increasing militarization, there was little consensus about the true relationship between war and civilization, and whether war would continue to be necessary in the future. The eminent sociologist Herbert Spencer argued that war had had its day.

HERBERT SPENCER
The Principles of Sociology

(1876–96)

The conclusion of profoundest moment to which all lines of argument converge, is that the possibility of a high social state, political as well as general, fundamentally depends on the cessation of war. After all that has been said it is needless to emphasize afresh the truth that persistent militancy, maintaining adapted institutions, must inevitably prevent, or else neutralize, changes in the direction of more equitable institutions and laws; while permanent peace will of necessity be followed by social ameliorations of every kind.

From war has been gained all that it had to give. The peopling of the Earth by the more powerful and intelligent races, is a benefit in great measure achieved; and what remains to be done, calls for no other agency than the quiet pressure of a spreading industrial civilization on a barbarism which slowly dwindles. That integration of simple groups into compound ones, and of these into doubly compound ones, which war has effected, until at length great nations have been produced, is a process already carried as far as seems either practicable or desirable. Empires formed of alien peoples habitually fall to pieces when the coercive power which holds them together fails; and even could they be held together, would not form harmoniously-working wholes: peaceful federation is the only further consolidation to be looked for. Such large advantage as war has yielded by developing that political organization which, beginning with the leadership of the best warrior has ended in complex governments and systems of administration, has been fully obtained; and there only remains for the future to preserve and remould its useful parts while getting rid of those no longer required. So, too, that organization of labour initiated by war – an organization which, setting out with the relation of owner and slave and developing into that of master and servant, has, by elaboration, given us industrial structures having numerous grades of officials, from head-directors down to foremen – has been developed quite as far as is requisite for combined action; and has to be hereafter modified, not in the direction of greater military subordination, but rather in the opposite direction. Again, the power of continuous application, lacking in the savage and to be gained only under that coercive discipline which the militant type of society establishes, has been already in large measure acquired by the civilized man; and such further degree of it as is needed, will be produced under the stress of industrial competition in free communities. Nor is it otherwise with great public works and developed industrial arts.

. . .

And though from early days when flint arrowheads were chipped and clubs carved, down to present days when armour-plates a foot thick are rolled, the needs of defence and offence have urged on invention and mechanical skill; yet in our own generation steam-hammers, hydraulic rams and multitudinous new appliances from locomotives to telephones, prove that industrial needs alone have come to furnish abundant pressure whereby, hereafter, the industrial arts will be further advanced. Thus, that social evolution which had to be achieved through the conflicts of societies with one another, has already been achieved; and no further benefits are to be looked for.

. . . while William James, though declaring himself essentially a pacifist, nevertheless maintained that martial virtues should always be with us.

WILLIAM JAMES
'The Moral Equivalent of War'

(1910)

I devoutly believe in the reign of peace and in the gradual advent of some sort of a socialistic equilibrium. The fatalistic view of the war function is to me nonsense, for I know that war-making is due to definite motives and subject to prudential checks and reasonable criticisms, just like any other form of enterprise. And when whole nations are the armies, and the science of destruction vies in intellectual refinement with the sciences of production, I see that war becomes absurd and impossible from its own monstrosity. Extravagant ambitions will have to be replaced by reasonable claims, and nations must make common cause against them. I see no reason why all this should not apply to yellow as well as to white countries, and I look forward to a future when acts of war shall be formally outlawed as between civilized peoples.

All these beliefs of mine put me squarely into the anti-militarist party. But I do not believe that peace either ought to be or will be permanent on this globe, unless the states, pacifically organized, preserve some of the old elements of army-discipline. A permanently successful peace-economy cannot be a simple pleasure-economy. In the more or less socialistic future towards which mankind seems drifting we must still subject ourselves collectively to those severities which answer to our real position upon this only partly hospitable globe. We must make new energies and hardihoods continue the manliness to which the military mind so faithfully clings. Martial virtues must be the enduring cement; intrepidity, contempt of softness, surrender of private interest, obedience to command, must still remain the rock upon which states are built – unless, indeed, we wish for dangerous reactions against commonwealths fit only for contempt, and liable to invite attack whenever a centre of crystallization for military-minded enterprise gets formed anywhere in their neighbourhood.

The war-party is assuredly right in affirming and reaffirming that the martial virtues, although originally gained by the race through war, are absolute and permanent human goods. Patriotic pride and ambition in their military form are, after all only specifications of a more general competitive passion. They are its first form, but that is no reason for supposing them to be its last form. Men now are proud of belonging to a conquering nation, and without a murmur they lay down their persons and their wealth, if by so doing they may fend off subjection. But who can be sure that *other aspects of one's country* may not, with time and education and suggestion enough, come to be regarded with similarly effective feelings of pride and shame? Why should men not some day feel that it is worth a blood-tax to belong to a collectivity superior in *any* ideal respect? Why should they not blush with indignant shame if the community that owns them is vile in any way whatsoever? Individuals, daily more numerous, now feel this civic passion. It is only a question of blowing on the spark till the whole population gets incandescent, and on the ruins of the old morals of military honour, a stable system of morals of civic honour builds itself up. What the whole community comes to believe in grasps the individual as in a vise. The war-function has grasped us so far; but constructive interests may some day seem no less imperative, and impose on the individual a hardly lighter burden.

10

Imagining the Next Century:
Regeneration

One of the most striking differences between the fin-de-siècle *and our current millennium was the enormous profusion of imagined twentieth centuries which it produced. Hundreds of books and magazines offered glimpses and projections of the 'New Century', extrapolating all the trends and elements which we have so far reviewed, and many more besides. Some offered a future of dystopian savagery, a return to barbarism or feudalism (such as Wells's* The War in the Air *and Jefferies's* After London*), but the majority offered templates for the renewal of humanity or, in the popular phrase of the time, 'Regeneration'.*

The preoccupations of this 'New Century' literature varied widely in tone from nation to nation. British images of the future were typically concerned with political structures and future government, a tone set early in Bulwer-Lytton's Utopian fantasy The Coming Race.

SIR EDWARD BULWER-LYTTON
The Coming Race

(1871)

When what we should term the historical age emerged from the twilight of tradition, the Ana were already established in different communities, and had attained to a degree of civilization very analogous to that which the more advanced nations above the earth now enjoy. They were familiar with most of our mechanical inventions, including the application of steam as well as gas. The communities were in fierce competition with each other. They had their rich and their poor; they had orators and conquerors; they made war either for a domain or an idea. Though the various states acknowledged various forms of government, free institutions were beginning to preponderate; popular assemblies increased in power; republics soon became general; the democracy to which the most enlightened European politicians look forward as the extreme goal of political advancement, and which still prevailed among other subterranean races, whom they despised as barbarians, the loftier family of Ana, to which belonged the tribe I was visiting, looked back to as one of the crude and ignorant experiments which belong to the infancy of political science. It was the age of envy and hate, of fierce passions, of constant social changes more or less violent, of strife between classes, of war between state and state. This phase of society lasted, however, for some ages, and was finally brought to a close, at least among the nobler and more intellectual populations, by the gradual discovery of the latent powers stored in the all-permeating fluid which they denominate Vril.

According to the account I received from Zee, who, as an erudite professor in the College of Sages, had studied such matters more diligently than any other member of my host's family, this fluid is capable of being raised and disciplined into the mightiest agency over all forms of matter, animate or inanimate. It can destroy like the flash of lightning; yet, differently applied, it can replenish or invigorate life, heal, and preserve, and on it they chiefly rely for the cure of disease, or rather for enabling the physical organization to re-establish the due equilibrium of its natural powers, and thereby to cure itself. By this agency they rend way through the most solid substances, and open valleys for culture through the rocks of their subterranean wilderness. From it they extract the light which supplies their lamps, finding it steadier, softer and healthier than the other inflammable materials they had formerly used.

But the effects of the alleged discovery of the means to direct the more terrible force of Vril were chiefly remarkable in their influence upon social polity. As these effects became familiarly known and skilfully administered, war between the Vril-discoverers ceased, for they brought the art of destruction to such perfection as to annul all superiority in numbers, discipline or military skill. The fire lodged in the hollow of a rod directed by the hand of a child could shatter the strongest fortress, or cleave its burning way from the van to the rear of an embattled host. If army met army, and both had command of this agency, it could be but to the annihilation of each. The age of war was therefore gone, but with the cessation of war other effects bearing upon the social state soon became apparent. Man was so completely at the mercy of man, each whom he encountered being able, if so willing, to slay him on the instant, that all notions of government by force gradually vanished from political systems and forms of law. It is only by force that vast communities, dispersed through great distances of space, can be kept together; but now there was no longer either the necessity of self-preservation or the pride of aggrandizement to make one state desire to preponderate in population over another.

The Vril-discoverers thus, in the course of a few generations, peacefully split into communities of moderate size. The tribe amongst which I had fallen was limited to 12,000 families. Each tribe occupied a territory sufficient for all its wants, and at stated periods the surplus population departed to seek a realm of its own. There appeared no necessity for any arbitrary selection of these emigrants; there was always a sufficient number who volunteered to depart.

. . .

The government of the tribe of Vril-ya I am treating of was apparently very complicated, really very simple. It was based upon a principle of recognized in theory, though little carried out in practice, above ground – viz., that the object of all systems of philosophical thought tends to the attainment of unity, or the ascent through all intervening labyrinths to the simplicity of a single first cause or principle. Thus in politics, even republican writers have agreed that a benevolent autocracy would ensure the best administration, if there were any guarantees for its continuance, or against its gradual abuse of the powers accorded to it. This singular community elected therefore a single supreme magistrate styled Tur; he held his office nominally for life, but he could seldom be induced to retain it after the first approach of old age. There was indeed in this society nothing to induce any of its members to covet the cares of office. No honours, no insignia of higher rank were assigned to it. The supreme magistrate was not distinguished from the rest by superior habitation or revenue. On the other hand, the duties awarded to him were marvellously light and easy, requiring no preponderant degree of energy or intelligence. There being no apprehensions of war, there were no armies to maintain; being no government of force, there was no police to appoint and direct. What we call crime was utterly unknown to the Vril-ya; and there were no courts of criminal justice.

*The generation after Bulwer-Lytton maintained his emphasis on politics,
but shifted from his aristocratic model of Platonic philosopher-kings to
a Utopia achieved by socialism.*

WILLIAM MORRIS
News from Nowhere

(1891)

'**N**ow,' said I, 'I have come to the point of asking questions which
I suppose will be dry for you to answer and difficult for you to explain;
but I have foreseen for some time past that I must ask them, will I nill
I. What kind of a government have you? Has republicanism finally
triumphed? or have you come to a mere dictatorship, which some
persons in the nineteenth century used to prophesy as the ultimate
outcome of democracy? Indeed, this last question does not seem so
very unreasonable, since you have turned your Parliament House into
a dung-market. Or where do you house your present Parliament?'

The old man answered my smile with a hearty laugh, and said: 'Well,
well, dung is not the worst kind of corruption; fertility may come of
that, whereas mere dearth came from the other kind, of which those
walls once held the great supporters. Now, dear guest, let me tell you
that our present parliament would be hard to house in one place,
because the whole people is our parliament.'

'I don't understand,' said I.

'No, I suppose not,' said he. 'I must now shock you by telling you
that we have no longer anything which you, a native of another planet,
would call a government.'

'I am not so much shocked as you might think,' said I, 'as I know
something about governments. But tell me, how do you manage, and
how have you come to this state of things?'

Said he: 'It is true that we have to make some arrangements about
our affairs, concerning which you can ask presently; and it is also
true that everybody does not always agree with the details of these
arrangements; but, further, it is true that a man no more needs an
elaborate system of government, with its army, navy and police, to force
him to give way to the will of the majority of his *equals*, than he wants

a similar machinery to make him understand that his head and a stone wall cannot occupy the same space at the same moment. Do you want further explanation?'

'Well, yes, I do,' quoth I.

. . .

'This is the way to put it,' said he: 'We have been living for a hundred and fifty years, at least, more or less in our present manner, and a tradition or habit of life has been growing on us; and that habit has become a habit of acting on the whole for the best. It is easy for us to live without robbing each other. It would be possible for us to contend with and rob each other, but it would be harder for us than refraining from strife and robbery. That is in short the foundation of our life and our happiness.'

. . .

Said I: 'I thought that I understood from something that fell from you a little while ago that you had abolished civil law. Is that so, literally?'

'It abolished itself, my friend,' said he. 'As I said before, the civil law courts were upheld for the defence of private property, for nobody ever pretended that it was possible to make people act fairly to each other by means of brute force. Well, private property being abolished, all the laws and all the legal "crimes" which it had manufactured of course came to an end. Thou shalt not steal, had to be translated into, Thou shalt work in order to live happily. Is there any need to enforce that commandment by violence?'

By the turn of the century, the Utopian socialist future had become a familiar model; but H. G. Wells, who addressed himself seriously and repeatedly to the genre of the Utopia, was unsatisfied both with the idea of human nature it assumed and with its view of a future society in static equilibrium. Confronting these problems, his Modern Utopia *finds itself entering more disturbing territory.*

H. G. WELLS
A Modern Utopia

(1905)

Were we free to have our untrammelled desire, I suppose we should follow Morris to his Nowhere, we should change the nature of man and the nature of things together; we should make the whole race wise, tolerant, noble, perfect – wave our hands to a splendid anarchy, every man doing as it pleases him, and none pleased to do evil, in a world as good in its essential nature, as ripe and sunny, as the world before the Fall. But that golden age, that perfect world, comes out into the possibilities of space and time. In space and time the pervading Will to Live sustains for evermore a perpetuity of aggressions. Our proposal here is upon a more practical plane at least than that.

. . .

The old Utopias – save for the breeding schemes of Plato and Campanella – ignored that reproductive competition among individualities which is the substance of life, and dealt essentially with its incidentals. The endless variety of men, their endless gradation of quality, over which the hand of selection plays, and to which we owe the unmanageable complication of real life, is tacitly set aside. The real world is a vast disorder of accidents and incalculable forces in which men survive or fail. A Modern Utopia, unlike its predecessors, dare not pretend to change the last condition; it may order and humanize the conflict, but men must still survive or fail.

Most Utopias present themselves as going concerns, as happiness in being; they make it an essential condition that a happy land can have no history, and all the citizens one is permitted to see are well looking and upright and mentally and morally in tune. But we are under the dominion of a logic that obliges us to take over the actual population of the world with only such moral and mental and physical improvements as lie within their inherent possibilities, and it is our business to ask what Utopia will do with its congenital invalids, its idiots and madmen, its drunkards and men of vicious mind, its cruel and furtive souls, its stupid people, too stupid to be of use to the community, its lumpish, unteachable and unimaginative people? And what will it do with the man who is 'poor' all round, the rather spiritless, rather incompetent low-grade man who on earth sits in the den of the sweater, tramps the streets under the banner of the unemployed, or trembles – in another man's cast-off clothing, and with an infinity of hat-touching – on the verge of rural employment?

These people will have to be in the descendant phase, the species must be engaged in eliminating them; there is no escape from that, and conversely the people of exceptional quality must be ascendant. The better sort of people, so far as they can be distinguished, must have the fullest freedom of public service, and the fullest opportunity of parentage. And it must be open to every man to approve himself worthy of ascendancy.

The way of Nature in this process is to kill the weaker and the sillier, to crush them, to starve them, to overwhelm them, using the stronger and more cunning as her weapon. But man is the unnatural animal, the rebel child of Nature, and more and more does he turn himself against the harsh and fitful hand that reared him. He sees with a growing resentment the multitude of suffering ineffectual lives over which his species tramples in its ascent. In the Modern Utopia he will have set himself to change the ancient law. No longer will it be that failures must suffer and perish lest their breed increase, but the breed of failure must not increase, lest they suffer and perish, and the race with them.

. . .

No doubt for first offenders, and for all offenders under five-and-twenty, the Modern Utopia will attempt cautionary and remedial treatment. There will be disciplinary schools and colleges for the young, fair and happy places, but with less confidence and more restraint than the schools and colleges of the ordinary world. In remote and solitary regions these enclosures will lie, they will be fenced in and forbidden to the common run of men, and there, remote from all temptation, the defective citizen will be schooled. There will be no masking of the lesson; 'which do you value most, the wide world of humanity, or this evil trend in you?' From that discipline at last the prisoners will return.

But the others; what would a saner world do with them?

Our world is still vindictive, but the all-reaching State of Utopia will have the strength that begets mercy. Quietly the outcast will go from among his fellow men. There will be no drumming of him out of the ranks, no tearing off of epaulettes, no smiting in the face. The thing must be just public enough to obviate secret tyrannies, and that is all.

There would be no killing, no lethal chambers. No doubt Utopia will kill all deformed and monstrous and evilly diseased births, but for the rest, the State will hold itself accountable for their being. There is no justice in Nature perhaps, but the idea of justice must be sacred in any good society. Lives that statesmanship has permitted, errors it has not foreseen and educated against, must not be punished by death. If the State does not keep faith, no one will keep faith. Crime and bad lives are the measure of a State's failure, all crime in the end is the crime of the community. Even for murder Utopia will not, I think, kill.

I doubt even if there will be jails. No men are quite wise enough, good enough and cheap enough to staff jails as a jail ought to be staffed. Perhaps islands will be chosen, islands lying apart from the highways of the sea, and to these the State will send its exiles, most of them thanking Heaven, no doubt, to be quit of a world of prigs. The State will, of course, secure itself against any children from those people, that is the primary object in their seclusion, and perhaps it may even be necessary to make these island prisons a system of island monasteries and island nunneries. Upon that I am not competent to speak, but if I may believe the literature of the subject – unhappily a not very well criticized literature – it is not necessary to enforce this separation.°

About such islands patrol boats will go, there will be no freedoms of boat-building, and it may be necessary to have armed guards at the creeks and quays. Beyond that the State will give these segregated failures just as full a liberty as they can have. If it interferes any further it will be simply to police the islands against the organization of serious cruelty, to maintain the freedom of any of the detained who wish it to

---

° See, for example, Dr W. A. Chapple's *The Fertility of the Unfit*.

transfer themselves to other islands, and so to keep a check upon tyranny. The insane, of course, will demand care and control, but there is no reason why the islands of the hopeless drunkard, for example, should not each have a virtual autonomy, have at the most a Resident and a guard. I believe that a community of drunkards might be capable of organizing even its own bad habit to the pitch of tolerable existence. I do not see why such an island should not build and order for itself and manufacture and trade. 'Your ways are not our ways,' the World State will say; 'but here is freedom and a company of kindred souls. Elect your jolly rulers, brew if you will, and distil; here are vine cuttings and barley fields; do as it pleases you to do. We will take care of the knives, but for the rest – deal yourselves with God!'

In continental Europe, visions of the future also flourished, but with a less insistent emphasis on political structures. Marinetti's Futurist Manifesto *is an exhilarating fantasia of possibilities opened up by technology and the modern era.*

F. T. MARINETTI
The Futurist Manifesto

(1909)

We have been up all night, my friends and I, beneath mosque lamps whose brass cupolas are bright as our souls, because like them they were illuminated by the internal glow of electric hearts. And trampling underfoot our native sloth on opulent Persian carpets, we have been discussing right up to the limits of logic and scrawling the paper with demented writing.

. . .

'Come, my friends!' I said. 'Let us go! At last Mythology and the mystic cult of the ideal have been left behind. We are going to be present at the birth of the centaur and we shall soon see the first angels fly! We must break down the gates of life to test the bolts and the padlocks! Let us go! Here is the very first sunrise on earth! Nothing equals the splendour of its red sword which strikes for the first time in our millennial darkness.'

We went up to the three snorting machines to caress their breasts. I lay along mine like a corpse on its bier, but I suddenly revived again beneath the steering wheel – a guillotine knife – which threatened my stomach. A great sweep of madness brought us sharply back to ourselves and drove us through the streets, steep and deep, like dried-up torrents. Here and there unhappy lamps in the windows taught us to despise our mathematical eyes. 'Smell,' I exclaimed, 'smell is good enough for wild beasts!'

And we hunted, like young lions, death with its black fur dappled with pale crosses, who ran before us in the vast violet sky, palpable and living.

. . .

'Let us leave good sense behind like a hideous husk and let us hurl ourselves, like fruit spiced with pride, into the immense mouth and breast of the world! Let us feed the unknown, not from despair, but simply to enrich the unfathomable reservoirs of the Absurd!'

As soon as I had said these words, I turned sharply back on my tracks with the mad intoxication of puppies biting their tails, and suddenly there were two cyclists disapproving of me and tottering in front of me like two persuasive but contradictory reasons. Their stupid swaying got in my way. What a bore! Pouah! I stopped short, and in disgust hurled myself – vlan! – head over heels in a ditch.

Oh, maternal ditch, half full of muddy water! A factory gutter! I savoured a mouthful of strengthening muck which recalled the black teat of my Sudanese nurse!

As I raised my body, mud-spattered and smelly, I felt the red-hot poker of joy deliciously pierce my heart. A crowd of fishermen and gouty naturalists crowded terrified around this marvel. With patient and tentative care they raised high enormous grappling irons to fish up my car, like a vast shark that had run aground. It rose slowly leaving in the ditch, like scales, its heavy coachwork of good sense and its upholstery of comfort.

We thought it was dead, my good shark, but I woke it with a single caress of its powerful back, and it was revived running as fast as it could on its fins.

Then with my face covered in good factory mud, covered with metal scratches, useless sweat and celestial grime, amidst the complaint of staid fishermen and angry naturalists, we dictated our first will and testament to all the living men on earth.

MANIFESTO OF FUTURISM

We want to sing the love of danger, the habit of energy and rashness.

The essential elements of our poetry will be courage, audacity and revolt.

Literature has up to now magnified pensive immobility, ecstasy and slumber. We want to exalt movements of aggression, feverish sleeplessness, the double march, the perilous leap, the slap and the blow with the fist.

We declare that the splendour of the world has been enriched by a new beauty: the beauty of speed. A racing automobile with its bonnet adorned with great tubes like serpents with explosive breath . . . a roaring motor car which seems to run on machine-gun fire, is more beautiful than the Victory of Samothrace.

We want to sing the man at the wheel, the ideal axis of which crosses the earth, itself hurled along its orbit.

The poet must spend himself with warmth, glamour and prodigality to increase the enthusiastic fervour of the primordial elements.

Beauty exists only in struggle. There is no masterpiece that has not an aggressive character. Poetry must be a violent assault on the forces of the unknown, to force them to bow before man.

We are on the extreme promontory of the centuries! What is the use of looking behind at the moment when we must open the mysterious shutters of the impossible? Time and Space died yesterday. We are already living in the absolute, since we have already created eternal, omnipresent speed.

We want to glorify war – the only cure for the world – militarism, patriotism, the destructive gesture of the anarchists, the beautiful ideas which kill and contempt for woman.

We want to demolish museums and libraries, fight morality, feminism and all opportunist and utilitarian cowardice.

We will sing of the great crowds agitated by work, pleasure and revolt; the multi-coloured and polyphonic surf of revolutions in modern capitals: the nocturnal vibration of the arsenals and the workshops beneath their violent electric moons: the gluttonous railway stations devouring smoking serpents; factories suspended from the clouds by the threat of their smoke; bridges with the leap of gymnasts flung across the diabolic cutlery of sunny rivers: adventurous steamers sniffing the horizon; great-breasted locomotives, puffing on the rails like enormous steel horses with long tubes for bridle, and the gliding flight of aeroplanes whose propeller sounds like the flapping of a flag and the applause of enthusiastic crowds.

It is in Italy that we are issuing this manifesto of ruinous and incendiary violence, by which we today are founding Futurism, because we want to deliver Italy from its gangrene of professors, archaeologists, tourist guides and antiquaries.

Italy has been too long the great second-hand market. We want to get rid of the innumerable museums which cover it with innumerable cemeteries.

. . .

The oldest among us are not yet thirty, and yet we have already wasted treasures, treasures of strength, love, courage and keen will, hastily, deliriously, without thinking, with all our might, till we are out of breath.

Look at us! We are not out of breath, our hearts are not in the least tired. For they are nourished by fire, hatred and speed! Does this surprise you? it is because you do not even remember being alive! Standing on the world's summit, we launch once more our challenge to the stars!

Your objections? All right! I know them! Of course! We know just what our beautiful false intelligence affirms: 'We are only the sum and the prolongation of our ancestors,' it says. Perhaps! All right! What does it matter? But we will not listen! Take care not to repeat those infamous words! Instead, lift up your head!

Standing on the world's summit we launch once again our insolent challenge to the stars!

Jules Verne's recently discovered Paris in the Twentieth Century *shares the Futurist vision of science and speed.*

JULES VERNE
Paris in the Twentieth Century

(written 1863)

It is evident that Paris had burst its precincts of 1843 and made incursions into the Bois de Boulogne, the Plains of Issy, Vanves, Billancourt, Montrouge, Ivry, Saint-Mandé, Bagnolet, Pantin, Saint-Denis, Clichy and Saint-Ouen. The heights of Meudon, Sèvres and Saint-Cloud had blocked its development to the west. The delimitation of the present capital was marked by the forts of Mont Valérien, Saint-Denis, Aubervilliers, Romainville, Vincennes, Charenton, Vitry, Bicêtre, Montrouge, Vanves and Issy; a city of one hundred and five kilometres in diameter, it had devoured the entire Department of the Seine.

Four concentric circles of railways thus formed the Metropolitan network; they were linked to one another by branch lines, which, on the Right Bank, extended the Boulevard de Magenta and the Boulevard Malesherbes and on the Left Bank, the Rue de Rennes and the Rue des Fossés-Saint-Victor. It was possible to circulate from one end of Paris to the other with the greatest speed.

. . .

This system consisted of two separate roadbeds on which the trains proceeded in opposite directions; hence there was no possibility of a collision. Each of these tracks was established along the axis of the boulevards, five metres from the housefronts, above the outer rim of the sidewalks; elegant columns of galvanized bronze supported them and were attached to one another by cast armatures; at intervals these columns were attached to riverside houses, by means of transverse arcades. Thus, this long viaduct, supporting the railway track, formed a covered gallery, under which strollers found shelter from the elements; the asphalt roadway was reserved for carriages; by means of an elegant bridge the viaduct traversed the main streets which crossed its path, and the railway, suspended at the height of the mezzanine floors, offered no obstacle to boulevard traffic.

. . .

Young Dufrénoy bought his ticket at the Grenelle station and ten minutes later got off at the Madeleine; he walked down the steps to the boulevard and made for the Rue Impériale, which had been constructed on the axis of the Opéra down to the Gardens of the Tuileries. Crowds filled the streets; night was beginning to fall, and the luxury shops projected far out onto the sidewalks the brilliant patches of their electric light; streetlamps operated by the Way System – sending a positive electric charge through a thread of mercury – spread an incomparable radiance; they were connected by means of underground wires; at one and the same moment, the hundred thousand streetlamps of Paris came on. Nonetheless a few old-fashioned shops remained faithful to the old means of hydrocarburated gas; the exploitation of new coal pits permitted its current sale at ten centimes per cubic metre; but the Company made considerable profits, especially by distributing it as a mechanical agent.

In fact, of the countless carriages which clogged the boulevards, a great majority were horseless; they were invisibly powered by a motor which operated by gas combustion.

. . .

These swift means of transport operated in streets less clogged than in the past, for a ruling of the Ministry of Police forbade any cart, dray or wagon to pass through the streets after ten in the morning, except for certain special routes.

These various improvements were certainly suited to this feverish century, during which the pressure of business permitted no rest and no delay.

What would one of our ancestors have said upon seeing these boulevards lit as brightly as by the sun, these thousand carriages circulating noiselessly on the silent asphalt of the streets, these stores as sumptuous as palaces, from which the light spread in brilliant patches, these avenues as broad as squares, these squares as wide as plains, these enormous hotels, which provided comfortable lodging for twenty thousand travellers, these wonderfully light viaducts, these long, elegant galleries, these bridges flung from street to street, and finally these glittering trains, which seemed to furrow the air with fantastic speed?

No doubt he would have been astonished; but the men of 1960 were no longer lost in admiration of such marvels; they exploited them quite calmly, without being any the happier, for, from their hurried gait, their peremptory manner, their American 'dash', it was apparent that the demon of wealth impelled them onward without mercy or relief.

The Eiffel Tower in construction: the technological fantasies of Marinetti and Verne being realized. (From *La Nature*, 1888.) (Courtesy of Mary Evans Picture Library)

In Germany, by contrast, ideas of regeneration and renewal tended to look to the past, seeking strength from the appeal to forgotten – or reinvented – traditions. Jung, in a letter to Freud, sees the destiny of psychoanalysis as the rekindling of the religious urge and the reinvention of Christianity.

C. G. JUNG
Letter to Freud

(written 1910)

2000 years of Christianity can only be replaced by something equivalent. An ethical fraternity, with its mythical Nothing, not infused by any archaic-infantile driving force, is a pure vacuum and can never evoke in man the slightest trace of that age-old animal power which drives the migrating bird across the sea and without which no irresistible mass movement can come into being. I imagine a far finer and more comprehensive task for ψ° than alliance with an ethical fraternity. I think we must give it time to infiltrate into people from many centres, to revivify among intellectuals a feeling for symbol and myth, ever so gently to transform Christ back into the soothsaying god of the vine, which he was, and in this way absorb those ecstatic instinctual forces of Christianity for the *one* purpose of making the cult and the sacred myth what they once were – a drunken feast of joy where man regained the ethos and holiness of an animal. That was the beauty and purpose of classical religion, which from God knows what temporary biological needs has turned into a Misery Institute. Yet what infinite rapture and wantonness lie dormant in our religion, waiting to be led back to their true destination! A genuine and proper ethical development cannot abandon Christianity but must grow up within it, must bring to fruition its hymn of love, the agony and ecstasy over the dying and resurgent god, the mystic power of the wine, the awesome anthropophagy of the Last Supper – only *this* ethical development can serve the vital forces of religion.

$^\circ$ ψ [psychoanalysis].

Meanwhile, the German mystic Guido von List found the template for renewal in a reinvention of the medieval societies of the Armanenschaft. His dreams of Aryan conquest made him a posthumous hero to the National Socialist movement.

GUIDO VON LIST
Die Armanenschaft der Ario-Germanen

(1908, 1911)

The most suitable young maidens – chosen on a strictly eugenic basis – were drawn from among the high Halgadom [temple] priestesses for the [ancient Germanic] mystery plays. They played the part of the divine brides in the procreation of temple-children and future leaders. This custom, however alien it may seem today, had the deeply serious purpose of creating and educating a noble race and would, if restored, be of inestimable value for the coming era.

. . .

The Arman [Ario-Germanic priest-king] knows how to read the future in the organic laws of change. He knows that the deplorable state of today's world is but the Twilight of the Gods (*Götterdämmerung*), the winter of the Aryan soul. The solar solstice, Yuletide, will follow and must follow the winter. He knows that beneath the weight of winter snow lies the grain sown by the Armans. These seeds will shoot forth like the bloodied points of spears through the melting mantle of snow, once Ostara (the goddess of spring) walks across the fields.

. . .

The ravens are still flying around the Untersberg [the refuge of the sleeping emperor Redbeard], whither the Armanist spirit looks for its rebirth. But the signs are multiplying, one sees the time is near when the great gate will open for the exodus of the reborn, for the 'Strong One from Above' who will come to end all strife with his just rule and to give the restored Armanic law to all peoples for the coming New Age.

We stand before the Dawn of the Gods, the new morning of the Aryan spirit. Already the mists are rising, already the magical solstice fires blaze upwards, the birth of a new sun.

. . .

Yes, the Aryo-German-Austrian battleships shall once more send sparks flying, Donar's lightning shall once more shoot forth sizzling from the giant guns of our dreadnoughts, our people's armies shall once more storm forth along the old Armanist roads to the south, west and north. The fetters of culture, so wantonly broken, will be fastened again upon the inferior castes and the ruling classes will reclaim those rights so slyly stolen from them. The lower classes will be restored to orderly conditions in which they can prosper.

> The gods awake with Albrad,
> The night sinks in the north by Nibelheim,
> Heimdall, the hornblower, striding across
> the resounding bridge up to Herian's castle,
> For coming to the circle of counsellors
> The Strong One from Above ends the strife,
> He settles everything with fair decisions
> Whatever he ordains shall endure for ever.

Sketch of a 'Wotanist pageant', public spectacles which stressed the renewal of the German people through the rediscovery of their Aryan roots. (Lithograph, Germany, c. 1895.) (Courtesy of Icon Productions)

In America, the nation's vigour, newness, rapid expansion and seemingly
inexhaustible resources produced a widespread literature of optimism
and the forthcoming 'American Century'. Edward Bellamy's influential
Looking Backward *imagines a New Century where all that is good in*
the present is transplanted into the more fertile soil of the future.

EDWARD BELLAMY
Looking Backward: 2000–1887

(1888)

'**F**eeling that the condition of the race was unendurable, they had
no clear hope of anything better. They believed that the evolution of
humanity had resulted in leading it into a *cul de sac*, and that there was
no way of getting forward. The frame of men's minds at this time is
strikingly illustrated by treatises which have come down to us, and may
even now be consulted in our libraries by the curious, in which laborious
arguments are pursued to prove that despite the evil plight of men, life
was still, by some slight preponderance of considerations, probably
better worth living than leaving. Despising themselves, they despised
their Creator. There was a general decay of religious belief. Pale and
watery gleams, from skies thickly veiled by doubt and dread, alone
lighted up the chaos of earth. That men should doubt Him whose breath
is in their nostrils, or dread the hands that moulded them, seems to us
indeed a pitiable insanity; but we must remember that children who
are brave by day have sometimes foolish fears at night. The dawn has
come since then. It is very easy to believe in the fatherhood of God in
the twentieth century.

'Briefly, as must needs be in a discourse of this character, I have
adverted to some of the causes which had prepared men's minds for
the change from the old to the new order, as well as some causes of the
conservatism of despair which for a while held it back after the time
was ripe. To wonder at the rapidity with which the change was completed
after its possibility was first entertained is to forget the intoxicating
effect of hope upon minds long accustomed to despair. The sunburst,
after so long and dark a night, must needs have had a dazzling effect.
From the moment men allowed themselves to believe that humanity

after all had not been meant for a dwarf, that its squat stature was not the measure of its possible growth, but that it stood upon the verge of an avatar of limitless development, the reaction must needs have been overwhelming. It is evident that nothing was able to stand against the enthusiasm which the new faith inspired.

. . .

'To put the whole matter in the nutshell of a parable, let me compare humanity in the olden time to a rosebush planted in a swamp, watered with black bog water, breathing miasmatic fogs by day, and chilled with poison dews at night. Innumerable generations of gardeners had done their best to make it bloom, but beyond an occasional half-opened bud with a worm at the heart, their efforts had been unsuccessful. Many, indeed, claimed that the bush was no rosebush at all, but a noxious shrub, fit only to be uprooted and burned. The gardeners, for the most part, however, held that the bush belonged to the rose family, but had some ineradicable taint about it, which prevented the buds from coming out, and accounted for its generally sickly condition. There were a few, indeed, who maintained that the stock was good enough, that the trouble was in the bog, and that under more favourable conditions the plant might be expected to do better. But these persons were not regular gardeners, and being condemned by the latter as mere theorists and daydreamers, were, for the most part, so regarded by the people. Moreover, urged some eminent moral philosophers, even conceding for the sake of the argument that the bush might possibly do better elsewhere, it was a more valuable discipline for the buds to try to bloom in a bog than it would be under more favourable conditions. The buds that succeeded in opening might indeed be very rare, and the flowers pale and scentless, but they represented far more moral effort than if they had bloomed spontaneously in a garden.

'The regular gardeners and the moral philosophers had their way. The bush remained rooted in the bog, and the old course of treatment went on. Continually new varieties of forcing mixtures were applied to the roots, and more recipes than could be numbered, each declared by its advocates the best and only suitable preparation, were used to kill the vermin and remove the mildew. This went on a very long time. Occasionally someone claimed to observe a slight improvement in the appearance of the bush, but there were quite as many who declared that it did not look so well as it used to. On the whole there could not be said to be any marked change. Finally, during a period of general despondency as to the prospects of the bush where it was, the idea of transplanting it was again mooted, and this time found favour. "Let us try it," was the general voice. "Perhaps it may thrive better elsewhere, and here it is certainly doubtful if it be worth cultivating longer." So it came about that the rosebush of humanity was transplanted, and set in sweet, warm, dry earth, where the sun bathed it, the stars wooed it, and the south wind caressed it. Then it appeared that it was indeed a rosebush. The vermin and the mildew disappeared, and the bush was covered with most beautiful red roses, whose fragrance filled the world . . .'

But this view of the American future wasn't universally shared. After the Battle of Wounded Knee, the Sioux led an extraordinary pan-tribal movement which predicted the return of America to its native population.

JAMES MOONEY
The Ghost-Dance Religion and the Sioux Outbreak of 1890

(1896)

The great underlying principle of the Ghost-dance doctrine is that the time will come when the whole Indian race, living and dead, will be reunited upon a regenerated earth, to live a life of aboriginal happiness, forever free from death, disease and misery. On this foundation each tribe has built a structure from its own mythology, and each apostle and believer has filled in the details according to his own mental capacity or ideas of happiness, with such additions as come to him from the trance. Some changes, also, have undoubtedly resulted from the transmission of the doctrine through the imperfect medium of the sign language.

. . .

As I had always shown a sympathy for their ideas and feelings, and had now accomplished a long journey to the messiah himself at the cost of considerable difficulty and hardship, the Indians were at last fully satisfied that I was really desirous of learning the truth concerning their new religion. A few days after my visit to Left Hand, several of the delegates who had been sent out in the preceding August came down to see me, headed by Black Short Nose, a Cheyenne. After preliminary greetings, he stated that the Cheyenne and Arapaho were now convinced that I would tell the truth about their religion, and as they loved their religion and were anxious to have the whites know that it was all good and contained nothing bad or hostile they would now give me the message which the messiah himself had given to them, that I might take it back to show to Washington. He then took from a beaded pouch and gave to me a letter, which proved to be the message or statement of the doctrine delivered by Wovoka to the Cheyenne and Arapaho delegates, of whom Black Short Nose was one, on the occasion of their last visit to Nevada, in August 1891, and written down on the spot, in broken English, by one of the Arapaho delegates, Casper Edson, a young man who had acquired some English education by several years' attendance at the government Indian school at Carlisle, Pennsylvania. On the reverse page of the paper was a duplicate in somewhat better English, written out by a daughter of Black Short Nose, a school girl, as dictated by her father on his return. These letters contained the message to be delivered to the two tribes, and as is expressly stated in the text were not intended to be seen by a white man. The daughter of Black Short Nose had attempted to erase this clause before her father brought the letter down to me, but the lines were still plainly visible. It is the genuine official statement of the Ghost-dance doctrine as given by the messiah himself to his disciples . . .

The Messiah Letter (free rendering)

When you get home you must make a dance to continue five days. Dance four successive nights, and the last night keep up the dance until the morning of the fifth day, when all must bathe in the river and then disperse to their homes. You must all do in the same way.

I, Jack Wilson, love you all, and my heart is full of gladness for the gifts you have brought me. When you get home I shall give you a good cloud [rain?] which will make you feel good. I give you a good spirit and give you all good paint. I want you to come again in three months, some from each tribe there [the Indian Territory].

There will be a good deal of snow this year and some rain. In the fall there will be such a rain as I have never given you before.

Grandfather [a universal title or reverence among Indians and here meaning the messiah] says, when your friends die you must not cry. You must not hurt anybody or do harm to anyone. You must not fight. Do right always. I will give you satisfaction in life. This young man has a good father and mother. [Possibly this refers to Casper Edson, the young Arapaho who wrote down this message of Wovoka for the delegation.]

Do not tell the white people about this. Jesus is now upon the earth. He appears like a cloud. The dead are alive all again. I do not know when they will be here; maybe this fall or in the spring. When the time comes there will be no more sickness and everyone will be young again.

Do not refuse to work for the whites and do not make any trouble with them until you leave them. When the earth shakes [at the coming of the new world] do not be afraid. It will not hurt you.

I want you to dance every six weeks. Make a feast at the dance and have food that everybody may eat. Then bathe in the water. That is all. You will receive good words again from me some time. Do not tell lies.

The mythology of the doctrine is only briefly indicated, but the principal articles are given. The dead are all risen and the spirit hosts are advancing and have already arrived at the boundaries of this earth, led forward by the regenerator in shape of cloud-like indistinctness. The spirit captain of the dead is always represented under this shadowy semblance. The great change will be ushered in by a trembling of the earth, at which the faithful are exhorted to feel no alarm. The hope held out is the same that has inspired the Christian for nineteen centuries – a happy immortality in perpetual youth. As to fixing a date, the messiah is as cautious as his predecessor in prophecy, who declares that 'no man knoweth the time, not even the angels of God'.

. . .

The manner of the final change and the destruction of the whites has been variously interpreted as the doctrine was carried from its original centre. East of the mountains it is commonly held that a deep sleep will come on the believers, during which the great catastrophe will be accomplished, and the faithful will awake to immortality on a new earth. The Shoshoni of Wyoming say this sleep will continue four nights and days, and that on the morning of the fifth day all will open their eyes in a new world where both races will dwell together forever. The Cheyenne, Arapaho, Kiowa and others, of Oklahoma, say that the new earth, with all the resurrected dead from the beginning, and with the buffalo, the elk and other game upon it, will come from the west and slide over the surface of the present earth, as the right hand might slide over the left. As it approaches, the Indians will be carried upward and alight on it by the aid of the sacred dance feather which they wear in their hair and which will act as wings to bear them up. They will then become unconscious for four days, and on waking out of their trance will find themselves with their former friends in the midst of all the old time surroundings.

. . .

All these tribes believe that the destruction or removal of the whites is to be accomplished entirely by supernatural means, and they severely blame the Sioux for having provoked a physical conflict by their impatience instead of waiting for their God to deliver them in his own good time.

*. . . and not all literary predictions shared Bellamy's Utopian optimism.
In* The Iron Heel, *Jack London focused in far greater detail on the
struggle and social collapse which must lie in the way of lasting progress.*

JACK LONDON
The Iron Heel

(1908)

The years of prosperity were now to be paid for. All markets
were glutted; all markets were falling; and amidst the general crumble
of prices the price of labour crumbled fastest of all. The land was
convulsed with industrial dissensions. Labour was striking here, there
and everywhere; and where it was not striking, it was being turned out
by the capitalists. The papers were filled with tales of violence and
blood. And through it all the Black Hundreds played their part. Riot,
arson and wanton destruction of property was their function, and well
they performed it. The whole regular army was in the field, called there
by the actions of the Black Hundreds. All cities and towns were like
armed camps, and labourers were shot down like dogs. Out of the vast
army of the unemployed the strike-breakers were recruited; and when
the strike-breakers were worsted by the labour unions, the troops always
appeared and crushed the unions. Then there was the militia. As yet,
it was not necessary to have recourse to the secret militia law. Only the
regularly organized militia was out, and it was out everywhere, and in
this time of terror the regular army was increased an additional hundred
thousand by the government.

Never had labour received such an all-round beating. The great
captains of industry, the oligarchs, had for the first time thrown their
full weight into the breach the struggling employers' associations had
made. These associations were practically middle-class affairs, and now,
compelled by hard times and crashing markets, and aided by the great
captains of industry, they gave organized labour an awful and decisive
defeat. It was an all-powerful alliance, but it was an alliance of the lion
and the lamb, as the middle class was soon to learn.

Labour was bloody and sullen, but crushed. Yet its defeat did not put
an end to the hard times. The banks, themselves constituting one of

the most important forces of the Oligarchy, continued to call in credits. The Wall Street group turned the stock market into a maelstrom where the values of all the land crumbled away almost to nothingness. And out of all the rack and ruin rose the form of the nascent Oligarchy, imperturbable, indifferent and sure. Its serenity and certitude was terrifying. Not only did it use its own vast power, but it used all the power of the United States Treasury to carry out its plans.

The captains of industry had turned upon the middle class. The employers' associations, that had helped the captains of industry to tear and rend labour were now torn and rent by their quondam allies. Amidst the crashing of the middle men, the small business men and manufacturers, the trusts stood firm. Nay, the trusts did more than stand firm. They were active. They sowed wind, and wind, and ever more wind; for they alone knew how to reap the whirlwind and make a profit out of it. And such profits! Colossal profits! Strong enough themselves to weather the storm that was largely their own brewing, they turned loose and plundered the wrecks that floated about them. Values were pitifully and inconceivably shrunken, and the trusts added hugely to their holdings, even extending their enterprises into many new fields – and always at the expense of the middle class.

Thus the summer of 1912 witnessed the virtual death-thrust to the middle class. Even Ernest was astounded at the quickness with which it had been done. He shook his head ominously, and looked forward without hope to the fall elections.

'It's no use,' he said. 'We are beaten. The Iron Heel is here. I had hoped for a peaceable victory at the ballot-box. I was wrong. Wickson was right. We shall be robbed of our few remaining liberties; the Iron Heel will walk upon our faces; nothing remains but a bloody revolution of the working class. Of course we will win, but I shudder to think of it.'

*Programmes for regeneration, it became clear, would require the seques-
tration and in some cases the sterilization of the undesirable or the
mentally deficient. The severity of such plans varied – while Britain
never implemented compulsory measures, parts of Germany and the
United States did. H. H. Goddard, director of research at the Vineland
Training School for Feeble-Minded Girls and Boys in New Jersey, was
a pioneer in the description of mental deficiency: he coined the term
'moron' from the Greek word for foolish.*

HENRY HERBERT GODDARD
Feeble-Mindedness: Its Causes and Consequences

(1914)

Our Institutions for these defectives are generally known as
Institutions for the Feeble-minded.

Since the introduction of the Binet Measuring Scale of Intelligence
and the grading of children by their mental age, a closer classification
has been followed. The American Association for the study of the
feeble-minded has adopted the following scheme: The term idiot is
used to designate those of mental age up to and including two years;
imbecile, those of from three to seven years, inclusive. For those from
seven to twelve a new term has been invented; they are now called
morons. The term moron, therefore, in America designates almost
exactly what is meant by 'feeble-minded' in England.

. . .

WHAT IS TO BE DONE? We have already seen that a large percentage
of paupers, criminals, drunkards, prostitutes and other ne'er-do-wells
are mentally defective. A study of the family history of feeble-minded
persons shows that at least two-thirds of feeble-minded people have
inherited their feeble-mindedness, and that this feeble-mindedness is
transmitted in accordance with the Mendelian formula. It has also
shown that the size of families among these defectives is at least twice as

great as among the general population. In other words the feeble-minded population contributing largely to our pauper, criminal, drunkard and prostitute classes is growing rapidly. It would seem from this that society cannot attack these problems in any more successful way than to attack one of the fundamental causes of the problem, namely: feeble-mindedness. And we must attack this from the standpoint of inheritability. It might be a defensible position to propose to go on as we are doing with the pauper and criminal, drunkard and prostitute, taking care of them until they die, if the present group were the end. But the instant we realize that these groups are continually being replenished, that our problem instead of growing less is actually growing greater, we discover how hopeless is the situation, unless we can accomplish more in the future than we have in the past. More than half of the states have given some attention to the question of feeble-mindedness, to the extent at least of building an Institution to care for them. But very few, possibly none, have as yet caught up with the problem, that is to say, they have not done enough to take care of the natural increase to say nothing of reducing the source of supply. The problem is a large one and the difficulties are great, but it would appear that we have not taken advantage of those things that are actually within our control.

. . .

Suppose now we go back to the general question – what shall we do with people of low intelligence? Colonize them, says one; sterilize them, says another; educate them, says a third. Each plan has its advocates and each has its difficulties. The first two seem to assume that the people of low intelligence are a different group and should be treated in a very special way; that those of us who are pleased to style ourselves intelligent have the right to deprive these people of something that we enjoy. The third plan suggests that these people are our equals in some things and that they can be educated as we have been educated.

It will be well to examine what facts we have before coming to a decision. Our facts at most are too few to warrant us in neglecting any. To begin with, no student of the problem will admit that these people constitute a different species of humanity. Some intelligence is possessed by all unless possibly the very lowest. It is a question of degree and a question of the need that the individual has of intelligence, in other words of his environment. If an individual cannot adapt himself to his environment, can we not adapt the environment to him? 'This is what colonization does,' says the advocate of this method. In theory this is true, in practice it is also often true, but not always. With certain high grades and under certain conditions there is an element of restraint, the colony becomes practically a prison; only under the wisest management, by the most broad-minded policy can this element of restraint be kept out of the mind of the high grade defective. And it is doubtful if it ever can be kept entirely away from the highest grade. Suppose then we are content to colonize as many as can be made contented in the colony, what of the others? It is for these that sterilization is supposed by many to be the panacea. But sterilization seems only to apply to a narrow zone; many of these high grades are regarded as being on the borderline, where it is of doubtful justice to take this action. Many other objections are urged.

We may accept the verdict that the facts, particularly those that are set forth in this study, show that we must colonize as many of the feeble-minded as we possibly can, that we must sterilize some and then we discover that we have only tithed the problem, we have not solved it. We still have left one expedient, that of educating them. 'But,' says someone, 'they cannot be educated, they have not mentality enough to take an education.' That depends upon our definition of education.

The group that cannot be colonized and many of those indeed who will eventually be colonized, and the group where we are in doubt about the propriety of sterilizing can be trained to a relatively high degree in certain directions. But again, says some one, they will always be vicious and dangerous and a menace to society. There are, however, no facts to prove this. That may sound strange in view of what has already been said in this volume. But it must be remembered that we have studied people, who in addition to their feeble minds, have had a bad environment, have been misunderstood or mistreated.

This article from the Daily Mirror *in 1904 reflects the broadly held view that regeneration would only take place if society was prepared to engineer it. (From Ives scrapbook.)*

LETHAL CHAMBERS FOR THE INSANE.

WHAT are we to do with the insane? It is a question that has troubled all communities ever since the complications of life produced insanity and Humanity forbade its victims being knocked on the head.

Just now the problem is, for us in England, more than usually acute. There are three or four persons in every thousand of our population who are certified to be either lunatics or idiots—that is, persons either born of unsound mind or driven mad by some cause, such as overwork, drink, or drugs. This is nearly double the per-thousand rate of fifty years ago.

In London alone, as the returns published to-day show, there are 24,000 insane people who have to be supported out of the rates. This shows an increase of just on a thousand in one year, and of 7,000 since 1890. Lunatics become, in fact, more and more numerous every day.

To shut them up is certainly better than letting them be at large. An insane person at liberty is not only a danger in the present. He is a danger to the future, for his children and his children's children may very likely spread into far-distant times the hideous disease which afflicts him.

But will the sane always be content to pay out large sums every year for the shutting-up of the insane? The doubt is aroused by a suggestion made only last week in the United States. A well-known doctor, who has made a special study of madness and crime, read a paper at a Prison Congress proposing that the permanently insane should be painlessly put to death.

At first sound this idea may seem brutal, impracticable. But as the world grows fuller, and the stress of life adds to the number of the insane, some solution of this kind is certain to be more and more insistently advocated.

The greatest care would have to be taken, of course, to defeat the designs of the wicked, who would try to get sane people out of the way by representing that they had lost their reason. With due precautions, however, we are not at all sure that the plan proposed by Dr. Hutch would not be much better all round than our present system.

Anyone whose mind has gone is as good as dead already. Can any good purpose be served by keeping his body alive?

Robert W. Chambers' The King in Yellow looks askance at a dynamic, regenerated future America with state-sanctioned euthanasia as its crowning achievement.

ROBERT W. CHAMBERS
The King in Yellow

(1895)

Toward the end of the year 1920 the Government of the United States had practically completed the programme, adopted during the last months of President Winthrop's administration.

. . .

The nation was prosperous. Chicago, for a moment paralyzed after a second great fire, had risen from its ruins, white and imperial, and more beautiful than the white city which had been built for its plaything in 1893. Everywhere good architecture was replacing bad, and even in New York, a sudden craving for decency had swept away a great portion of the existing horrors. Streets had been widened, properly paved and lighted, trees had been planted, squares laid out, elevated structures demolished and underground roads built to replace them. The new government buildings and barracks were fine bits of architecture, and the long system of stone quays which completely surrounded the island had been turned into parks which proved a godsend to the population. The subsidizing of the state theatre and state opera brought its own reward. The United States National Academy of Design was much like European institutions of the same kind.

. . .

When, after the colossal Congress of Religions, bigotry and intolerance were laid in their graves and kindness and charity began to draw warring sects together, many thought the millennium had arrived, at least in the new world, which after all is a world by itself.

But self-preservation is the first law, and the United States had to look on in helpless sorrow as Germany, Italy, Spain and Belgium writhed in the throes of Anarchy, while Russia, watching from the Caucasus, stooped and bound them one by one.

. . .

It was, I remember, the 13th day of April 1920, that the first Government Lethal Chamber was established on the south side of Washington Square, between Wooster Street and South Fifth Avenue. The block which had formerly consisted of a lot of shabby old buildings, used as cafés and restaurants for foreigners, had been acquired by the Government in the winter of 1898. The French and Italian cafés and restaurants were torn down; the whole block was enclosed by a gilded iron railing, and converted into a lovely garden with lawns, flowers and fountains. In the centre of the garden stood a small, white building, severely classical in architecture, and surrounded by thickets of flowers. Six Ionic columns supported the roof, and the single door was of bronze. A splendid marble group of 'The Fates' stood before the door, the work of a young American sculptor, Boris Yvain, who had died in Paris when only twenty-three years old.

The inauguration ceremonies were in progress as I crossed University Place and entered the square. I threaded my way through the silent throng of spectators, but was stopped at Fourth Street by a cordon of police. A regiment of United States lancers were drawn up in a hollow square around the Lethal Chamber. On a raised tribune facing Washington Park stood the Governor of New York, and behind him were grouped the Mayor of New York and Brooklyn, the Inspector-General of Police, the Commandant of the state troops, Colonel Livingston, military aid to the President of the United States, General Blount, commanding at Governor's Island, Major-General Hamilton, commanding the garrison of New York and Brooklyn, Admiral Buffby of the fleet in the North River, Surgeon General Lanceford, the staff of the National Free Hospital, Senators Wyse and Franklin of New York, and the Commissioner of Public Works. The tribune was surrounded by a squadron of hussars of the National Guard.

The Governor was finishing his reply to the short speech of the Surgeon-General. I heard him say: 'The laws prohibiting suicide and providing punishment for any attempt at self-destruction have been repealed. The Government has seen fit to acknowledge the right of man to end an existence which may have become intolerable to him, through physical suffering or mental despair. It is believed that the community will be benefited by the removal of such people from their midst. Since the passage of this law, the number of suicides in the United States has not increased. Now that the Government has determined to establish a Lethal Chamber in every city, town and village in the country, it remains to be seen whether or not that class of human creatures from whose desponding ranks new victims of self-destruction fall daily will accept the relief thus provided.' He paused, and turned to the white Lethal Chamber. The silence in the street was absolute. 'There a painless death awaits him who can no longer bear the sorrows of this life. If death is welcome let him seek it there.' Then quickly turning to the military aid of the President's household, he said, 'I declare the Lethal Chamber open,' and again facing the vast crowd he cried in a clear voice: 'Citizens of New York and of the United States of America, through me the Government declares the Lethal Chamber to be open.'

The new century saw the first sterilization law passed in Indiana, targeting the 'unimproveable' [sic]. This set a precedent for the subsequent sterilization plans adopted in Germany under National Socialism.

Sterilization Law of Indiana

(1907)

The bill was introduced on 29 January 1907, by Representative Horace D. Read, of Tipton, Ind.

It passed the House 19 February 1907 – 59 ayes, 22 noes; the Senate 6 March 1907 – 28 ayes, 16 noes.

It was approved 9 March 1907, by Governor J. Frank Hanley.

It appears on the Indiana laws of 1907 as Chapter 215, on page 377; Burns' Indiana Statutes 1908, sec. 2232.

An act to prevent procreation of confirmed criminals, idiots, imbeciles, and rapists; Providing that superintendents or boards of managers of institutions where such persons are confined shall have the authority and are empowered to appoint a committee of experts, consisting of two physicians, to examine into the mental condition of such inmates.

WHEREAS, heredity plays a most important part in the transmission of crime, idiocy and imbecility:

THEREFORE, BE IT ENACTED BY THE GENERAL ASSEMBLY OF THE STATE OF INDIANA, that on and after the passage of this act it shall be compulsory for each and every institution in the state, entrusted with the care of confirmed criminals, idiots, rapists and imbeciles, to appoint upon its staff, in addition to the regular institutional physician, two (2) skilled surgeons of recognized ability, whose duty it shall be, in conjunction with the chief physician of the institution, to examine the mental and physical condition of such inmates as are recommended by the institutional physician and board of managers. If, in the judgement of this committee of experts and the board of managers, procreation is inadvisable, and there is no probability of improvement of the mental and physical condition of the inmate, it shall be lawful for the surgeons to perform such operation for the prevention of procreation as shall be decided safest and most effective. But this operation shall not be performed except in cases that have been pronounced unimproveable: *Provided*, That in no case shall the consultation fee be more than three dollars to each expert, to be paid out of the funds appropriated for the maintenance of such institution.

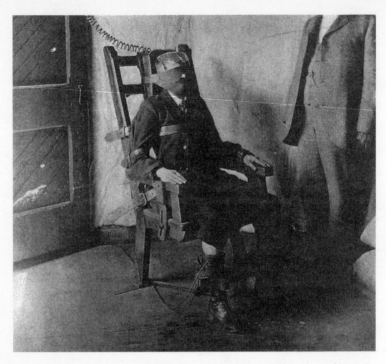

New technology for social control: one of the first electric chairs (1908).

Coda

BENEDICT MOREL
Treatise on Degenerations of the Human Race

(1857)

The plan which I have adopted is vast but I am determined to pursue it to the end. The confidence which sustains me does not arise from any exaggerated idea of my own strength but from a lively and profound faith which strengthens and animates me. I believe that the study of the cause of degenerations and of their treatment is one of the most important, useful and suggestive that can occupy the mind of a physician and that it is the duty of each, according to his power and ability to aid in preventing the generalization of the evils pointed out. And thus to have before him, as the programme of his labours, the intellectual, moral and physical amelioration of man. Or if the term be preferred his REGENERATION.

CHARLES DARWIN
On the Origin of Species

(1859)

It is interesting to contemplate a tangled bank, clothed with many plants of many kinds, with birds singing on bushes, with various insects flitting about and with worms crawling through the damp earth and to reflect that these elaborately constructed forms, so different from each other and dependent on each other in so complex a manner, have all been produced by laws acting around us . . . Thus, from the war of nature, from famine and death, the most exalted object which we are capable of conceiving, namely, the production of the higher animals, directly follows. There is grandeur in this view of life, with its several powers, having been originally breathed by the Creator into a few forms or into one; and that, whilst this planet has gone cycling on according to the fixed law of gravity, from so simple a beginning endless forms most beautiful and most wonderful have been, and are being, evolved.

Permissions

Every effort has been made to trace or contact copyright holders. The editors and publishers would like to apologize in advance for any inadvertent use of copyright material, and thank the following publishers and agents who have kindly given their permission to reproduce copyright material. Penguin would be pleased to rectify any omissions brought to their notice at the earliest opportunity.

Robert Baden-Powell: extract from *Scouting for Boys* (Horace Cox, 1908). Reprinted by permission of The Scout Association; James Crichton-Browne: extract from *The Doctor's After Thoughts* (Ernest Benn, 1932). Reprinted by permission of A & C Black (Publishers) Ltd; Arthur Conan Doyle: extracts from 'The Poison Belt' from *The Professor Challenger Stories* (John Murray, 1952), extract from *The Sign of Four* from *Sherlock Holmes: The Complete Long Stories* (John Murray, 1929), extract from 'Return' from *Sherlock Holmes: The Complete Short Stories* (John Murray/Jonathan Cape), copyright © 1996 The Sir Arthur Conan Doyle Copyright Holders. Reprinted by kind permission of Jonathan Clowes Ltd, London, on behalf of Andrea Plunket, Administrator of the Sir Arthur Conan Doyle Copyrights; Théodore Flournoy: extracts from *From India to the Planet Mars: A Case of Multiple Personality with Imaginary Languages*, edited by Sonu Shamdasani (Princeton University Press, 1994), © 1994 by Princeton University Press. Reprinted by permission of the publishers; James Frazer: extract from *The Golden Bough* (Macmillan, 1907–15). Reprinted by permission of A. P. Watt Ltd on behalf of Trinity College, Cambridge; Sigmund Freud: extract from *The Freud–Jung Letters: Correspondence Between Sigmund Freud and C. G. Jung*, translated by Ralph Manheim and R. F. C. Hull, edited by William McGuire (Hogarth Press/Routledge & Kegan Paul, 1974). Reprinted by permission of Random House UK Ltd; extracts from 'Case Histories 1, "Dora" and "Little Hans"', extract from 'Civilization, Society and Religion: Group Psychology, Civilization and Its Discontents and Other Works', extracts from 'Studies on Hysteria' from *The Standard Edition of the Complete Psychological Works of Sigmund Freud*, translated and edited by James Strachey (Hogarth Press, 1951). Reprinted by permission of Sigmund Freud Copyrights, the Institute of Psycho-Analysis and Random House UK Ltd; C. G. Harrison: extracts from *The Transcendental Universe* (Temple Lodge, 1993). Reprinted by permission of the publishers; A. E. Housman: 'The laws of God, the laws of

PENGUIN ()CLASSICS

www.penguinclassics.com

- *Details about every Penguin Classic*

- *Advanced information about forthcoming titles*

- *Hundreds of author biographies*

- *FREE resources including critical essays on the books and their historical background, reader's and teacher's guides.*

- *Links to other web resources for the Classics*

- *Discussion area*

- *Online review copy ordering for academics*

- *Competitions with prizes, and challenging Classics trivia quizzes*

PENGUIN CLASSICS ONLINE

READ MORE IN PENGUIN

In every corner of the world, on every subject under the sun, Penguin represents quality and variety – the very best in publishing today.

For complete information about books available from Penguin – including Puffins, Penguin Classics and Arkana – and how to order them, write to us at the appropriate address below. Please note that for copyright reasons the selection of books varies from country to country.

In the United Kingdom: Please write to *Dept. EP, Penguin Books Ltd, Bath Road, Harmondsworth, West Drayton, Middlesex UB7 ODA*

In the United States: Please write to *Consumer Sales, Penguin Putnam Inc., P.O. Box 12289 Dept. B, Newark, New Jersey 07101-5289.* VISA and MasterCard holders call 1-800-788-6262 to order Penguin titles

In Canada: Please write to *Penguin Books Canada Ltd, 10 Alcorn Avenue, Suite 300, Toronto, Ontario M4V 3B2*

In Australia: Please write to *Penguin Books Australia Ltd, P.O. Box 257, Ringwood, Victoria 3134*

In New Zealand: Please write to *Penguin Books (NZ) Ltd, Private Bag 102902, North Shore Mail Centre, Auckland 10*

In India: Please write to *Penguin Books India Pvt Ltd, 11 Community Centre, Panchsheel Park, New Delhi 110017*

In the Netherlands: Please write to *Penguin Books Netherlands bv, Postbus 3507, NL-1001 AH Amsterdam*

In Germany: Please write to *Penguin Books Deutschland GmbH, Metzlerstrasse 26, 60594 Frankfurt am Main*

In Spain: Please write to *Penguin Books S. A., Bravo Murillo 19, 1° B, 28015 Madrid*

In Italy: Please write to *Penguin Italia s.r.l., Via Benedetto Croce 2, 20094 Corsico, Milano*

In France: Please write to *Penguin France, Le Carré Wilson, 62 rue Benjamin Baillaud, 31500 Toulouse*

In Japan: Please write to *Penguin Books Japan Ltd, Kaneko Building, 2-3-25 Koraku, Bunkyo-Ku, Tokyo 112*

In South Africa: Please write to *Penguin Books South Africa (Pty) Ltd, Private Bag X14, Parkview, 2122 Johannesburg*

READ MORE IN PENGUIN

Penguin Twentieth-Century Classics offer a selection of the finest works of literature published this century. Spanning the globe from Argentina to America, from France to India, the masters of prose and poetry are represented by Penguin.

If you would like a catalogue of the Twentieth-Century Classics library, please write to:

Penguin Press Marketing, 27 Wrights Lane, London W8 5TZ

(Available while stocks last)

READ MORE IN PENGUIN

A CHOICE OF TWENTIETH-CENTURY CLASSICS

Ulysses James Joyce

Ulysses is unquestionably one of the supreme masterpieces, in any artistic form, of the twentieth century. 'It is the book to which we are all indebted and from which none of us can escape' T. S. Eliot

The First Man Albert Camus

'It is the most brilliant semi-autobiographical account of an Algerian childhood amongst the grinding poverty and stoicism of poor French-Algerian colonials' J. G. Ballard. 'A kind of magical Rosetta stone to his entire career, illuminating both his life and his work with stunning candour and passion' *The New York Times*

Flying Home Ralph Ellison

Drawing on his early experience – his father's death when he was three, hoboeing his way on a freight train to follow his dream of becoming a musician – Ellison creates stories which, according to the *Washington Post*, 'approach the simple elegance of Chekhov.' 'A shining instalment' *The New York Times Book Review*

Cider with Rosie Laurie Lee

'Laurie Lee's account of childhood and youth in the Cotswolds remains as fresh and full of joy and gratitude for youth and its sensations as when it first appeared. It sings in the memory' *Sunday Times*. 'A work of art' Harold Nicolson

Kangaroo D. H. Lawrence

Escaping from the decay and torment of post-war Europe, Richard and Harriett Somers arrive in Australia to a new and freer life. Somers, a disillusioned writer, becomes involved with an extreme political group. At its head is the enigmatic Kangaroo.

READ MORE IN PENGUIN

A CHOICE OF TWENTIETH-CENTURY CLASSICS

Belle du Seigneur   Albert Cohen

Belle du Seigneur is one of the greatest love stories in modern literature. It is also a hilarious mock-epic concerning the mental world of the cuckold. 'A *tour de force*, a comic masterpiece weighted with an understanding of human frailty ... It is, quite simply, a book that must be read' *Observer*

The Diary of a Young Girl   Anne Frank

'Fifty years have passed since Anne Frank's diary was first published. Her story came to symbolize not only the travails of the Holocaust, but the struggle of the human spirit ... This edition is a worthy memorial' *The Times*. 'A witty, funny and tragic book ... stands on its own even without its context of horror' *Sunday Times*

Herzog   Saul Bellow

'A feast of language, situations, characters, ironies, and a controlled moral intelligence ... Bellow's rapport with his central character seems to me novel writing in the grand style of a Tolstoy – subjective, complete, heroic' *Chicago Tribune*

The Go-Between   L. P. Hartley

 Discovering an old diary, Leo, now in his sixties, is drawn back to the hot summer of 1900 and his visit to Brandham Hall ... 'An intelligent, complex and beautifully-felt evocation of nascent boyhood sexuality that is also a searching exploration of the nature of memory and myth' Douglas Brooks-Davies

Orlando   Virginia Woolf

Sliding in and out of three centuries, and slipping between genders, Orlando is the sparkling incarnation of the personality of Vita Sackville-West as Virginia Woolf saw it.

READ MORE IN PENGUIN

A CHOICE OF TWENTIETH-CENTURY CLASSICS

Collected Stories Vladimir Nabokov

Here, for the first time in paperback, the stories of one of the twentieth century's greatest prose stylists are collected in a single volume. 'To read him in full flight is to experience stimulation that is at once intellectual, imaginative and aesthetic, the nearest thing to pure sensual pleasure that prose can offer' Martin Amis

Cancer Ward Aleksandr Solzhenitsyn

Like his hero Oleg Kostoglotov, Aleksandr Solzhenitsyn spent many years in labour camps for mocking Stalin and was eventually transferred to a cancer ward. 'What he has done above all things is record the truth in such a manner as to render it indestructible, stamping it into the Western consciousness' *Observer*

Nineteen Eighty-Four George Orwell

'A volley against the authoritarian in every personality, a polemic against every orthodoxy, an anarchistic blast against every un-questioning conformist . . . *Nineteen Eighty-Four* is a great novel, and it will endure because its message is a permanent one' Ben Pimlott

The Complete Saki Saki

Macabre, acid and very funny, Saki's work drives a knife into the upper crust of English Edwardian life. Here are the effete and dashing heroes, Reginald, Clovis and Comus Bassington, tea on the lawn, the smell of gunshot and the tinkle of the caviar fork, and here is the half-seen, half-felt menace of disturbing undercurrents . . .

The Castle Franz Kafka

'In *The Castle* we encounter a proliferation of obstacles, endless conversations, perpetual possibilities which hook on to each other as if intent to go on until the end of time' Idris Parry. 'Kafka may be the most important writer of the twentieth century' J. G. Ballard

READ MORE IN PENGUIN

A CHOICE OF TWENTIETH-CENTURY CLASSICS

The Garden Party and Other Stories Katherine Mansfield

This collection reveals Mansfield's supreme talent as an innovator who freed the short story from its conventions and gave it a new strength and prestige. 'One of the great modernist writers of displacement, restlessness, mobility, impermanence' Lorna Sage

The Little Prince Antoine de Saint-Exupéry

Moral fable and spiritual autobiography, this is the story of a little boy who lives alone on a planet not much bigger than himself. One day he leaves behind the safety of his childlike world to travel around the universe where he is introduced to the vagaries of adult behaviour through a series of extraordinary encounters.

Selected Poems Edward Arlington Robinson

Robinson's finely crafted rhythms mirror the tension the poet saw between life's immutable circumstances and humanity's often tragic attempts to exert control. At once dramatic and witty these poems lay bare the tyranny of love and unspoken, unnoticed suffering.

Talkative Man R. K. Narayan

Bizarre happenings at Malgudi are heralded by the arrival of a stranger on the Delhi train who takes up residence in the station waiting-room and, to the dismay of the station master, will not leave. 'His lean, matter-of-fact prose has lost none of its chuckling sparkle mixed with melancholy' *Spectator*

The Immoralist André Gide

'To know how to free oneself is nothing; the arduous thing is to know what to do with one's freedom' André Gide. Gide's novel examines the inevitable conflicts that arise when a pleasure-seeker challenges conventional society, and raises complex issues of personal responsibility.

READ MORE IN PENGUIN

A CHOICE OF TWENTIETH-CENTURY CLASSICS

Enemies Isaac Bashevis Singer

Singer's first 'New York' novel is a bleak and brilliant love story, a study of people profoundly estranged from each other and from themselves. 'A brilliant, unsettling novel ... he works out a bizarre plot with perfect naturalness and aplomb' *Newsweek*

The Man Within Graham Greene

'One of our greatest authors ... Greene had the sharpest eyes for trouble, the finest nose for human weaknesses, and was pitilessly honest in his observations' *Independent*. 'No serious writer of this century has more thoroughly invaded and shaped the public imagination than Graham Greene' *Time*

Guilty Men 'Cato'

Published a month after the evacuation of Dunkirk, and conceived by three journalists, Michael Foot, Peter Howard and Frank Owen, this impassioned polemic singled out the leaders MacDonald, Baldwin and, above all, Chamberlain, who, through their policy of appeasement in the face of Hitler's aggression, had brought the country to the brink of disaster. 'A polemic of genius' Peter Clarke

The Victim Saul Bellow

Leventhal is a man uncertain of himself, never free from the nagging suspicion that the other guy might be right. So when a down-at-heel stranger accuses him of ruining his life, he half believes it, and cannot stop himself becoming trapped in a mire of self-doubt. 'A masterful and chilling novel' *The Times*

Wide Sargasso Sea Jean Rhys

Jean Rhys's literary masterpiece was inspired by Charlotte Brontë's *Jane Eyre*, and is set in the lush, beguiling landscape of Jamaica in the 1830s. 'A tale of dislocation and dispossession, which Rhys writes with a kind of romantic cynicism, desperate and pungent' *The Times*

READ MORE IN PENGUIN

Published or forthcoming:

Wars Edited by Angus Calder

'Soon there'll come – the signs are fair –
A death-storm from the distant north.
Stink of corpses everywhere,
Mass assassins marching forth.'

Wars dominated life in Europe in the first half of the twentieth century
and have haunted the second, as the terrible legacy of guilt and grief is
worked through. In this powerful and original anthology, Angus
Calder brings together writings which emphasize that, despite the
camaraderie and heroism of war, it is really about killing and being
killed.

It concentrates on why men fight wars and how something we can call
'humanity' somehow survives them. Primo Levi, Robert Graves,
Wilfred Owen, W. B. Yeats, Anna Akhmatova , Seamus Heaney,
Kurt Vonnegut, Marguerite Duras, Jacques Brel, Bertolt Brecht,
Sorley Maclean and Miklos Radnoti are among the many writers
represented; all offer a vivid sense of what war at the sharp end is
really like.

READ MORE IN PENGUIN

Published or forthcoming:

Utopias   Edited by Catriona Kelly

Russian modernism began with the triumph of the symbolist style and survived until the Stalinist terror of the late 1930s. This was an age bristling with visions of glorious or terrifying futures, with manifestos for new artistic movements and furious feuds between them.

This richly illustrated anthology brings together Bakhtin's celebrated analysis of 'carnival culture'; reflections by painter and stage designer Léon Bakst and film director Sergei Eisenstein; and major texts by Babel and Bulgakov, Mayakovsky and the Mandelstams, Akhmatova and Tsvetaeva, Nabokov and Pasternak, as well as many works by less well-known, but equally talented, figures. Supportive or subversive of the Soviet régime, baldly realistic or boldly experimental, they capture the essence of an astonishingly fertile and stimulating literary era.

'Modernism everywhere entailed a drastic, dangerous breach with the past; in Russia it gained an extra impetus from an entire society's efforts to modernise itself. *Utopias* tells the whole whirlygig story . . . This is *Dr Zhivago* for highbrows!' Peter Conrad

READ MORE IN PENGUIN

Published or forthcoming:

Artificial Paradises   Edited by Mike Jay

Taking Baudelaire's now famous title as its own, this anthology reveals the diverse roles mind-altering drugs have played throughout history. It brings together a multiplicity of voices to explore the presence – both secret and public – of drugs in the overlapping dialogues of science and religion, pleasure and madness, individualism and social control. From Apuleius's *Golden Ass* to Hunter S. Thompson's frenzied *Fear and Loathing in Las Vegas*, via Sartre's nightmarish experiences with mescaline and Walter Benjamin's ecstatic wanderings on hashish, *Artificial Paradises* is packed full of the weird, the wonderful and the shocking.

'This is a superb anthology – scholarly, penetrative, mind-expanding. It's probably the best of its kind' Ian McEwan

'Excellent . . . shows how drugs permeate the very fabric of our history and culture' Irvine Welsh

READ MORE IN PENGUIN

Published or forthcoming:

Movies Edited by Gilbert Adair

At the turn of the millennium cinema permeates all of our lives. From the Lumière brothers' first public film screening at the end of the nineteenth century to the technical wizardry at the end of the twentieth, it has both recorded and created our history. Its images and icons are part of our collective consciousness. We are all film buffs now.

But does the end of the century also herald the 'End of Cinema'? Has mainstream, formulaic, big-budget moviemaking triumphed over all other alternatives? Covering subjects as diverse as avant-garde cinema, B-movies, blue movies, bad movies and Nazi propaganda, with texts by filmmakers and non-specialists – Orson Welles, Fellini, Updike on Burton and Taylor, Mailer on Marilyn – this is a refreshing corrective to the Hollywood bias.

'An anthology to destroy in a weekend – and open up your life. Start dipping Friday night, and by Sunday lunch you're seeing the links between Manny Farber and Sergei Eisenstein, Mickey Mouse and Modernism . . . a superb, unexpected collection of thoughts, wonders and outrages, making you want to read – and see – more' David Thomson

READ MORE IN PENGUIN

Published or forthcoming:

Titanic   Edited by John Wilson Foster

RMS *Titanic* sank to the bottom of the Atlantic during a night of rare calm, but the tragedy caused shock waves on both sides of the ocean and has continued to haunt our imaginations ever since.

The human drama of the disaster still has much of the power to excite and appal that it had in 1912, inspiring novels, films, plays, paintings and music. This anthology draws from more than eight decades of literature about the great ship, combining journalism, essays, fiction, poems, letters, songs and transcripts of hearings. It relives the event through the accounts of survivors, witnesses and commentators, with contributions from major writers of the time such as Joseph Conrad, H. G. Wells, Thomas Hardy, George Bernard Shaw and Sir Arthur Conan Doyle.

But beyond that it also shows how the sinking of *Titanic* was a cultural phenomenon which fulfilled the anxieties of its time – the frictions of class, race and gender, the hunger for progress and machine efficiency, and the arrogant assumptions of the Mechanical Age.